AMERICAN INDIAN LITERARY NATIONALISM

American Indian Literary Nationalism

Jace Weaver

Craig S. Womack

Robert Warrior

Foreword by Simon J. Ortiz

Afterword by Lisa Brooks

University of New Mexico Press | Albuquerque

Foreword © 2005 by Simon J. Ortiz
Text © 2006 by the University of New Mexico Press
All rights reserved. Published 2006
Printed in the United States of America
12 11 10 09 08 07 06   1 2 3 4 5 6 7

LIBRARY OF CONGRESS CATALOGING-IN-PUBLICATION DATA
Weaver, Jace, 1957–
    American Indian literary nationalism /
Jace Weaver, Craig S. Womack, Robert Warrior ;
foreword by Simon J. Ortiz ; afterword by Lisa Brooks.
        p. cm.
    Includes bibliographical references and index.
    ISBN-13: 978-0-8263-4073-3 (pbk. : alk. paper)
    ISBN-10: 0-8263-4073-3 (pbk. : alk. paper)
    1. Indian literature—United States—History and criticism.
2. American literature—Indian authors—History and criticism.
3. Indians of North America—Intellectual life.
4. Indians of North America—Ethnic identity.
I. Womack, Craig S. II. Warrior, Robert Allen. III. Title.
    PM157.W42 2006
    810.9'897—dc22
                                2006018224

o

"Cook's Mountains" by P. K. Page reprinted from *The Hidden Room*
(in two volumes) by P. K. Page by permission of the Porcupine's Quill.
Copyright © P. K. Page, 1997.

Excerpt from "Perhaps the World Ends Here" reprinted from *The
Woman Who Fell From the Sky* by Joy Harjo. Copyright © 1994 by
Joy Harjo. Used by permission of W. W. Norton & Company, Inc.

Simon J. Ortiz poem in Preface reprinted from *From Sand Creek*
by permission of the author.

Excerpt from "I Lost My Talk" reprinted from *We Are the Dreamers:
Recent and Early Poetry* by Rita Joe. Used by permission of the publisher.

"First Rule" reprinted from Maurice Kenney, *On Second Thought:
A Compilation* (University of Oklahoma Press, 1995) with permission
of the publisher.

o

Book design and type compostition by Kathleen Sparkes
Body type is Sabon 10.5/14, 26P
Display type is Helvetica Neue and Cezanne

Contents

o

Foreword

Speaking-Writing
Indigenous Literary Sovereignty

Almost every morning, I get up early and I go running. I go running in order to physically exercise, to stay fit, to maintain my health, and to contemplate and meditate upon my relationship with the natural world that encompasses and supports my physical reality. To put it another way, by running as physical exercise I also conduct and engage in a spiritual practice. This is not so farfetched an idea when I consider it in the context of spiritual tradition at Acoma Pueblo, my Indigenous home community. Running is considered a spiritual discipline on certain ritual occasions. I don't necessarily adhere to or consider my morning running—or jogging, as you might call it—exercise as ritual occasion exclusively, but I do consider it an expression that has a spiritual discipline and dimension to it. As I go outside I have cornmeal in my hand, and when I am outdoors before I begin to run, I say a brief prayer with the cornmeal. I usually say, "Grandmothers and grandfathers, and mothers and fathers of this land, culture, and community, thank you for this morning and the life of this morning. Please recognize and accept me, a person of the Eagle Clan and a child of the Antelope Clan. Please help me and all others in the course of this day. Thank you." And then I set off in my usual running stride that is never overly vigorous but tempered, measured, focused. And meditative since I am closely aware of the climate, the street conditions—sometimes there is snow in winter!—and the time of day, which is usually pretty early in the morning and there's not much light except for Toronto street lighting. Physically I am very alert as I focus on my feet and legs meeting the hard asphalt and cement streets and sidewalks. My meditation then is a deliberate awareness of my physical activity as well as the mental and emotional awareness of the relationship I am experiencing with the world around me. As expression, my physical exercise of running is equivalent to speaking and writing. I choose to run, and I choose to speak and write.

✺

For Indigenous peoples of the United States and Canada, English language writing is relatively recent and new. It's been just about three hundred years that Indigenous people have written in English. Except for petroglyphs on natural stone, the technology of "writing," i.e., the means of putting oral communication into visual script, is also relatively recent in human cultural history. In today's human cultural world, the principal and main method of expressing and conveying knowledge, information, and rhetorical impressions is still oral language. And it continues to be the source of written language, i.e., of writing.

Indigenous American people are among the world's foremost advocates of oral language, usually referred to as oral tradition, even though there's some evidence Indigenous languages are less existent today than yesteryear. Nonetheless, Indigenous oral tradition cannot be disregarded when considering today's writing by Indigenous poets, novelists, playwrights, essayists, critical theorists, and so forth. In fact, this volume features three highly regarded Indigenous writer-intellectuals living and working in the Americas today. There's no question Jace Weaver, Robert Warrior, and Craig Womack consider their various writings as originating in the oral tradition of their ancestral cultural Indigenous heritages.

Although formally schooled in Western cultural learning systems, the Indigenous literary topics and matters they address in their works cannot be anything but literature that originates in Indigenous oral tradition. Three hundred years may seem like a long time but Indigenous American oral tradition and the knowledge-experience it conveys is ageless when we Indigenous people consider it as the basis of our human cultural Existence. And this Existence is the main reason and purpose social-cultural change and modernization for Indigenous people. Although I didn't think about it back then, now it is something that is dismaying because the more we use English in speaking and writing, the more we are losing our Indigenous languages and I am convinced this is not a good change. When I think about it, this is why I get up early in the morning, even when it is freezing cold and snowy in Toronto, and go running not simply as physical exercise but also because I am keenly tuning and aligning myself with the natural process of the universe around me so that I am respondent to it intellectually, aesthetically, emotionally, physically. And the brief prayer I say before I begin my run is in the Acoma Keres language, and during my run I find myself thinking and feeling as much as possible in Acoma Keres also.

The consciousness of ourselves as Indigenous cultural beings is very important to our Existence as speaking-writing Indigenous people. In fact, cultural consciousness as Indigenous people *is* the bottom line. And that, more than anything else, has to do crucially with our cultural sovereignty as Indigenous people. While it's true to some extent—some people will even say many Native languages have completely vanished—that Indigenous languages are spoken less than they were five hundred years ago, there is, nonetheless, a vital sense of cultural continuity maintained because of Indigenous cultural consciousness. "Indians are still Indians," I've heard people say on more than a few occasions. The dynamic of cultural identity is not wholly dependent upon spoken oral language, because orality or oral tradition is more than conveyance of oral language. In fact, Indigenous identity is more than what is provided by oral tradition; Indigenous identity simply cannot be dependent only upon Indigenous languages no matter how intact the languages are. Because identity has to do with a way of life that has its own particularities, patterns, uniqueness, structures, and energy. Because Indigenous identity cannot simply be attributed to only one quality, aspect, or function of culture. Because identity has to be relevant and pertinent to other elements and factors having to do with land, culture, and community of Indigenous people. For example, Acoma people are not identified as Aacqumeh hanoh simply because they are fluent speakers of the Acoma Keres language. They are Aacqumeh hanoh whether or not they speak the language. There are some people, even within the Acoma Pueblo community, who will say otherwise, but such sentiments have more to do, unfortunately, with internalized colonialism, i.e., going along with how Indigenous people are perceived by outsiders and the federal government.

The U.S. federal government has instituted policy that defines "Indians." Thereafter, Native Americans have followed too often the dictates of federal policy so that tribal governments implement blood quantum standards in establishing Indigenous identity. As a result, this contradicts the fact that Existence is maintained wholly by cultural consciousness. And then there is the popular notion by a large segment of Euro-American society and culture that there are no more Indians or no more real Indians: they're gone; they don't have a distinct culture anymore; they don't speak Indian so I don't know how they could really be Indian! And it's factually true that Indians were decimated by Spanish, British, and French colonialism early in the settlement of the Americas—in the "early contact period" as some historians would have it—and recent U.S., Mexican, Brazilian, Peruvian, Guatemalan, Canadian, and other national governments in the Americas have shown no mercy in warring against and subsequently subduing Indigenous American people whose lands and resources they have coveted.

Nevertheless, despite horrendous measures arrayed and deployed by colonizers to achieve the physical annihilation, disappearance, and/or subservience of Indigenous people, "Indians are still Indians." Throughout the Americas, issues and concerns about land, culture, and community abound especially where Indigenous communities have resisted physical removal and annihilation, destructive assimilation and acculturation, and the outright loss of land, resources, and human capital. This means Indigenous people have completely relied upon their Indigeneity to state their case for sovereignty in cultural and self-governance matters. "Indians are still Indians" is not an empty statement but a basic assertion and stand in securing the rightful position they have as human beings.

But it is not enough that Indians are still Indians. Although it's usually a very positive stand to take, it may be a case of taking being Indigenous for granted. We can't take Indigeneity for granted. It is hard and tough enough to be Indigenous, especially against such heavy political, social, and cultural odds. On the other hand, it is too easy to be Indigenous, especially to be the very image of the Indian who is a foil and fool to the dominant culture and society. Too much is at stake for easy, convenient images to adequately and appropriately represent Indigenous people, much less to bring attention to conditions and circumstances that need to be brought to light. Indigenous writers and poets such as myself can undertake this task to the best of our abilities by creating and composing literature. We have to; there is not much choice. This is what Robert Warrior, Jace Weaver, and Craig Womack are saying. Work conscientiously, honestly, passionately, and creatively with what we have as Indigenous poets, novelists, playwrights, critics, storytellers. What we have as Indigenous people is what we are: north, west, south, east throughout the Americas from North to Central to South America, we are wealthy with many languages, Indigenous tribal histories, experience; we have no lack of cultural resources; we are enduring and resilient communities from one end of the hemisphere to the other.

While there is valid concern about the gradual loss and diminishment of Indigenous languages throughout the Indigenous hemisphere, there is, on the other hand, the opportunity to make use of English, Spanish, and French languages—and other languages of the modern world—even as we recognize they are colonial languages that have been used against us and too often we have been victimized and oppressed by them. We have to acknowledge and face historical facts; there is no use or sense in denying that colonialism has not affected us in very serious and critical ways; in fact, it is self-defeating to do so. Colonialism has driven us to the verge of vanishing; at times, in fact, we have succumbed and accepted banishment and invisibility! However, as said above, we are still "Indians"—although the term I've insisted on throughout this piece is the term Indigenous.

English has been a knotty problem for us. Like I said, it has become the most common language for many of us because of constant use and habit, since it is the language of the prominent culture and society around us and we are constantly faced with it. Indigenous people in Mexico, Central America, and South America face the same situation with Spanish, perhaps even more drastically and traumatically than we do with English language use in the United States and Canada. However, we can make use of English. But we must determine for ourselves how English is to be a part of our lives socially, culturally, and politically. We have every power within ourselves to do that, to make that determination and not to have that determination made for us. While English—and other colonial languages—may be the "enemy's language," it can be helpful and useful to us just like any other languages we have the opportunity to learn.

There is no reason for us not to speak-write in languages other than our own. My late mother and father were both fluent in speaking English; my father also spoke some Spanish, and my brother Petuuche presently does fluently. I never for a second thought my parents were less Aacqumeh hanoh for being able to speak fluently in English. Yet too often I find Indigenous people, including Acomas, holding and expressing a view that constantly speaking English threatens and jeopardizes our cultural identity as Indigenous people. We have to be careful and watchful not to get into that internalized colonized mode of thought or else we'll be limited by that kind of thinking.

Although we have to make sure we do not compromise ourselves by inadvertently speaking-writing what we don't want to mean (because English carries a lot of Western social-cultural baggage), English language writing can work to our advantage when we write with a sense of Indigenous consciousness. In *Wasase: Indigenous Pathways of Action and Freedom*, Gerald Taiaiake Alfred firmly urges such a stance: "These words are an attempt to bring forward an indigenously rooted voice of contention, unconstrained and uncompromised by colonial mentalities. A total commitment to the challenge of regenerating our indigeneity, to rootedness in Indigenous cultures, to fundamental commitment to the centrality of our truths—this book is an effort to work through the philosophical, spiritual, and practical implications of holding such commitments." Indigeneity—living by the ways of Indigenous peoples of the Americas—is so important. Does this sound like one of those elder women and men of our people, who we may have heard sometime in our lives? *We must remember the people; we must remember the way they lived with the land, culture, and community.* Can you hear them?

Simon J. Ortiz
Toronto, Ontario

Preface

[*N*ationalism is a term on a short list, one that also includes sovereignty, culture, self-determination, experience, and history, that is central to understanding the relationship between the creative expression of Native American literature and the social and historical realities that such expression embodies.] It is also, of course, a term that describes a phenomenon that has given rise, on the one hand, to modern democracy and the thirst for liberation of oppressed people around the world, and, on the other hand, some of the worst forms of political repression and xenophobia in human history. In this book, we seek to enliven discussions of what nationalism can and should mean within contemporary scholarship on Native literature.

As three authors who produced books on Native American literature within a five year period in the 1990s at a time when full-length works of literary criticism by Native scholars were still relatively rare, it was perhaps inevitable that we would come to be thought of together. "The three W's" of Native American literature, Clara Sue Kidwell called us. Yet in spite of our similarities, those three books were also quite different. Robert Warrior's book *Tribal Secrets* (1995) is about Native intellectual history, focusing on two important Indian writers, one Osage and one Sioux, and their views on sovereignty. *That the People Might Live* by Jace Weaver (1997) was a broad examination of Native written literatures from 1768 to the present and their relationship to Native community. Craig Womack's *Red on Red* (1999) argued for closer examination of the literatures of individual tribal traditions, using his own Muskogee Creek Nation as the primary example.

These interventions in Native literary criticism share a concern for developing Native criticism in conversation with both historical and contemporary Native intellectual work. In this way, the work we did in our separate projects explored the contours of what critical discourse by Native scholars could and should look like. Each for our part envisioned more vigorous intellectual exchange that would include voices from the Native intellectual past, present, and future. Fortunate for three scholars whose agendas and projects have become linked as part of an ongoing conversation, we have enjoyed each other's company intellectually, professionally, socially, and personally. Two of us have known each other since graduate school and two of us work together at the same institution in the same English department and Native American Studies program.

Our friendships with each other have been as important to us as the intellectual concerns we share, but we have not walked in lockstep since *Tribal Secrets*, *That the People Might Live*, and *Red on Red*. Warrior coauthored a history of the radical Indian activism of the 1960s and 1970s, *Like a Hurricane* (with Paul Chaat Smith). Weaver's next monograph, *Turtle Goes to War*, deals with constitutional law; a collection of his own essays published the year before took on the interdisciplinary nature of Native American Studies, containing pieces not only on literature and law but also on religion. Womack wrote a novel. Even so, our interest in the development of Native literary criticism has continued.

We first discussed working together on a project like the present one about four years ago, but other responsibilities and other projects pulled us away from it. The delay has made the book more timely. In developing as we do here concepts relating to Native American literature and nationalism, we each wanted to acknowledge and honor the foundational contribution of Simon Ortiz in his 1981 *MELUS* essay, "Towards a National Indian Literature: Cultural Authenticity in Nationalism" (included herein as an appendix). That essay is now a quarter-century old.

Ortiz's essay is a major statement from one of our major statesmen. In Ortiz's case one does not easily separate the man from his writings. Countless numbers of Native people, many who will never know Ortiz is a well-known writer, have been greeted by him at airports and bus stations and cafes, for no other reason than Simon loves meeting Indian people. This love is also evident in poems about traveling throughout America looking for Indians. No less than in his creative work, Ortiz's compassion breaks through in the non-fiction writing of "Towards a National Indian Literature" and reveals itself in sentences such as the one that concludes the essay: "It is the voice of countless other non-literary Indian women and men of this nation who live a daily life of struggle to achieve and maintain meaning which gives the most authentic character to a national Indian literature" (12).* Ortiz's exemplary humanism is evident everywhere in his stories and equally so in his life. He is a great critic as well as a great human being whose compassion extends across many lines of gender, race, and class. His important phrase "fight back," as much as anything, has to do with a profound love for America. He is our best example that a nationalist is not the same thing as an isolationist.

It is not necessary to state the obvious, the cultural authority with which Ortiz speaks, his deep connections to Acoma language, thought, tradition, politics, history. These manifest themselves throughout his writing and in his very bearing. What perhaps can be said is the way the essay deviates from the pessimism of others similarly grounded in home cultures who proclaim the imminent demise of Native ceremony, stories, language; the doom and gloom school too often assumed as the authentic voice of those most culturally intact. Ortiz represents the necessity of wedding traditionalism to intellectual rigor. To those who would put Native languages on the endangered species list, Ortiz replies,

> Along with their native languages, Indian women and men have carried on their lives and their expression through the use of the newer languages, particularly Spanish, French, and English, and they have used these languages on their own terms. This is the crucial item that has to be understood, that it is entirely possible for a people to retain and maintain their lives through the use of any language. (10)

---

*Simon J. Ortiz, "Towards a National Indian Literature: Cultural Authenticity in Nationalism," *MELUS* 8.2 (1981): 7–12.

Crucial, indeed. Ortiz, brilliantly, lays claim to English as an Indian language instead of the omnipresent cliche that Indian people are the victims of English. Claiming English as an Indian language is one of the most important, if not *the* most important step toward insuring Indian survival for future generations. This does not mean other Indian languages should be forgotten; it means *more* should be included, learned, mastered. Ortiz has gifted us with an artist's perspective on linguistic preservation that will always involve the creation of new languages. Remembering the older languages becomes no less important in Ortiz's schema; at the same time the profound Indianness of English is celebrated. This lays the groundwork to challenge the notion of the radical incommensurability between Indian languages and English, and, concurrently, the idea that when Indians write novels, poems, stories, and plays they are automatically, by default, engaged in an act of hybridity because of the supposed European origins of language and literary endeavors. Ortiz's essay is one of the important beginning points for our own arguments in this book. Ortiz seems to see nothing particularly un-Indian about novel writing and other acts of authorship. Using a religious argument to make his point, he draws a corollary between Native literature and Acoma feast days:

> Obviously, there is an overtone this is a Catholic Christian ritual celebration because of the significance of the saints' names and days on the Catholic calendar. But just as obviously, when the celebration is held within the Acqumeh community, it is an Acqumeh ceremony. It is Acqumeh and Indian (or Native American or American Indian if one prefers those terms) in the truest and most authentic sense. This is so because this celebration speaks of the creative ability of Indian people to gather in many forms of the socio-political colonizing force which beset them and to make these forms meaningful in their own terms. In fact, it is a celebration of the human spirit and the Indian struggle for liberation.
>
> Many Christian religious rituals brought to the Southwest (which in the 16th century was the northern frontier of the Spanish New World) are no longer Spanish. They are now

Indian because of the creative development that the native people applied to them. Present-day Native American or Indian literature is evidence of this in the very same way. (8)

Ortiz follows this quote by showing how Acoma people have *transformed* Catholicism into something Indian, the concept of transformation being markedly different than that of hybridization because Ortiz claims it as an Indian phenomenon rather than descending into a relativistic abyss in which Indian experience can be claimed by no one and everyone. In fact, the word "authenticity" occurs over and over again in the essay. Most critics, when confronted with the concept of authenticity, throw their hands up in the air and back away, claiming the impossibility of discussing the topic. Ortiz confronts the subject head on, recognizing the important fact that authenticity is a major concern among Native people whatever philosophical traps it might entail. Ortiz goes on to evocatively illustrate the provocative role of parody of the Spanish soldiers and Catholic priests, then tells about the Acoma songs and prayers that must be a part of their procession into the village:

> It is necessary that there be prayer and song because it is important, and no one will forget then; no one will regard it as less than momentous. It is the only way in which event and experience, such as the entry of the Spaniard to the Western Hemisphere, can become significant and realized in the people's own terms. And this, of course, is what happens in literature, to bring about meaning and meaningfulness. (9)

Ortiz, then, in the face of a burgeoning literature in 1981, (not a beginning literature since Indians had been writing in English since the 1770s and other languages centuries before contact in mesoamerica) provides the very justification for its existence and how it can be viewed as Indian. While we have certainly tried to expand on Ortiz's arguments in this volume, it is doubtful we can improve on them. This remarkable essay is central to any serious consideration of Indian literary nationalism.

Since we first considered the idea for this book, the need for something that furthers Ortiz's agenda has become to us more urgent. Though we are hardly alone in taking up the challenge Ortiz set of a Native nationalist literature and criticism (Paula Gunn Allen and Elizabeth Cook-Lynn come to mind from an earlier generation of scholars, and there are also voices like Daniel Justice, James Cox, and Lisa Brooks, who authored the Afterword to this volume, among the rising class), we still believe far too few have engaged it. Further, a backlash has developed against nationalist approaches to Native literature by those, both Native and non-Native, who find them either impossible to maintain, theoretically untenable, or simply too confrontational. We, of course, as will become clear in these pages, disagree with such analyses.

The University of Nebraska Press's publication of *Toward a Native American Critical Theory* by Elvira Pulitano galvanized our resolve actually to do the project. Pulitano, trained at the University of New Mexico by the late Louis Owens, embraces the footloose, rootless, mixed-blood hybridity that people too casually take away from Owens's work, in which both everyone and no one is Indian. It becomes impossible to espouse a Native perspective. In her attempt to articulate a "Native American critical theory," she rejects nationalist approaches to Native literature in favor of doctrinaire postmodernism. This flawed text is relatively unimportant in and of itself. Yet it, like the work of her mentor before her, has begun to be taken up methodologically by those opposed to literary nationalism and by others who pay lip service to Native sovereignty, but seem to have little or no attachment to the centrality of Native nationhood to contemporary Native people. Virtually all of these scholars use a freewheeling hybridity like that Pulitano advances as a means to validate their own identities. It seems to us the book is indicative of a wider backlash against literary nationalism, which is also often part and parcel of a rejection of tribal political sovereignty, as well.

Yet while Pulitano's book may have been the catalyst that finally ignited our collective fuse, and though each of us, in our own way, addresses her text—Craig Womack most directly and extensively—this book you hold in your hands takes up themes and issues much more important than this one piece of scholarship. It deals with the broader issues of Native literary nationalism we have all been wrestling with throughout our careers. As we make clear herein, we believe that being a nationalist is a legitimate perspective from which to approach Native American literature and criticism. We believe that such a methodology is not only defensible but that it is also crucial to supporting Native national sovereignty and self-determination, which we see as an important goal of Native American Studies generally. At the same time, however, we do *not* believe that it is the only possible approach to Native literature, and the nationalism we advance herein is not exclusionary. As we show, both Natives and non-Native allies who support tribal national sovereignty and nationalist readings of Native literature are welcome at our table. Moreover, we realize that many will see tensions even between us as authors. While we could have tried to reconcile our ideas in light of one another's claims, we decided to let divergent viewpoints stand in the hope of a literary nationalism that endorses *free expression* as much as uniformity of opinion.

More than three and a half decades into the academic legitimation of Native American literature, we are among those who see a continuing need for more Native voices articulating literary criticism and for better, clearer thinking about what links that literature to communities. We are not ashamed to say we love both. Concomitantly, we believe that the intellectual health of Native communities and the quality of critical discourse that emerges alongside Native literature requires attention to the ways Native scholars articulate and deploy the methods and parameters of a "Native critical theory" or a "Native American literary criticism."

In 1968, at the dawning of the Black Power movement, Stokely Carmichael declared, "For once, black people are going to use the words they want to use—not just the words whites want to hear. And they will do this no matter how often the press tries to stop the use of the slogan [Black Power] by equating it with racism or separatism." All three of us have been accused either directly or indirectly of promoting both, largely, we think, because we remain committed to an old and persisting dream in which indigenous groups in the Americas author their own destinies as distinct peoples with a discrete political status in this world. So long as that dream continues, we will remain committed to doing the best intellectual work we can to undergird and foster it.

That dream
shall have a name
after all,

and it will not be vengeful
but wealthy with love
and compassion
and knowledge.
And it will rise
in this heart
which is our America.
        —Simon J. Ortiz,
        From Sand Creek

I LOST MY TALK

I lost my talk
The talk you took away.
When I was a little girl
At Shubenacadie school.

You snatched it away:
I speak like you
I think like you
I create like you
The scrambled ballad,
    about my word.

Two ways I talk
Both ways I say,
Your way is more powerful.

So gently I offer my
    hand and ask,
Let me find my talk
So I can teach you about me.
    —Rita Joe[1]

Blatant colonialism mutilates you without pretense:
It forbids you to talk, it forbids you to act, it forbids you
to exist. Invisible colonialism, however, convinces you
that serfdom is your destiny and impotence is your nature;
it convinces you that it's not possible to speak, not possible
to act, not possible to exist.
    —Eduardo Galeano[2]

Aboriginal literature and creative arts need to be expanded
and infused with their unique Indigenous vision.... We must
not mistake enthusiastic reception by the white middle-class
as a measure of literary or artistic success of Aboriginal artists.
Popularity may mean the Aboriginal work harmonizes
with the archaic racial stereotypes of Eurocentric society.
If it does not, then most white readers are likely to
disbelieve and discredit the creative work.
    —Howard Adams[3]

Chapter One
Splitting the Earth
First Utterances and Pluralist Separatism

I. "Hello, Englishmen!"

"Salaam Alaykum." As preposterous as it might seem, those may be the first words Natives ever heard uttered by Christopher Columbus. Although, at this late date, we will never be able to know with certainty, the notion is not as odd as it appears at first blush. Arabic was the lingua franca of the era. It was assumed that any person engaged in commerce would speak it, and Columbus believed he had reached the Indies—that is to say, Asia. His interpreter was fluent in it. The charts that Columbus took on his voyage had been drafted by Moorish cartographers. In fact, his entire enterprise was only possible because the Moors had been forced off the Iberian Peninsula after years of bloody warfare.[4]

Reversing the gaze, historically we know that the first words spoken by an Indian to the would-be colonists of Plimouth Plantation were, "Hello, Englishmen!" They were reportedly uttered by Squanto, who had been captured and sold into slavery abroad before escaping and returning to his Patuxet people, becoming in the process perhaps one of the first modern cosmopolitans.[5]

Taken together, these two first utterances and the events surrounding them (which could be replicated many times over) reflect the truth that much of the received history of this place has been a mono-cultural imposition on what, from the very inception, was a multicultural encounter.

Almost five hundred years after Columbus befuddled no-doubt-curious indigenes on a beach in the Caribbean with his elocution, Acoma poet and scholar Simon Ortiz, in a very different kind of first utterance, laid the groundwork for a Native American literary nationalism in his seminal article "Towards a National Indian Literature: Cultural Authenticity in Nationalism," published in the Summer of 1981 in *MELUS*. Despite the importance of Ortiz's call for recognition of Native American literature as a distinctive discourse, nearly twenty-five years later, most non-Native literary critics continue to remain blind to the unique character of Native American literature and either oblivious or hostile to the work of their fellow critics who are themselves Indian about that literature. They remain most interested in those indigenes who provide them with an entrée into Native culture, who appear to offer initiation into a hidden world of tribal wisdom.

Too often non-Native critics want their Natives to be Squanto, kidnapped and traduced and coming home speaking the language of the colonizer; la Malinche, translator and concubine, progenitress of a fictive, thoroughly *mestizaje raza* of Mexico; or Pocahontas, sacrificing her body and her health on the altar of mediation, becoming in the process the guarantor of indigeneity for the Lees, the Randolphs, the Symingtons, and others who call themselves, utterly devoid of irony, the First Families of Virginia. They prefer Sarah Winnemucca to Red Cloud, Gertrude Bonnin to Richard Fields.[6]

In his book *Ethnocriticism*, Arnold Krupat observed that "what might be called an 'indigenous' criticism for Indian literatures remains to be worked out." By "Indian literatures," he was referring to the "traditional Indian expression" of orature, excluding "poetry and fiction . . . work *written* in English for publication."[7] Yet even if one were to expand his definition to encompass written literatures, Krupat's statement would still have been accurate. Though Ortiz's challenge was more than a decade old at the time, criticism of Native literature by Natives had proceeded only sporadically and spasmodically. Paula Gunn Allen's wide-ranging *The Sacred Hoop: Recovering the Feminine in American Indian Traditions*, a landmark (for all its essentialism), had been published in 1986. But

Louis Owens's *Other Destinies: Understanding the American Indian Novel* appeared in 1992, the same year as *Ethnocriticism*. The following year, Jeannette Armstrong edited *Looking at the Words of our People: First Nations Analysis of Literature*. In it Kimberley Blaeser wrote:

> Recognizing that the literatures of Native Americans have a
> unique voice and that voice has not always been adequately
> or accurately explored in the criticism that has been written
> about the literature, I have begun in the last few years to be
> attentive to other ways of talking about the literature of the
> First Peoples. Particularly, I have been alert for critical methods
> and voices that seem to arise out of the literature itself (this as
> opposed to critical approaches applied from already established
> critical language or attempts to make the literature fit already
> established genres and categories of meaning). So far, I have
> uncovered only fitful attempts to fashion this interpretive
> method or give voice to this new critical language."[8]

Howard Adams relates an incident that took place at the University of Saskatchewan at almost the same historical moment as Blaeser's statement. Cree playwright Tomson Highway was scheduled to speak. The leaflet for his appearance stated, "He reads Dostoevsky, plays Chopin on the piano and sprinkles his conversations with references to classical Greek drama." Adams comments, "This suggests the presenters were fearful an outstanding Canadian Aboriginal could not attract an audience without being allied with famous European artists and people."[9] This may be right, but it sounds more like a sideshow barker's pitch: "Step right up, ladies and gentlemen, and see the chimpanzee who signs Chekhov! See the monkey who types with his feet!" It is little different than those on the Chautauqua circuit who came to gape in amazement at E. Pauline Johnson, the savage who wrote poetry and prose a century past, or decades before that those who went to see Elias Boudinot lecture—"with curiosity and anticipation the audience prepared to listen to an Indian direct from the wild."[10] Such an ongoing fascination with Native cultures perceived as exotic remains an impediment to critics who advocate Native national literatures.

The early 1990s are not that long ago in chronological time, but in scholarly terms, they are aeons ago in some ways. At the time Krupat and Blaeser spoke about the lack of a Native American literary criticism, Kenneth Lincoln's announcement of the "Native American Renaissance" in literature was barely twenty years old, though Native American written literatures in English already went back more than two centuries. Since then, however, there has developed a rich and varied literary criticism by Native scholars, including not only Allen, Owens, and Blaeser but also figures as diverse as Elizabeth Cook-Lynn, Gerald Vizenor, Thomas King, Lee Maracle, Kateri Akiwenzie Damm, Armand Ruffo, Greg Sarris, Kathryn Shanley, Geary Hobson, and Daniel Justice (many of whom were writing earlier, as well), to name but a very few. In addition, the major works of all three authors of this book came after this moment I single out in the early nineties.

In some ways that moment is distant. In other ways, little has changed. Despite the ever-increasing output, Native criticism often remains curiously invisible. Susan Berry Brill de Ramirez, for instance, in her *Contemporary American Indian Literatures and the Oral Tradition*, despite citing several Native critics, deploys Krupat's statement quoted above seven years on, in 1999.[11] It is in some ways hardly surprising that non-Natives would continue to replicate this discourse of lacking with regard to Native literary criticism. Amer-Europeans have always most regarded Native cultures as static and unchanging. They want them to remain flies in amber, beautiful, pristine, and ultimately cold, dead, and sterile. Sadly, however, it is not only non-Natives that seemingly remain mired in that 1992–93 instant, ignorant of much that has come since.

A few years ago, a young woman was introduced to me at a conference on Native American literature. She identified herself as Native and said that she was writing her dissertation on Native literature, applying Craig Womack's critical model from *Red on Red*. When we met, she said that *people at the conference* had told her that she should read Robert Warrior's and my books—what did I think? Encounters with under-informed graduate students are not peculiar to Native American Studies (NAS), but probably only in NAS do you have persons involved as advisors who know little or nothing about the state of the field, so that doctoral work becomes essentially unsupervised research. A junior

Native scholar (though senior to me in age) recently reviewed my book *Other Words*, calling it a "good first step along the Red Road," although I was publishing in the field before he got his PhD.[12]

Gros Ventre critic Sidner Larson, in his book, *Captured in the Middle: Tradition and Experience in Contemporary Native American Writing*, suggests a way to "move forward" what he contends is a stalled Native American criticism. He recommends "supplementing scholarly analysis with dialogues as much as possible to avoid single-author texts."[13] Though, given the multiplicity of Native voices now being raised regarding indigenous literature, we—the authors of this book—are somewhat baffled by his contention that we are somehow stymied, we agree unequivocally on the need for dialogue. Perhaps he was referring to the ignorance to which I just referred. It is difficult to build up a nationalist criticism if its proponents and would-be fellow travelers engage in unsupervised research and remain ignorant of the work of others in the field. As Native critics, we all have an obligation to know each other's work and to be in conversation with each other (even if we do not cite each other explicitly). The answer (if "answer" is the right word) in Native American literary criticism, as it is in all of discourse, is more discourse, not less—more quality discourse. In this book and our articulation of American Indian Literary Nationalism, we are not only responding to Ortiz and Blaeser. In the way we approach the project, we are also attempting to rise to Larson's challenge to engage in collaborative work as well. In so doing, however, we are acutely aware that we are going against another central tenet of Larson's analytical approach.

Larson writes, "I am intrigued by a transformative project that seeks to influence culture by means other than militant or nationalist approaches." He then states, "I have American Indian academic colleagues and nonacademic friends who are cultural nationalists, which means they are often militant and confrontational. Certainly there is much cause for activism in the American Indian world, and I am grateful there are those willing to do the necessary work of demanding redress of the theft and genocide committed against American Indians. In fact, their good work allows me to emphasize the things different cultural peoples have in common . . . "[14] Larson says he is particularly concerned about the increasing penchant of Native scholars to criticize other Natives. Are we still so fragile in Native American Studies that we can brook no criticism of each other's theories and opinions? To be sure, not all Native critics are literary nationalists, as Larson's example illustrates. Yet as I wrote in my book *Native American Religious Identity: Unforgotten Gods*, "Critique . . . is not dismissal. And our communities arrive at an approximation of truth and right action as they always have, through honest sharing, discussion, and consensus."[15] The hour is late in the history of imperialism and colonialism. We see no advantage in eschewing confrontation, but we do not see all criticism as confrontation. At the same time, we recognize, as does Larson, that there is more that unites us as Native persons and scholars, both experientially and intellectually, than divides us.

At its most profound, literary nationalism is not a confrontation, not a tearing down, but an upbuilding. We believe this is what sets us apart from our fellow critics who seem to expend all their energy in exposing and attacking "the evil White man" and his "racist hegemony" over publishing and universities and so forth. While we do not avoid confrontation and while we will continue to critique those critics, both Native and non-Native, with whom we disagree or whom we see as misguided or, worse, destructive of Native agency and self-determination, we would rather commit considerable energy to the explication of specific Native values, readings, and knowledges and their relevance to our contemporary lives. This difference in focus is crucial to American Indian Literary Nationalism.

The colonial process has always depended upon division and the power to bestow names. Most of our peoples are known popularly today by names they did not call themselves. Ani yv' wiya became Cherokee. Anishinaabe became Ojibway or Chippewa or Cree. Dakota, Lakota, and Nakota became Sioux. As Gerald Taiaiake Alfred states, "The imposition of labels and definitions of identity on indigenous people has been a central feature of the colonization process from the start."[16] Or as Maori scholar Linda Tuhiwai Smith puts it succinctly in her book *Decolonizing Methodologies: Research and Indigenous Peoples*, "Fragmentation is not a phenomenon of postmodernism as many might claim. For indigenous peoples fragmentation has been the consequence of imperialism."[17]

It was, of course, not only peoples who were renamed and thus changed and recast; it was also the place itself. In Tasmania, where

George Augustus Robinson, the government appointed "saviour" of Tasmanian Aborigines, christened natives with new names like Queen Elizabeth, King George, Washington, Milton, Romeo, Andromache, Hector, Nimrod, Cleopatra, and, most provocatively, Colombus and Friday, the land itself also received new divisions and a nomenclature deemed more appropriate. As Palawa artist Julie Gough writes:

> This act of naming was the European means of deliberately (linguistically then actually) displacing the original tenants in order to claim ownership and control. The land and the people had therefore no past, (re)emerging with names at the same time that the settlers had titled their new properties and districts in Tasmania. These provinces were, derivatively, named after 'home'—England: 'Kent,' 'Buckingham,' 'Cumberland,' 'Dorset,' 'Devon,' 'Westmoreland,' 'Glamorgan,' 'Somerset,' 'Pembroke,' 'Monmouth,' 'Cornwall' and 'Hobarton.' In fact, to become the promised land rather than purely the familiar, towns and places were called 'Paradise,' 'Golconda,' 'Jericho,' 'Bagdad,' 'Stonehenge,' 'Jerusalem,' 'Tiberius' and 'Mangalore,' to suggest a sense of history that the land here was not recognised by the settler/invader culture to have.[18]

Such a process was replicated over the entire colonized world. In North America, names such as Bethlehem, Salem ("Jerusalem"), and Antioch sprouted on the landscape. What Wallace Stegner so eloquently dubbed "a geography of hope" was for indigenous peoples a geographic erasure.

Canadian poet P. K. Page's familiar "Cook's Mountains," about the Glass House Mountains in Australia, runs:

By naming then he made them.
They were there
before he came
but they were not the same.
It was his gaze
that glazed each one.
He saw

the Glass House Mountains in his glass.
They shone.

And still they shine.
We saw them as we drove—
sudden, surrealist, conical
they rose
out of the rain forest.
The driver said,
"Those are the Glass House Mountains up ahead."

And instantly they altered to become
the sum of shape and name.
Two strangenesses united into one
more strange than either.
Neither of us now
remembers how they looked before they broke
the light to fragments as the driver spoke. .

Like mounds of mica
hive-shaped hothouses,
mountains of mirror glimmering
they form
in diamond panes behind the tree ferns of
the dark imagination,
burn and shake
the lovely light of Queensland like a bell
reflecting Cook upon a deck
his tongue
silvered with paradox and metaphor.[19]

Named in Captain Cook's imperial gaze, of course, if one reads closely, is more than a single topographic feature. It is also an entire place, once/still Aboriginal, Queensland—the Queen's land. Conquest is written with a word and the stroke of the pen.

Whenever I read or hear Page's reverie, I think of the Glass Mountains back home in Oklahoma in Cheyenne territory. Those were named because an English surveyor saw the silica-rich mesas and proclaimed, "They shine just like glass." Surely they glimmered for Indians just as they did for that purveyor of names and as they still do today, even though most modern-day Oklahomans are ignorant of the "genuine" name—a heavily accented British, pronounced "gloss." Those mountains are glossed by a language utterly foreign to them, that White/white frost covering the name spoken by those who first loved them and held them sacred.

In describing the poem in his powerhouse-turn 2002 Sedgewick Lecture, W. H. New said, "The point about metaphors is that they have the power to make us see things in a particular way, and of course once we see them that way we sometimes have to free ourselves from the metaphor in order to understand how in some loose sense we're being politically constrained." New continues:

> What's wrong with metaphors of simple colonial reflection is more or less the same thing that the Cherokee-German-Greek-American-Canadian writer Thomas King rails against in "Godzilla vs. Post-Colonial." As King makes clear, the term "postcolonial"... is not free from the rumble of political assumption and political desire. The chronological linearity suggested by one reading of the *post* in postcolonial, King affirms—like the limited authority granted the branch/daughter/fragment figures—implicitly assumes a hierarchical relation between here and there, near and far, now and then. In the case of aboriginal peoples, "postcolonial" (in King's reading of the term) also suggests that there was no *precolonial*, no culture or cultures in place prior to the arrival of English (or French, or any other European language) to which contemporary people might look back with pride or on whose integrity they might in some measure continue rewardingly to draw. Like P. K. Page's Captain Cook in Queensland, the imperial language *un-names* even as it names anew.[20]

To push/deconstruct New's notion of metaphor a bit more: it was before autochthonous notions of the temporal were pushed aside, and time was chopped into uniform measured parcels, recorded from Greenwich, and this place was judged far from that colonial center.

Before going on with any with discussion of American Indian Literary Nationalism, there is a fallacious but persistently invoked issue that must be addressed. This is the question of whether Amer-Europeans can or should do Native American Studies. No matter how many times we say otherwise, certain whites contend that those of us who claim a national-ist stance do not want non-Natives doing Native American Studies. Robert Dale Parker, for instance, in discussing Craig Womack's *Red on Red*, has written, "Just as I do not find Womack's arguments for essentialism con-vincing or well informed about critical debates around essentialism, so I can't abide his implication that non-Native critics cannot contribute help-fully to the discussion of Native American literature."[21] I do not read Womack's work this way: rather I see him simply saying that in reading literature one should privilege internal cultural readings. Notice that it is nothing that Womack says explicitly to which Parker is reacting. Rather, it is his "implication"—actually Parker's own highly charged inference.

Daniel Justice, who also approaches Native literatures from a nation-alist direction, writes: "To ground one's work within Indigenous episte-mologies is not a necessarily exclusivist act that seeks an idealized cultural purity. Rather, it is, at its core, a deeply realistic and life-affirming act." He then quotes Womack on this very point:

> I would like to think . . . that I have not written *Red on Red*
> in a rejectionist mode but that, to the contrary, I seek to
> examine these histories to search for those ideas, articulated
> by Indian people, that best serve a contemporary critical
> framework. More specifically, in terms of a Creek national
> literature, the process has been based on the assumption
> that it is valuable to look toward Creek authors and their
> works to understand Creek writing. My argument is not
> that this is the *only* way to understand Creek writing
> but an important one given that literatures bear some
> kind of relationship to communities, both writing
> communities and the community of the primary culture,
> from which they originate.

Justice then continues, "Intellectual sovereignty doesn't presume an insistence on tribal-centered scholarship as the *exclusive* model of sensitive or insightful analysis. It does, however, privilege an understanding of community as being important to a nuanced reading of the text. This notion is rarely questioned in other areas of inquiry—after all, historical and cultural context is generally seen as essential to any substantive understanding of Shakespeare's plays—but the reactionary howl of 'essentialism' rises up when we try to apply similar methods to minority literatures."[22]

Parker himself states, "'Scholars who write about an ethnic group to which they do not belong,' notes bell hooks, 'rarely discuss in the introductions to their work the ethical issues of their race privilege.' I am white and lament, as hooks notes, some people may unwittingly attribute greater authority to the work of white scholars. I would rather that people approached my work with extra skepticism. There is a great deal that some Native critics will understand that I would never appreciate. But just as my failures cannot reduce to my whiteness, so to reduce Native scholars' insights to their Nativeness would demean the work it took to reach those insights."[23]

Let me be explicit and I hope (for the last time) coruscatingly clear: I have never said, nor have I ever heard any responsible Native scholar say, that non-Natives should not do Native American Studies, much less the study of Native American literature, any more than Natives should prescind from bringing their own insights to literature by anyone else. (The late Louis Owens was, among his other accomplishments as a creative writer and critic of Native literature, a talented Steinbeck scholar.) It is not our intent simply to superinduce Native scholars for white ones. We need simpatico and knowledgeable Amer-European critical allies. Alan Velie, Lavonne Ruoff, Karl Kroeber, Bill New, and the late Elaine Jahner come to mind. In the rising generation, Michael Elliot, Maureen Konkle, and James Cox have each made important interventions and doubtless will make more. And all these names stand amidst many others. We *want* non-Natives to read, engage, and study Native literature. The survival of Native authors, if not Native people in general, depends on it. But we do not need modern literary colonizers. We only ask that non-Natives who study and write about Native peoples do so with respect and a sense of responsibility to Native community. The same applies to Native scholars. We ask no more from others than we ask of ourselves, but neither do we expect less.

Some years ago, I appeared with Cornel West on a television program on multiculturalism, moderated by Charlayne Hunter-Gault. I made the point that we welcome allies (given our numbers, we need as many as we can get), so long as they don't come as cultural tourists or, worse, cultural voyeurs—or doing Native literature because they need to make their name, or need a job and see Native American Studies (possibly coupled with a distant and dimly known Native ancestry) as the chance at employment, or because they perceive multiculturalism or diversity to be the academic currency of the day. West agreed with me, adding, "I don't care if a white sister wants to sing 'Precious Lord.' I just don't expect it to sound like Mahalia."

Too often, non-Native critics have no real knowledge of, let alone commitment to, Native communities. They simply want to read Native texts without ever engaging, let alone encountering, Native peoples. In this they are little different than early anthropologists who exploited their indigenous "informants," and saw themselves as adding the value for increase in the "universal" body of knowledge, even as they burnished the luster of their own careers. If one is to study and write about Native Americans and their literatures, one must be prepared to listen to and respect Native voices and, in keeping with the traditional Native ethic of reciprocity, not take without giving something back.

In 1829, with the death of Shawnadithit, the Beothuk of Newfoundland were proclaimed extinct. Her withering expiration from consumption has become an iconic moment in the settler-colony history of Canada. For years, she was known only by a portrait of a girl with vacant eyes. Poet Al Pittman ascribes a wan, thanatic agency to the image, her martyr-like eyes those of someone waiting for her own surcease:

> *knowing that beyond all kindred deaths*
> *yours will matter most.*

The image, we now know, was that, not of her, but of her aunt, Demasduwit, or Mary March (so-called for the month in which she was captured).[24]

In a statement that could apply equally to "American" literature, W. H. New writes:

> The time is not so distant when the "Native" was a
> conventional figure in Canadian literature—but not a voice
> (or a figure allowed separate voices). If Native characters
> spoke, they spoke in archaisms or without articles, in the
> sham eloquence of florid romance or the muted syllables of
> deprivation. If Native characters moved, they moved according
> to European schedules of arrangement, as faithful friends or
> savage foes, or as marginal figures the mighty could afford to
> ignore. Over the course of time, even historical individuals
> turned from persons into signs. As far as textbooks were
> concerned, fictions were as acceptable as fact. Shananditti
> became a figure of curiosity, though few admitted to start
> with that this position was artificially constructed. It was
> genocide that made her *the last of the Beothuks*, and therefore
> tragic. (But, says the literary echo, also "romantic": *the last
> of the Mohicans* was a phrase ready to hand, ready to explain
> the "reality" away.)[25]

Terry Goldie points out that white Canadians, when challenged by scholars "about the inaccuracies of theories of an active genocide," by their reaction "made it clear that they wished to maintain their guilt; they did not wish to be absolved or forgiven."[26] Pittman, in his poem "Shanadithit," admits that his love for Shawnadithit has nothing to do with the woman herself as she was

> *or might have been in those few*
> *of your own dead-end days.*

Similarly, Chauncey Yellow Robe, in his prologue to the 1930 film *The Silent Enemy*, states:

> This picture is the story of my people. I speak for them
> because I know your language. In the beginning the Great

Spirit give us this land. The wild game was ours to hunt.
We were happy when game was plenty. In years of famine
we suffered.

Soon we will be gone. Your civilization will have
destroyed us. But by your magic we will live forever. We
thank the white men who help us to make this picture. They
came to our forest. They share our hardships. They listened
to our old men around the campfire. We told them the stories
our grandfathers told us. That is why this picture is real.

Look not upon us as actors. We are living our own life
today as we live it yesterday. Everything you see is as it always
has been: our buckskin clothes, our birch bark canoes, our
wigwams, and our bows and arrows. All were made by my
people just as they always have done.

Only six of these Indians have ever seen a motion picture.
Many of them are still in the forest, hunting game which is
ever growing less. Still they feel the great drummer of the
North, this struggle for meat, a never-ending fight against
the silent enemy.[27]

The aged Rosebud Sioux, playing an Anishinaabe chief in the film but
introduced as himself here, assures the theater-going audience as to the
verisimilitude—indeed absolute accuracy—of what they are about to
see. He then *re*assures them that it is nonetheless past. He thanks them
for the fact that the Indian, though imminently vanishing, will always
live thanks to the white man's technology ("magic"). They will be seen,
and they will move, but theirs will be nonetheless a cryogenic survival,
frozen forever in silver nitrate. *The Silent Enemy* was originally made
without sound, but the emergence of talkies while the movie was still in
production led to the addition of Yellow Robe's monologue as a mar-
keting device. After he waves his symbolic goodbye, the film and the
Indians in it lapse into silence.

The ultimate imperative of settler colonialism is the "construction of
margins"—"to displace one language of perception with a self-justifying
substitute."[28] Natives, it seems, in the audition of settler colonizers are permitted first utterances and dying words but nothing in between.

II. "Let a Thousand Separatisms Bloom"

American Indian Literary Nationalism does not have two different senses. It does, however, have two prongs. The first relates to the consideration of Native American literary output as separate and distinct from other national literatures. The second deals with a criticism of that literature that supports not only its distinct identity but also sees itself as attempting to serve the interests of indigenes and their communities, in particular the support of Native nations and their own separate sovereignties. This is an essential component of what I have identified as communitism, a word of my own coinage from the words "community" and "activism" and signifying a proactive commitment to Native community.

First in my monograph *That the People Might Live*, and later in my book *Other Words*, I argue for Native American literature as something apart from American literature (or, by extension, from Canadian literature or any other national literature of the Americas). Amid a larger set of arguments, I quote Bill Ashcroft, Gareth Griffiths, and Helen Tiffins, from their now much overworked text on postcolonial literatures, *The Empire Writes Back*: "Indigenous writing has suffered many of the general historical problems of post-colonial writing, [including] being incorporated into the national literatures of the settler colonies as an 'extension' rather than as a separate discourse."[29] I write:

> Such incorporation denies Native literature recognition
> of its own distinct existence, specific differences, and
> independent status as literary production and, as Owens
> contends, retards consideration of Native works in their
> own cultural contexts. The very fact that Thomas King,
> E. Pauline Johnson (Mohawk), Peter Jones (Anishinaabe),
> and George Copway (Anishinaabe)—among others—
> can be, and have been claimed at various times and for
> various purposes as part of the national literatures of
> both the United States and Canada says that something
> more important and complex is occurring in Native
> literature, something that merits recognition as a
> separate discourse.[30]

Writings by Native Americans might be considered American literature, if that term is taken as meaning simply literature produced within
the geographic boundaries that today comprise the United States (though
this feeds an indigenizing impulse on the part of Amer-Europeans, and
I believe it begs other important issues). Although we might concede
this, neither James Fenimore Cooper's *Leather-Stocking Tales*, nor Helen
Hunt Jackson's *Ramona*, nor Arnold Krupat's *Woodsmen, or Thoreau
and the Indians* can ever be Native American literature, any more than
Peter Høeg's *Smilla's Sense of Snow* is Greenlander Inuit literature, or
James Hilton's *Lost Horizon* can be considered Tibetan literature, or
"Merchant of Venice" included among Jewish drama simply by reason
of the presence of Shylock. Native American literature, it must be said
finally (and we would have thought it was obvious), is literature of, from,
by Native Americans, not *about* them—or, worse yet, *set* among them.

The primary problem with a film like *Dances with Wolves* is neither its depictions of indigenes nor its perpetuation of the "tragic mistake doctrine" that absolves imperial power structures of culpability in
genocide—though, obviously, these are indeed problematic. Rather, it is
simply that many filmgoers don't comprehend that ultimately it is a film
about two Amer-Europeans, Kevin Costner's stalwart Lt. Dunbar and
his white captive paramour. Similarly, the recent *Windtalkers*, by Hong
Kong action director John Woo now working in the United States, was
promoted as an account of the Navajo codetalkers of World War II; in
reality, however, it is the story of Nicholas Cage's white Marine sergeant,
with Natives simply serving as props, the means of his spiritual redemp-
tion. From Cooper to Louis L'Amour and Tony Hillerman the thread is
one of a journey of self-discovery by Amer-Europeans along an indigenizing path that must lead through Indian Country. It is a phenomenon
that Paiute writer Adrian Louis lampoons in "Edwin's Letter About *A
Man Called Horse*," writing, "This man named Horse wanted to be an
Indian more than anything. It just wasn't fair, he thought, that Indianness
was wasted on Indians who did not appreciate their noble status."
Louis's Edwin says, "Americans are hungry for Indian lore as long as
they never have to smell a real live Indian."[31]

In the book of his Sedgewick Lecture, *Grandchild of Empire: About
Irony, Mainly in the Commonwealth*, Bill New discusses the distinction

between the literatures of settler colonies and those of their indigenes. He writes that the assumptions

behind the distinction "Settler/Subjugated" are ... open to analysis. Among these assumptions are those derived from any given society's social values. How these are established sets up still more questions: What priority, for example, does a society attach to ancestral rights and property rights? to occupation and ownership? to claim and displacement, movement by force or necessity and movement by free choice? to identification by means of exile and identification with reference to home? to centrality or marginality, colour, gender, language, belief and general access to opportunity? Whatever pattern emerges from answers to these questions will spell out a society's organization and—in a very general way—affect and contextualize its literary culture.[32]

As each of us has illustrated, Native literature proceeds from different assumptions and embodies different values from American literature.

This brings us to the second prong of American Indian Literary Nationalism, that of criticism. Just as Native American literature by definition can only be produced by Native writers, so Native American literary criticism (in contrast to criticism of Native American literature) must be in the hands of Native critics to define and articulate, from resources *we* choose. It must be simply a criticism of our own. This, it seems to me, is the essence of intellectual sovereignty. Mohawk critic Gerald Taiaiake Alfred puts the matter succinctly when he notes, "Our deference to other people's solutions has taken a terrible toll on indigenous peoples."[33]

Despite what to us seems a self-evident fact, some non-Natives persist not only in evaluation of our literatures and in judging our criticism but in prescribing how we must go about our own business. As New writes in his editorial introduction to *Native Writers and Canadian Writing*, "Sometimes people are willing to listen only to those voices that confirm the conventions they already know. The unfamiliar makes them fear. Or makes them condescend. Neither fear nor condescension encourages listening. And no one who does not listen learns to hear."[34]

For example, in spite of their acknowledgment of the damage resulting from indigenous literatures "being incorporated into the national literatures of the settler colonies as an 'extension' rather than as a separate
discourse," Ashcroft, Griffiths, and Tiffin also have attempted, as
Chadwick Allen points out in *Blood Narrative*, "to discipline supposedly wayward indigenous activists and writers for not following the techniques that orthodox postcolonial theory prefers, most prominently,
ambivalence, hybridity, pastiche, and fragmentation."[35] While admit-
ting some validity to their critique, Allen contends there is "also an element of barely concealed paternalism." He responds:

> Indigenous minority discourses pose a problem for those
> postcolonial theories that designate "essentialism,"
> "nativism," "nationalism," and so forth as anachronistic
> politics, because indigenous minority discourses often
> emphasize land and treaty rights and because they often insist
> on persistent racial, cultural, and linguistic distinctiveness
> despite other changes over time. They provoke charges of a
> retrograde "essentialism," in particular, because orthodox
> postcolonial critics often fail to understand how discourses
> that intersect with the controversial blood/land/memory
> complex, including the discourse of treaties, might appear
> cogent for indigenous activists and writers. A number of
> critics of orthodox postcolonial theory have argued, in other
> contexts, that nationalism, tribalism, and sovereignty are not
> simply matters of individual identity and the development of
> self-esteem or exercises in "word play." But these terms have
> a particular resonance for indigenous minority writers and
> activists in the early contemporary period. Their right to assert
> an indigenous nationalism or sovereignty distinct from and
> potentially in opposition to that of settler-invaders had been
> not only historically suppressed but also perennially
> disavowed—and it continues to be disavowed today.[36]

In her book *Toward a Native American Critical Theory*, Elvira
Pulitano, an Italian scholar who studied in the United States with the

late Louis Owens and now teaches in Switzerland, chastises Native nationalist critics, in a vein similar to Ashcroft, Griffiths, and Tiffin. She criticizes them for their failure to acknowledge their hybridity and for their refusal to engage and utilize the tools of high theory and postcolonial discourse. She sets herself the task of discussing the work in critical theory produced by Native Americans, outlining its foundations and parameters. Even the title of the monograph, probably one of the most misguided texts and one potentially most pernicious to indigenous agency published in Native American literary studies in a decade, bespeaks of the same "barely concealed paternalism" Allen observed in Ashcroft, Griffiths, and Tiffin.

Pulitano identifies two different emerging strands within Native literary criticism, the "separatist" (or nationalist) and the "dialogic." To explicate these two approaches, she examines the work of six contemporary critics: Paula Gunn Allen, Robert Warrior, Craig Womack, Greg Sarris, Gerald Vizenor, and Louis Owens. She explicitly excludes non-Native critics (Krupat, Velie, Jahner, James Ruppert), except, of course, herself (and those, in turn, like Krupat, whom she quotes extensively in a highly mediated fashion). Though she professes to appreciate the importance of all her exemplars, she clearly prefers the relative inclusiveness of her dialogic critics (who discuss a "mixed-blood" positionality or multiple identities) to those who take a more recognizable nationalist stance. On the first page, she asks a series of crucial questions: "Is there such a thing as a Native American critical theory? If so, how should we define it? As a non-Native critic, am I entitled to define it? Does my 'speaking about' necessarily mean 'speaking for'?" Only on the book's penultimate page does she fully admit her ideological agenda, writing, "As a non-Native critic presenting this material from the outside, but implicating and exposing my own readerly position as well, it appears quite natural for me to embrace the crosscultural dialogic approach of Sarris, Owens, and Vizenor, rather than the separatist stances of Allen, Warrior, and Womack."37 "Well, hello, Englishmen," Squanto said again.

Despite her self-acknowledged status as an outsider/outlander, Pulitano does not hesitate to be prescriptive. Ex cathedra statements abound. Far from simply discussing emerging critical dialogue, she gives herself permission to contest divergent Native points of view and to determine which are "valid." She becomes within the four corners of her text the arbiter of the worthy.[38]

In particular, Pulitano spanks her three nationalists (Allen, Warrior, and Womack) for their refusal to engage high theory. She accuses them of running the risk of essentialism and of promoting romantic notions of "Indianness," since they are inextricably imbricated in Western culture and academic discourse. Her discussion, however, shows her to be the one engaged in romanticism and essentialism. Concerns about purity, legitimacy, validity, and authenticity run like red threads through the discussion, the words themselves and their variations appearing repeatedly. In discussing Warrior's *Tribal Secrets*, she queries how his subjects, John Joseph Mathews and Vine Deloria, Jr., can provide a basis for a "valid" Native intellectual tradition when both were highly educated and their experiences were so cosmopolitan.[39] Apparently, the more educated an Indian is in a Western institutional sense and the better traveled, the less "authentic."

Pulitano contends that what marks all her six subjects is their attempt to bring the orality of Native traditions into the world of written criticism, but she immediately excludes Warrior from this in a footnote because his "critical strategy follows a more traditional Western rhetorical pattern."[40] She criticizes Womack for his "Creekcentric" approach in *Red on Red* because once "oral tradition enters into dialogue with the rhetorical systems of the Western tradition" it becomes impossible to discuss "an authentic Native perspective." Womack's approach, she avers, "means turning Native identity into a textual commodity that continues to perpetuate fabricated versions of Indianness."[41] Yet, despite postmodern claims of fragmented, fractionated, and multiple identities, Native identity is not freewheeling and infinitely refracted. One cannot, for instance, dream oneself Indian while possessing no Native ancestry. Not even the most louche critic would contend so.[42]

In her book *Race and Time*, Janet Gray writes, "For all we might do to deconstruct race, to expose its lack of essence, the historical experience of race does not go away—not from the past, not from the present. Critical methods can expose how race gets made in its historical forms, but only as a kind of formalist fantasy does that exposure reduce race to an idea that has no use."[43] For instance, in a similar vein, Henry Louis Gates observes:

> To declare that race is a trope, however, is not to deny its palpable force in the life of every African-American who tries to function every day in a still very racist America. In the face of Anthony Appiah's and my own critique of what we might think of as "black essentialism," Houston Baker demands that we remember what we might characterize as the "taxi fallacy."
>
> Houston, Anthony, and I emerge from the splendid isolation of the Schomburg Library and stand together on the corner of 135th Street and Malcolm X Boulevard attempting to hail a taxi to return to the Yale Club. With the taxis shooting by us as if we did not exist, Anthony and I cry out in perplexity, "But sir, it's only a trope."[44]

To return to Gray, she critiques Walter Benn Michaels's contention that race "is either an essence or an illusion" and "the concept of a raced 'cultural identity' as masked essentialism." (Tell that to three prominent Black academics standing in Harlem trying to catch a cab.) Gray writes, "One chooses and does not choose to have a particular racial identity, and differing identities cannot be reduced to formal theoretical equivalence. 'Belonging is long and painful, but it is belonging nonetheless,' [Himani] Bannerji writes. To belong is to live with the consequences of the history of 'illusions' about race."[45]

Pulitano is hardly alone among non-Native critics in becoming trapped in what I have termed the "delicate gymnastics of authenticity."[46] There is something more grounded in Native identity that such scholars cannot admit. And it is here that Pulitano sells short, especially, Vizenor. As Krupat perceptively observes, "In one place or another, Vizenor has written that the tribes are dead; Indians are inventions, or simulations; Indians are *Indians*, or post-Indians; and so on. Such remarks might be read as rejections of an 'Indian' identity in favor of some 'emergent hybridity.' But the identity Vizenor has elaborately been defining and redefining has at base the deep and unmistakable roots of 'tribal' values—which can and indeed must be taken along wherever one may go—to the cities, to

Europe, to China, anywhere."[47] Though Vizenor champions what he calls "crossbloods," he nonetheless champions them as *Natives* rather than "hybrids." While we all have specific differences, there is more that unites critics that Pulitano identifies with the "separatist" school with those she places in the "dialogic" box than divides us. We are all seeking an appropriate language of Native American criticism. To appropriate a metaphor from African-American religious discourse, we all seek to cobble shoes that fit our feet (for some, perhaps, sewing soft deerskin moccasins) as opposed to the hard discomfort of "tight-shoe night" back in Oklahoma.[48]

Though the theoretical approach is quite different, Susan Berry Brill de Ramirez's *Contemporary American Indian Literatures and the Oral Tradition* exhibits affinities with Pulitano's book in certain important ways. As I noted above, Pulitano draws together her six Native subjects because of their supposed attempt to bring the orality of Native traditions into the world of written criticism. Similarly, as the title of her book indicates, Brill hones in on orality. At the outset of her monograph, she states that she agrees with Warrior's contention in *Tribal Secrets* that "the preoccupation in American Indian Studies with oral traditions to the serious detriment of serious engagement with more theoretical work by Native intellectuals" has hobbled the discipline. Yet on the previous page, she writes, "My decision to approach American Indian literatures from an oral center comes from a conviction that oral storytelling is foundational to these literatures and, in fact, all literatures."[49] She forges boldly ahead in her pursuit of traces of orature despite her professed agreement with Warrior. Robert Dale Parker writes, "Many others have already noted the central role of oral storytelling in Indian culture and literature, and I do not wish to undermine their insights. Instead I reread those insights through the broader lenses of modernist nostalgia and its drive to construct the oral as a touchstone and core of Indian distinctiveness. That nostalgia helps open the door to naïve identification of orality with Indianness in a world or print literacy that condescends to orality, even as condescension is the tacit accomplice of romanticized exaltation."[50] In her epilogue on James Welch's *Winter in the Blood*, Brill concludes, "Our world and our lives are continually changing, and therefore, our stories need to change and evolve, too. As literary scholars, we tell our own stories/scholarship to provide helpful pathways into various literatures for ourselves, our colleagues, our students. This volume tells the story of a new role for literary scholars that actually is the resurrection of the age-old role of storytellers."[51] In her focus on orality, she not only engages in ethnostalgia, but she also ignores the reality that storytelling needs no "resurrection." Native storytellers never disappeared or ceased their telling.

On the issue of theory, Brill would seem to part company with Pulitano. She quotes Elizabeth Cook-Lynn: "The truth is, American Indian fiction and the American Indian novel, in particular, has been the captive of western literary theory." And, later, "It is important that the parameters of the discipline be defined, examined, redefined, and reexamined according to the experiences of American Indians themselves and in the context of a shifting and developing body of knowledge." Brill concludes, "A conversive strategy is an important step in this direction."[52]

Up to this point Brill is cruising smoothly down Larson's Good Red Road—she points out both potentials and pitfalls. I'm right behind her. Then she takes a bizarre ninety-degree turn onto New Mexico State Highway 602 toward Gallup, turning her text into a kind of critical captivity narrative.[53] Brill writes:

> What underlies the concerns of American Indian literatures
> scholars is the inevitable silence of Native peoples themselves
> within critical approaches informed by the Western tradition.
> Some Native writers and critics, such as Gerald Vizenor
> (Anishinaabe), have reinformed such strategies to fit their
> work—Vizenor, for example, using poststructural criticism
> in his discussion of the post-Indian trickster figures common
> in some contemporary Native literatures. Sarris moves in the
> direction of a conversive criticism in his struggle to arrive
> at a criticism that is more relational and informed by both
> Western and Native traditions. However, the absence of
> Native voices within the critical endeavor bespeaks of
> the struggle of scholars who study Native texts. Krupat
> forthrightly acknowledges, "the danger I run as an
> ethnocritic is the danger of leaving the Indian" silent
> entirely in my discourse. I don't know of any way securely

to avoid this danger." ... [A] conversive method informed by Wittgenstein's philosophical method points the way in/to American Indian literatures through conversive engagement with those literary works.[54]

The way into Native literatures and thought-worlds without erasing Natives is through Ludwig Wittgenstein. You know, that Karl May really understood Indians!

Brill, of course, is talking about a means of entry for non-Natives. It says nothing about Native Americans and their desires, needs, or viewpoints. For Brill, "conversive" conveys the twin senses of "conversion and conversation in which literary scholarship becomes a transformative and intersubjective act of communication." She concludes, "The transformative aspect of conversive language use is intertwined with the spiritual idea of conversion—not in the sense of sectarian conversion, but in the sense of growth, renewal, and healing that are part of the sacred."[55]

Conversation and conversion. What if we do not want to be in conversation to educate what Brill terms the Amer-European "listener-reader?" What if we want to have a conversation just among ourselves over a cup of coffee at the kitchen table—must Amer-European critics be included? What if that conversation is taking place in Cherokee, or Muskogee, or Osage; are we under an obligation to translate? J. M. Bridgeman discusses New's central principle of irony. In a comment that could equally apply to conversivity, she writes, "Irony, like colonization, like liberation, is, to a certain extent, a state of mind. It may be used consciously or emerge unconsciously, in the work of the writer or in the mind of the reader. It may be full-frontal or tongue-in-cheek. It may be there for everyone to read and chuckle at, or reserved for customers only."[56] Non-Native critics seem to invite us to the table as long as, for their benefit, we, like the returnee Squanto, speak the King's English. What if we do not want to come to the table at all? What if we see it as sometimes better to kick the legs out from under the table than sit at it? Although we acknowledge the need for allies, what exactly is entailed in conversion, and why must we be concerned with it? Indigenous religious traditions are not, unlike Christianity, proselytizing or evangelical faiths. They do not seek converts. As Sioux holy man Sitting Bull said,

"He put in your heart certain wishes and plans, in my heart he put other and different desires. Each man is good in his sight. It is not necessary for eagles to be crows."[57]

Smith writes, "When I read texts, for example, I frequently have to orientate [sic] myself to a text world in which the centre of academic knowledge is either in Britain, the United States or Western Europe; in which words such as 'we,' 'us,' 'our,' 'I' actually exclude me."[58] In like fashion, from the other side of the "racial/cultural" divide, in his early-seventies article "The Liberal as Fall Guy," Peter L. Berger satirically asks readers to pity the poor liberal, noting "that white liberals had barely succeeded in convincing themselves and a good many other people that Negroes were just like everybody else, when they were told in tones of vehement denunciation that blacks were like nobody else under the sun (and least of all like white liberals)." Similarly, Women's Liberation meant for them that women were just like men, and they only later discovered that "women are not like men in the least." Berger laments, "Racial liberalism yesterday becomes racism today; sexual emancipation at 2:00 has turned into sexism by cocktail time."[59] When some Western readers/critics, accustomed to being at the center, read Native American nationalist criticism, they cannot fathom being marginalized, or even excluded, themselves. The attitude is epitomized in Brill's monograph, where she writes, "As this book clarifies, a conversive literary scholarship engages with literary works, as scholars (1) learn to listen to voices previously silenced or otherwise critically altered through criticism's preconceived interpretive strategies, thereby gaining access in/to a range of literary works otherwise seemingly impenetrable; (2) serve as storyteller-guides teaching readers to listen to the words, worlds, realities, and histories within the literatures; and (3) demonstrate the transformative power of stories as manifested in the scholar's own interactions with particular literary works."[60] The transformative power of Native stories as manifested in the Amer-European scholar's "own interaction with particular literary works."

In his famous essay "Power and Racism," Stokely Carmichael wrote that whenever he discussed the nationalism of Black Power with well-meaning whites, they inevitably asked, "What about me?"[61] They never recognized that, in so doing, they were returning the subject of the conversation to themselves. An insistence by non-Natives that Native American critics embrace high theory or postcoloniality because of our mutual hybridity or that we mediate our texts to make them accessible to them comes across as a whinging "What about us?" It is a radical turn to the (non)Native.

Krupat acknowledges in *Red Matters* the pitfalls inherent in such an approach: "The danger is very real. Several recent writers have noted the possibility of a second erasure of Native agency..., in Julie Cruikshank's words, 'first by colonial force, then by postcolonial analyses,' ostensibly sympathetic to Natives but quite careless of their actual desires."[62] Alfred notes, "Despite all the wisdom available within indigenous traditions, most Native lives continue to be lived in a world of ideas imposed on them by others."[63] James Cox concurs, writing, "Much recent scholarly work in Native Studies addresses a consistent flaw in many articles and books published on writing by Native Americans: the scholar's lack of familiarity with tribal and Native intellectual contexts. The most serious scholarly transgression involves writing about Native literature without privileging, or even acknowledging, the work of Native scholars and other Native creative writers." He continues that such studies without the benefit of a critical framework based on Native intellectual output are "a form of academic colonialism: as discussions between primarily non-Natives about Native Americans, they ignore and erase Natives from the contemporary academic landscape."[64]

In *Grandchild of Empire*, New reproduces a 1948 cartoon by David Low. It shows a line of variously dressed "postcolonial" subjects coming down the stairs of a boardinghouse and taking keys from a board labeled "British Commonwealth." To the side, Britannia reaches for the board, saying, "I'm sure you children won't object if Mother has a latchkey, too."[65] If New, as the postcolonial progeny of settler colonizers, is a grandchild of empire, Natives are the stepchildren of empire. Too often, we are treated as Cinderella, and the stepsisters continue to insist on running the household.

A decade before Pulitano or Brill, Kim Blaeser wrote:

> While I believe these theories [Bakhtin, Lacan, Derrida]...
> have been helpful, they still have the same modus operandi

when it comes to Native American literature. The literature is approached within an already established theory, and the implication is that the worth of the literature is essentially validated by its demonstrated adherence to a respected literary mode, dynamic or style. Although the best scholars in native studies have not applied the theories in this colonizing fashion but have employed them, the implied movement is still that of colonization: authority emanating from the mainstream critical center to the marginalized native text.[66]

Smith discusses what James Cox terms "the real-world implications" of differing Native and Amer-European narrative strategies, pointedly stating:

[W]riting and theory are very intimidating ideas for many indigenous students. Having been immersed in the Western academy which claims theory as thoroughly Western, which has constructed all the rules by which the indigenous world has been theorized, indigenous voices have been overwhelmingly silenced. The act, let alone the art and science, of theorizing our own existence and realities is not something which many indigenous people assume is possible. Frantz Fanon's call for the indigenous intellectual and artist to create a new literature, to work in the cause of constructing a national culture after liberation still stands as a challenge. While this has been taken up by writers of fiction, many indigenous scholars who work in the social and other sciences struggle to write, theorize and research as indigenous scholars."[67]

Just as we begin to produce theories in the humanities in response to Fanon's challenge, some non-Native critics would silence us yet again, saying, in effect, that we're not doing it right!

Non-Native critics object to a nationalist or separatist approach for the same reason that conservatives decry multiculturalism as rending the fabric of our E Pluribus Unum society: it flies in the face of the assimilationist myth of the melting pot that they or their parents or their grandparents—or their distant forebears—embraced. Hybridity, postmodernism, and postcoloniality are the twenty-first-century "smelting pot" in which diverse metals become alloyed into one. Such critics want death without dying, change without upheaval, revolution without violence. They want an omelet without breaking eggs. By contrast, Amer-European scholar James Cox works in a very different mode from those non-Native critics who would dictate external methodologies for our work, who would continue to exclude, silence, or devalue our perspectives. In his monograph, *Muting White Noise*, in the chapters that deal with Native authors, his readings "rely heavily, at times almost exclusively, on Native sources." He writes, "I use this strategy out of respect for Native voices and in an effort to avoid perpetuating, implicitly or explicitly, an academic version of colonialism: the presumption that non-Natives know more about or what is most important to Native people."[68]

Certainly one cannot deny the historical reality of cultural change. As both Pulitano and the subjects of her analysis point out, Native cultures have always been highly adaptive, and they continue to evolve constantly. To acknowledge the truth of hybridity, however, does not mean that we are globally merging into a single McCulture in which we must all consume the same Happy Meal, using the same critical utensils, and then excrete the same McCriticism. Since 1492, hybridity has been an attribute of both "races," Native and Amer-European. Its positive aspects, however, are often presented as unidirectional. For Europeans or Amer-Europeans to hybridize with Natives is to become more American, more indigenized. For Natives, it seems, it is to become less Native. Alfred avers that those Natives who "yield to the assimilationist demands of the mainstream . . . abandon any meaningful attachment to an indigenous cultural and political reality. And in so doing they are lost to the rest of us." Why should we, he queries, "look away from our own wisdom and let other people answer the basic questions for us?"[69]

At precisely what point did hybridity make it impossible to express a Native perspective? Was it at the moment of first contact? Was it when Squanto mastered English? Was it when the first mixed-blood child was born? Was it when they learned of Christianity, and in some cases converted? Was it when Tenskwatawa had a vision in his nativist raising-up movement that Indians should give up everything they got from whites except guns and horses? Or was it when Big Foot's frozen and contorted corpse was photographed on the killing field of Wounded Knee, signaling an end to the Ghost Dance? Native interest in incorporating elements from other cultures long predated European encounter. Vast trading networks carried goods throughout North America, and trade argots were developed to facilitate commerce—all before any had seen a white man. Natives showed themselves adept at adopting and adapting anything that seemed to be useful or to have power. Yet each new item, tool, or technology was used to strengthen, not weaken, their people. The question remains unanswered: at what point did they become incapable of expressing a separate cultural/national perspective?

Metaphors abound for the effect of mandating Natives confess their hybridity and employ Western theories or postcoloniality. In a new multicultural version of the discarded melting pot hypothesis, some non-Native critics desire Natives to dissolve into a soup of hybridity (in which they too, of course, can share), embracing our mixed-blood identities. They hope that, as the pregnant Hester Prynne character says dejectedly in Peter De Vries's *Slouching Toward Kalamazoo*, "There is a destiny that ends our shapes." Or perhaps they envision postmodern and postcolonial theories together as the mighty pulverizing engine to break up the tribal mass that allotment, in the end, failed to be.

For "postcolonial" peoples, Smith refers to the "unfinished business of decolonization."[70] To press everyone into a hybrid or mixed-blood mold is to consummate finally the as yet uncompleted enterprise of colonialism. Or as Julie Gough states so eloquently and succinctly: "Hybridity... is a potentially dangerous notion, a scientific disclaimer of authenticity or originality, a reactionary term that Western societies allocate to other cultures in order to develop the binary codings necessary to elevate Self and subjugate Other: East and West, Black and White, Pagan and Christian.... By accepting the label 'hybrid'... Indigenous people relinquish the power to name themselves."[71] Following the path that Pulitano, especially, advocates can only lead to the dissolution of our governments and the destruction of our traditions. Any claim to self-determination or any form of separatism will disappear. The "Indian Problem" will have achieved the final resolution reached for in Termination. We will have been defined out of existence.

The historical precedent here has been provided by Gough's own native Tasmanians.

In *Old Melbourne Memories*, published in 1884, novelist Rolf Boldrewood describes their demise: "They pined away slowly, and but a few years since the last female of the race died. The prosaic, joyless prosperity told on health and spirits. It was wholly alien to the constitution of the wild hunters and warriors who had been wont to traverse pathless woods, to fish in the depths of sunless forest streams, to chase the game of their native land through the lone untrampled mead, or the hoar of primeval forests which lay around the snow-crested mountain range." Critic Terry Goldie comments, "The people of 'wont,' 'mead,' and 'primeval' are of the past. The people of 'wild,' 'pathless,' and 'untrampled' would not be of the future."[72]

The Tasmanians were declared extinct despite the reality, as Goldie points out, of the continued existence of mixed-blood Tasmanians "who continue to live on islands off Tasmania [and] have every right to be considered Tasmanian Aborigines." As Smith sums up, "In Tasmania, where experts had already determined that Aborigines were 'extinct,' the voices of those who still speak as Aboriginal Tasmanians are interpreted as some political invention of a people who no longer exist and who therefore no longer have claims."[73] Canada, too, engaged in its own attempts at definitional extermination.[74]

We are being pushed into a postmodern boarding school, where, instead of Christian conversion and vocational skills, assimilation requires that we all embrace our hybridity and mixed-blood identities, and high theory replaces English as the language that must be spoken. To give in runs the risk of producing yet another lost generation, out of touch with, and unable to talk to, Native community. Of those so-called "lost generations" of the boarding and residential schools, Isabelle Knockwood writes, "When little children first arrived at the school we would see bruises on their throats and cheeks that told us they'd been caught speaking [their Native language]. Once we saw the bruises begin to fade, we knew they'd stopped talking."[75] Notice: not stopped talking "Indian," but simply stopped talking. Like Knockwood's students at Shubenacadie, and like Rita Joe in the epigrammatic poem that begins this chapter, we all need to find our talk.

Australian Aborigines, who endured a similar process of coercive educational assimilation, are more honest in their descriptors. No "lost generations" for them. Theirs were "stolen generations." To reject a non-Native imposition of hybridity and Western theoretical discourse—to contend that Native American literature stands outside the American canon—and to affirm American Indian Literary Nationalism is to say that never again will we cooperate, nor will be stand by and acquiesce, in the theft of another intellectual generation.

Though it will seem little more than academic bafflegab to many, if not most, non-Native critics, to make such an argument is not actually to reject Western theory. Gerald Vizenor, for example, uses postmodernism more skillfully than most, if not all, of its Amer-European adherents. As Smith states:

> The development of theories by indigenous scholars which
> attempt to explain our existence in contemporary society
> (as opposed to the 'traditional' society constructed under
> modernism) has only just begun. Not all these theories claim
> to be derived from some 'pure' sense of what it means to be
> indigenous, nor do they claim to be theories which have been
> developed in a vacuum separated from association with civil
> and human rights movements, other nationalist struggles or
> other theoretical approaches. What is claimed, however is that
> new ways of theorizing by indigenous scholars are grounded
> in a real sense of, and sensitivity towards, what it means to
> be an indigenous person.[76]

Alfred elaborates, "Experience . . . has shown that cultural revival is not a matter of rejecting all Western influences, but of separating the good from the bad and fashioning a coherent set of ideas out of the traditional culture to guide whatever forms of political and social development—including the good elements of Western forms—are appropriate to the contemporary reality."[77]

This is not a case, to borrow once more Audre Lourde's much appropriated phrase, of the master's tools never dismantling the master's house. A hammer and a crowbar are damn fine tools to have if one is disassembling a house, no matter what their provenance (and the child of a slave can learn to use them as easily as the children of the master). If outright demolition is one's goal, a wrecking ball would do better, regardless of its manufacturer. The problem comes when someone says that you must use the hammer and the crowbar, and they must be used just the way the authors of the instruction manual dictate.

Howard Adams writes, "[W]e can understand within a colonial society the function of a colonizer's language is to promote intellectual and cultural domination. For Natives, English and French are imperialist languages. Although most of us speak one or another of the colonizer's languages, it does not mean that we embrace all his culture or ideology."[78] This presents the question of whether literature can truly be considered Native if it employs Western languages or literary forms. This is a question I have already visited in *That the People Might Live*. While there are those who would argue that works written in English (for example) in a form like the novel for publication are something apart from Native American literature, for me the answer is manifest: there is "still something 'Indian' about it regardless of its form or the language in which it speaks." Goldie would agree, writing, "[I]s it possible for the [Native] writer to take a European form such as the novel and use it successfully to describe his or her own people? When this question has been addressed to me my usual reaction has been to attempt to deflect it. Regardless of Arnoldian claims for the freedom of the disinterested liberal critic, I question the right of any person to judge another's representation of his or her own culture."[79]

John Moss, a Mohawk, in discussing the work of Tomson Highway, a Cree, states, "His English echoes with the cadences of another language—not only the images but the sounds themselves—the music of another world. He brings Cree to English the way Chinua Achebe plays out the inflections of the Ibo language and doomed Biafra into English, transforming the syntax of imperial subjugation into something new and so vital that the language itself is transformed into the voice of the people whose lives it organized nearly to extinction." He continues, "I think it is Cree that I hear, but I do not speak Cree myself. Nor Ibo. But Highway, like Achebe, shifts the walls of my English labyrinth. He opens my way as his reader to worlds I could never have known otherwise."[80]

I think of Ray Young Bear, who through the lyricism of *Remnants of the First Earth* artfully grants readers an entrée into a Mesquakie world. Or Gerald Vizenor in *Bear Island: The War at Sugar Point*, in which I imagine I hear not only Anishinaabe but the rhythm of the first environment, that of a Native mother's heartbeat within the womb, of the drum.

In the first section of this chapter, I referred to Simon Ortiz's essay "Towards a National Indian Literature: Cultural Authenticity in Nationalism" as a first utterance on a par with the allophonic greetings of Columbus and Squanto. I am aware that this is not, of course, literally the case. He was not the first Native to write about Native literature, nor was he the first to do so in a nationalist stance. Nothing springs forth full-grown like Athena from the head of Zeus. Everything has precedents, and one can find nationalistic comments on indigenous self-representation in the writings of Samson Occom and William Apess. In that 1981 essay, Ortiz laid not only the groundwork for American Indian Literary Nationalism, but also for the recognition of the integrity of Indian literature in English through his argument for indigenous transformations of colonial impulses. Risking becoming trapped in what Warrior terms the "rhetoric of ancientness and novelty," as far as I know, Ortiz was the first to refer to a "National Indian Literature" and to bring into its discussion the issues of "authenticity" and "nationalism."[81] And it is on this point of "authenticity" of form and language that he proves most helpful.

Ortiz asks his reader to imagine a fiesta for a Catholic saint's day at Acoma Pueblo. In the syncretic ritual, persons bearing the name of the particular saint (Pedro/Peter, for instance) "throw from housetops gifts like bread, cookies, crackerjacks, washcloths, other things, and the people catching and receiving dance and holler the names. It will rain then and the earth will be sustained." Writes Ortiz:

> Obviously, there is an overtone that this is a Catholic Christian celebration because of the significance of the saints' names and days on the Catholic calendar. But just as obviously, when the celebration is held within the Acqumeh community, it is an Acqumeh ceremony. It is Acqumeh and Indian (or Native American and American Indian if one prefers those terms) in the truest and most authentic sense. This is so because this

celebration speaks of the creative ability of Indian people to gather in many forms of the socio-political colonizing force which beset them and to make these forms meaningful in their own terms.

He concludes:

Like the drama and characters described above, the indigenous peoples of the Americas have taken the languages of the colonialists and used them for their own purposes. Some would argue that this means that Indian people have succumbed or become educated into a different linguistic system and have forgotten or have been forced to forsake their native selves. This is simply not true. Along with their native languages, Indian women and men have carried on their lives and their expression through the use of newer languages, particularly Spanish, French, and English, and they have used these languages on their own terms. This is the crucial item that has to be understood, that it is entirely possible for a people to retain and maintain their lives through the use of any language. There is not a question of authenticity here; rather it is the way that Indian people have creatively responded to forced colonization. And this response has been one of resistance; there is no clearer word for it than resistance.[82]

Just as today Christianity can be for some a Native religion, English is a Native language. Removal, diaspora, "exile, isolation, categorical enclosure"—hybridity, heteroglossia, crossblood, mixed-blood. Beyond the words, as New reminds us, "the politics is in the voice."[83] For Ortiz, in the syncretism of the ceremony can be observed "the primary element of a nationalistic impulse to make use of foreign ritual, ideas, and material in their own—Indian—terms. Today's writing by Indian authors is a continuation of this elemental impulse."[84]

The issue of power cannot be ignored here. Arnold Krupat, in discussing the critical work of Jana Sequoya (now Jana Sequoya Magdaleno), writes, "For all that ethnocriticism wishes to engage on an equal footing with Native literary practice, it cannot help but do so in a context of vastly unequal power relations. Thus, for all that the ethnocritic may decently and sincerely attempt to inquire into and learn from the Otherness of ongoing Indian literary performances, the sociopolitical context being what it is, she or he cannot help but threaten to swallow, submerge, or obliterate these performances. This is not to say that nothing can be done; but goodwill or even great talent alone cannot undo the current differential power relations between dominant and subaltern cultural production."[85]

Pulitano quite rightly points out the syncretisms of the Ghost Dance of 1889–90. Its transmission, as Vizenor writes in *Manifest Manners*, was enabled by the shared use of English. The movement also borrowed elements of Christianity—perhaps the ultimate hybrid collaboration. Yet these were choices made by Natives themselves. They were wholly in their hands to define. And by doing so, these choices, events, experiences, ceremonies, texts, bodies, and languages *became* indigenous, regardless of their origin(s). Hybridity works best as a choice rather than an imposition, such as Pulitano demands—which itself contradicts the very nature of the dialogist project.

Native American critics may use the tools of critical theory or not, as they choose. They may elect to do so in some instances and not in others, depending upon their particular goals and audiences. Contrary to what some critics, whether Native or non-Native, may believe, nationalism or separatism and the use of Western forms or theories (depending, of course, on which ones) are not antithetical or contradictory. As Mohawk Robbie Robertson's Virgil Caine says, "Ya take what ya need and ya leave the rest." To say otherwise is to once again attempt to trap the fly in amber, to set up a hierarchical distinction between "pure" and "impure" Native expression. W. H. New writes:

Power declares; it doesn't readily listen. In conventional circles, in the early years of the twentieth century, Pauline Johnson was accepted as a performer, and accepted as a poet only to the degree that the performance—complete with Mohawk "costume"—was patronizingly being praised. In retrospect, it is hard not to think that these same communities subsequently (and readily) accepted Grey Owl as an "Indian" because he was theatrical *like Johnson*—that he was praised because he fit the model that convention had made familiar. The model confirmed expectations. It nevertheless left the reality unquestioned, and therefore unmet.[86]

To put the matter somewhat differently, in the living room of the home where I drafted most of this chapter, my wife and I have only art by Native artists on the walls, an exclusionary act that was solely our choice. At the same time, on the mantel, Thucydides' *History of the Peloponnesian War* nestles next to *The Papers of Chief John Ross*, an act of hybridity—but again our choice alone.[87] In justifying himself to the Athenian people, Pericles declared, "I wanted a just society, but I didn't think it was possible if I gave up the empire. It may have been wrong to take it, but empires, no matter how gained, are dangerous things to let go." The Greek leader's statement is true, it seems, not only in geopolitics but in academia, as well.

The Shoshone become "Snakes," and the Salish are labeled Flatheads. The "shiny mountains" of the Cheyenne are passed down to settler/ invaders with a gloss. Survey any map of North America. From Devil's Tower in Wyoming to Devil's Canyon in Oklahoma to Devil's Lake in Wisconsin, it's a sure bet that any site today known as "devil's" anything was and is sacred to Native Americans. The ability to name is the power to define and control. Kathie Irwin pointedly argues, "We don't need any- one else developing the tools which will help us to come to terms with who we are. We can and will do this work. Real power lies with those who design the tools—it always has. This power is ours." Smith responds, "Contained within this imperative is a sense of being able to determine priorities, to bring to the centre those issues of our own choosing, and to discuss them amongst ourselves."[88]

In *Rutherford v. United States*, Luther Bohanon, the Oklahoma fed- eral judge who was the subject of my first book, wrote, "Freedom of choice necessarily includes freedom to make a wrong choice, and there is much force to an argument that matters of the type herein under discus- sion should be left ultimately to the discretion of the persons whose lives are directly involved."[89] For over a century, at least, well-meaning whites have sought to deny—often successfully—Natives and their national governments the capacity to make choices that appear wrong in their more enlightened/Enlightenment eyes. Native Americans need the experience of making our own mistakes in literary criticism. Even a faulty criticism is more interesting than a "correct" one directed by a literary overseer. That is what sovereignty and self-determination are all about.

Blaeser, in her previously cited essay, avers, "The critical language of Mikhail Bakhtin and Walter J. Ong may be profitably applied to Native American literature, but as [Louis] Owens' Uncle Luther [in *The Sharpest Sight*] reminds us, we must first 'know the stories of our people' and then 'make our own story too.' And he warns, we must 'be aware of the way they change the story we already know' for only with that awareness can we protect the integrity of the Native American story. One way to safeguard that integrity is by asserting a critical voice from within the tribal story itself."[90]

In his seminal manifesto of the "Red Power" era, *The Unjust Society* (1969), Harold Cardinal described the "buckskin curtain" that separated Native peoples from the dominant culture. It was, he said, a divide of "indifference, ignorance and, all too often, plain bigotry." Obviously a riff on the Churchillian articulation of the Iron Curtain during the Cold War, Cardinal's Buckskin Curtain suggests something opaque and substantial. But though Cardinal named a reality, his Buckskin Curtain is far from solid. It is more akin to W. E. B. Du Bois's "Veil," a diaphanous barrier that, according to historian Jonathan Holloway, even as it "worked to segregate . . . was also translucent and, as such, it gave blacks the 'gift' of seeing white America while simultaneously remaining invisible to white America. As often as not, this gift was a curse."[91] Both Veil and Buckskin Curtain are equally constructs of empire.

Today well-meaning Amer-Europeans want desperately to pierce the Veil. They want us to rend the Buckskin Curtain for them, and they are wounded when we say we have grown to like it just fine as a way of maintaining a demarcation, much like a border between nation-states. The more Natives attempt to live out sovereignty, the greater the backlash. If a Native nation asserts its treaty rights, howls of balkanization and "special rights" go up. If the Hopi or the Yoeme close their doors to outside scholars and attempt to achieve some degree of control over representations of their traditions, cries of the death of "academic freedom" ring throughout the landscape. If we contend that literature is not a universal category but something specific to given peoples, if we assert American Indian Literary Nationalism, there are those critics who will accuse of a destructive separatism and an effort to suppress all other voices.

What then exactly is American Indian Literary Nationalism, and what does the criticism that flows from it look like? What are its goals and parameters?

On the one hand, though we, the authors of this book, coin the term, it is not for us to say. As I have already said, ideally "our communities arrive at an approximation of truth and right action as they always have, through honest sharing, discussion, and consensus."[92] For me, American Indian Literary Nationalism is processual. I liken it to Warrior's intervention in *Tribal Secrets*, in which he advances the idea of "intellectual sovereignty" (a trope we revisit herein). Although he creates the concept, he nonetheless leaves it somewhat undefined, a vessel awaiting additional meaning to be poured in through discussion. We hope to provoke a dialogue through which the community will determine the exact goals and parameters of such a nationalism. We thus mean to be suggestive rather than prescriptive.

The conversation we hope will ensue places an obligation upon all of us to know and engage each other's work. This might seem obvious. Any scholar should know and keep up with the field. It is especially incumbent upon us as Native scholars, however, to know the work of other Natives. And unfortunately, the way Native literature is too often taught and the work of doctoral students supervised results in each new dissertation reading as if it were produced in a vacuum. Knowing better the work of those who have thought and worked before will result in better new work and spare us the feeling that we exist in isolation, in an environment in which we must reinvent the wheel ourselves each time. The resultant dialogue will move our criticism forward, just as Sid Larson desires in his evocatively titled *Captured in the Middle*.

Having said that the final definition of American Indian Literary Nationalism must await a collaborative effort beyond the confines of the four corners of this book, in our effort to move forward the conversation we hope to spark, including among the three of us, I will suggest some things about its elements.

American Indian Literary Nationalism takes as a given, as Chad Allen has said, that settler colonialism in North America is "deep and enduring." As I put it in *Native American Religious Identity*, "Only the most winsome dreamer and the most prophetic visionary believe that Amer-Europeans are going anywhere."[93] The colonizers have settled in to stay. To acknowledge this reality, however, is not to acquiesce in it. The challenge is both theoretical and practical.

Smith notes, "Many indigenous intellectuals actively resist participating in any discussion within the discourse of post-coloniality. This is because post-colonialism is viewed as the convenient invention of Western intellectuals which reinscribes their power to define the world." This is not the venue in which to rehearse an indigenous critique of postcolonial theory—a theory, as I have alluded to earlier, that tends to exclude indigenes and then lectures them for not participating. The relevant point here is that, as I have written elsewhere, there is a troubling temporal aspect to most postcolonial discourse—"postcolonial" truly means a time *after* colonialism, and for the indigenes of the Anglo-colonial settler colonies that time has not yet come.[94]

Vizenor, in *Manifest Manners*, deploys the term "paracolonial." "Para-," from the Greek, meaning "beside," "near," or "beyond," it sometimes refers to "alteration" or "modification." Paracolonialism suggests the difference between colonialism here and classic "blue-water" colonialism; it thus may serve as a synonym for settler colonialism. I would go further and suggest yet another new word: "pericolonialism." "Peri-," also Greek, is defined as "around," "through," "beyond," "having an intensive force." Pericolonialism therefore acknowledges the thorough, pervading nature of settler colonialism and marks it as something that, for indigenes, must be gotten around, under, or through.[95] It, like Vizenor's coinage, shifts the temporal metaphor (postcolonial) to a spatial one, something that must be overcome here, in this place.

In his study of both Maori and Native American literatures, *Blood Narrative*, Chad Allen says that although Louis Owens's and Arnold Krupat's efforts in the direction of postcolonialism "are important first steps for gauging the relevance of postcolonial theory for American

Indian—or, more generally, Fourth World—literature, both run a considerable risk of simply grafting indigenous minority literatures onto existing postcolonial models, developed in response to radically different colonial or postcolonial histories, rather than pursuing rigorous independent study of indigenous minority literatures and their relevant contexts."[96] Such "grafting" is an old story, the prototypical example of which is the inclusion of Native American literature within American literature, thus giving settler colonizers a formal, if not actual, indigeneity, as they trace their national literature uninterrupted back to an autochthonous past.

A basic tenet of American Indian Literary Nationalism, it seems to me, is a defense of Native literatures against such co-optation and incorporation. I quoted Kim Blaeser above to the effect "that the literatures of Native Americans have a unique voice and that voice has not always been adequately or accurately explored in the criticism that has been written about the literature." As Womack states, "Native literatures deserve to be judged by their own criteria, in their own terms, not merely in agreement with, or reaction against, European literature and theory"—or as a precursory adjunct of white settler literary output.[97]

Native American literature is a separate national/local literature from that produced by immigrants. As Womack argues, the output of each tribal nation is yet still another localized national literature. While it might logically be argued that only the latter are "validly" separate literatures, I would contend that, since the very moment of colonization, accelerating (as Cherokee anthropologist Robert Thomas argued) during the reservation period, and reaching final culmination during Termination and Relocation, a separate, distinct acknowledgment of something more than singular tribal identity coalesced.

I noted above that literature is not a universal category but rather something specific to a given people. The broader one extends any category, the more amorphous and meaningless it becomes. One need take only the ultimate, all-encompassing category of "world literature." On its face, such a term includes, quite literally—everything. Yet few instructors, if any, teach such a course unless it excludes her or his own particular national literature (or that of the place where their institution is located). A case in point, the *Norton Anthology of World Literature*, which, though it speaks a few times of "American," contains little or no American literature; it does, however, contain Native American orature. Thus, in the United States, "world literature" excludes "American" literature while including everything else, rendering the former normative while "othering" the "everything else." Two other examples: "North American literature" and "multicultural literature." Does the first term encompass all of North America, or is it limited to the United States and Canada? *Ad arguendum*, if the second, must the literature be in English, or would it include francophone writings? Again, if the latter, what about the separatist Quebecois literature? At the Universidad Autonoma de Madrid, where there is a North American Literature program, a website shows the reading list looking like a Who's Who of Amer-European heavyweights, plus Ralph Ellison, Toni Morrison, and Louise Erdrich. Nary a Canadian, not even Margaret Atwood, Alice Munro, or Mordecai Richler, is in sight. The problem with "multicultural literature" should be clear: it becomes a meaningless othering ground for writings by non-whites: African American, Asian American, Latino/a, and American Indian. My point is that one can make up any geographic, ethnic, or other category one wishes—from something as all encompassing as world literature to, reductio ad absurdum, the "literature of West 86th Street." In every instance, however, one must interrogate oneself as to what is at stake—what is gained and what is lost—by any given category, not only intellectually and pedagogically, but politically and ideologically as well. In the case of American Indian Literary Nationalism, we believe, ultimately, what is at stake is nothing less than Native identity, definitional and actual sovereignty—identity "constituted by the historical continuity of relatively open-ended processes of self-definition by community members that relate to both what they take themselves to be and how they define their interests or ends over time."[98] It is about the ability of Natives and their communities to be self-determining rather than selves determined.

James (Sákéj) Youngblood Henderson notes, "Eurocentric thought does not claim to be a privileged norm. This would be an argument about cultural relativism, which asserts that values are about specific cultural contexts. Instead, Eurocentric thought claims to be universal and general." In *Ethnocriticism*, Krupat limns what might be called "the fallacy of aesthetic universalism," writing, "The first type of esthetic universalism holds that for all the differences in cultural custom all over the world, art is nonetheless, essentially the same everywhere." It reinforces the claim that literature is universal and available/accessible to all, reviving Arnoldian notions. Henderson writes, "Universality is really just another aspect of diffusionism, and claiming universality often means aspiring to domination. Universality creates cultural and cognitive imperialism, which establishes a dominant group's knowledge, experience, culture, and language as the universal norm. Dominators or colonizers reinforce their culture and values by bringing the oppressed and the colonized under their expectations and norms."[99] As much as postmodern and postcolonial practitioners believe they are deconstructing such power relations, they too often merely reinscribe metanarratives even as they proclaim the end of metanarrative; this is especially true when they maintain that subaltern subjects must employ their tools and techniques if they are to be heard and participate in the larger literary discussion. The study of American literature involves and proceeds from different critical assumptions than the study of Native American literature. And we contend that the norms in the second instance should derive from internal sources within the Native community itself.

Ortiz writes:

[I]t is not the oral tradition as transmitted from ages past alone which is the inspiration and source for contemporary Indian literature. It is also because of the acknowledgment by Indian writers of a responsibility to advocate for their people's self-government, sovereignty, and control of land and natural resources; and to look also at racism, political and economic oppression, sexism, supremacism, and the needless and wasteful exploitation of land and people, especially in the U.S., that Indian literature is developing a character of nationalism which it indeed should have. It is this character which will prove to be the heart and fibre and story of an America which has heretofore too often feared its deepest and most honest emotions of love and compassion. It is this story, wealthy without an illusion of dominant power and capitalistic abundance, that is most authentic.[100]

For me, the goals of American Indian Literary Nationalism are consonant with those of Native American Studies more broadly, the studying and teaching about Native peoples from an indigenous perspective and supporting Native Americans in their struggles. It "provides space for further dialogue within a framework that privileges the indigenous presence."[101] As the name implies and Ortiz makes explicit, American Indian Literary Nationalism attempts to serve the goal of sovereignty for Native nations.

Two objections may be raised at this juncture. The first and assuredly most common—that in so stating I move from scholarship to advocacy—is nothing more than a red herring and can be dealt with easily. In *Turtle Goes to War*, I wrote, "Commenting on *l'affaire Dreyfus*, future French Prime Minister Georges Clemenceau said, 'Military justice is to justice as military music is to music.' The quote has become famous. It was used in 1970 as the title of a book on courts-martial by Robert Sherrill. It is often assumed that Clemenceau, as a journalist and passionate defender of Alfred Dreyfus, meant that both military justice and military music were bad imitations of justice and music, respectively. This may be. The statement is also true, however, in another sense. Both military justice and music serve ends narrower than either justice or music in their broader meanings." As I state elsewhere in that monograph, "I do not believe that there is any scholarship that is value-neutral. All scholarship, every academically attested to 'fact,' serves some political agenda."[102] In this regard, I thus agree with the postmodernists and postcolonialists. I simply believe that, with regard to the indigenous, most of them are either naïve or disingenuous about the logical implications and potential consequences of their work.

The second objection is, to my way of thinking, thornier and, as one generated from within Native community, deserving of a considered and careful response. It relates to the use of the word "sovereignty." The term came into vogue in both Native political and academic circles two decades ago and since then has only grown in importance, assuming in many circles an almost unassailable status. Despite this, Vine Deloria, Jr., indisputably a founder of, and remaining one of the most important voices in, contemporary Native American Studies questioned the term, though he himself employed it early on.[103] One of the most vociferous critics of the use of the word in recent years has been Gerald Taiaiake Alfred. A critique of the concept takes up a considerable portion of his book *Peace, Power, Righteousness: An Indigenous Manifesto*.

Alfred considers "sovereignty" a European concept that "must be eradicated from politics in Native communities." He writes, "A crucial feature of the indigenous concept of governance is its respect for individual autonomy. This respect precludes the notion of 'sovereignty'— the idea that there can be a permanent transference of power or authority from the individual to an abstraction of the collective called 'government.'" He sees it as something that is statist and delegated. In an interview contained in the book, Audra Simpson, another Mohawk and then-graduate student, echoes Alfred's conceptualization, saying, "Now, sovereignty—the authority to exercise power over life, affairs, territory— this is not inherited. It's not part of being, the way our form of nationhood is. It has to be conferred, or granted—it's a thing that can be given and thus can be taken away."[104] Alfred prefers "self-determination" or "nationhood" to "sovereignty" as a term.

I do not question for a moment the need for a nuanced reading and interpretation of sovereignty. But let's not forget, we are arguing over a word in English here. "Self-determination" and "nation" are equally "foreign" concepts. And they are equally indigenous. Sovereignty is not delegated, conferred, or granted. As Justice writes, "The U.S. government didn't *create* Cherokee nationhood or sovereignty."[105] Rather, sovereignty in international law is an inherent attribute of peoples or nations. Each of our peoples had some sort of notion of sovereignty traditionally, though the concept might better be described in translation as "peoplehood," or, better, "peopleness," or, better still, simply Cherokee, Mohawk, Navajo, or what have you. Nonetheless, each tribal "nation" had a clear sense of who was "us" and what was our defined place (territory), and each had leaders that exercised power not because they themselves were sovereign but because the people permitted it.[106] The United States did not create Native sovereignty, but, as Justice points out, "by recognizing the existence of such, the U.S. has acknowledged the fundamental right of Cherokees (and other indigenous nations) to negotiate in the political arena as more than scattered ethnic or social constituencies, but as national bodies: peoples defined as much by their political relationship to one another as by their kinship ties and genealogies. Not all Cherokees are enrolled tribal citizens, but the number of those whose citizenship is acknowledged by their respective nations is considerable, and that formal relationship carries with it significant political and cultural weight."[107]

Justice sees one of his aims as a Native literary critic as "to realign reader expectation of nationhood and what it means in Indigenous contexts, which differ significantly from discussions about the coercive nationalism of industrialized nation-states." Such a goal seems to be exactly what Alfred calls for when he declares, "We need to create a meaning for 'sovereignty' that respects the understanding of power in indigenous cultures, one that reflects more of the sense embodied in such Western notions as 'personal sovereignty' and 'popular sovereignty.' Until then, 'sovereignty' can never be part of the language of liberation."[108] This, it seems to me, is the core of Warrior's "intellectual sovereignty." Though we must always be careful in our use of language (I myself have suggested that "sovereignty" has become a retronym.[109]), to continue to wrangle over the utility of the term "sovereignty" is to become unnecessarily stuck, engaging in a kind of navel gazing. It is to argue over how many fancydancers can dance fit on the head of a pin.

Harold Cardinal makes clear in *The Rebirth of Canada's Indians* that sovereignty is the absolute right of a people to make decisions about the matters affecting their lives and the lives of their children. It is the freedom to make wrong choices. Daniel Justice, who uses the terms "sovereignty" and "nationhood" interchangeably, sees his own approach as "grounded in the firm belief that Indigenous nationhood is a necessary ethical response to the assimilationist directive of imperialist nation-states, and that Native people are well qualified to speak on these matters without the need of non-Native translation or interpretation." He writes:

> Indigenous nationhood, in this case, challenges the assimilative
> foundations of state nationalism by its assertion of an inherent
> distinctiveness based on tradition, culture, language, and
> relationship to the world and its various peoples. Fundamental
> to this distinction is the ability of Indigenous nationalism
> to extend recognition to other sovereignties without that
> recognition implying a necessary need to consume, displace,

or become absorbed by those nations.

Indigenous nationhood is more than simple political independence or the exercise of a distinctive cultural identity; it is also an understanding of a common social interdependence within the community, the tribal web of kinship rights *and* responsibilities that link the people, the land, and the cosmos together in an ongoing and dynamic system of mutually affecting relationships.[110]

After *That the People Might Live* appeared, my friend Alan Velie accused me of "pluralist separatism." In *Turtle Goes to War*, I professed to a lack of understanding as to what exactly he meant by the phrase. I wrote that it evoked to my mind "Let a thousand separatisms bloom" or "Let there be two, three, many separatisms." Despite my incomprehension, I said that I embraced the term.[111] I still do. Pluralism has been defined as "a public arrangement in which distinct groups live side by side in conditions of mutual recognition and affirmation."[112] American Indian Literary Nationalism espouses a kind of separatism, but it *is* a pluralist separatism. In this it mirrors the pluralistic aspects of the broader Native community. Though it is popular to refer to Native America, it is perhaps more correct to refer to Native *Americas*, in the plural.

It may be the pluralist separatism, in the United States, of more than 550 federally recognized tribes. There, only Indians and blacks have been constitutionally othered. Unlike any other racial or ethnic minority, Native American tribes are separate sovereign nations. As flawed as it was, the treaty process confirmed this status. Native nations are separate sovereigns, but they are sovereigns within the federal system of the United States. They are "nations within a nation" or, perhaps more accurately still, "nations within a nation-state."[113] And, of course, nations can only exist, can only define themselves, in relation to other nations.

It may be the separatism of Native American literature separate from American literature. I first discussed this issue in *That the People Might Live*, and I have already revisited briefly herein. Robert Berner, in his essay "What is an American Indian Writer?", makes the case for subsuming all literatures produced within these geographic confines into "American" literature based upon our mutual hybridity:

[T]he human encounter with the physical and spiritual reality represented by the landscape and the Indian must be understood not only in terms of the application to it of the mind of Europe but also the strong hearts and physical stamina of the African slaves whose presence in the American psyche is just as strong as the other elements and whose culture has affected American culture as a whole in numberless ways. To be an American is, whether he knows it or not, simultaneously to be a European *and* an African *and* an Indian living in the American landscape....

[I]f we learn to rise above the superficialities of race when we define the elements of our literature, if we learn, that is, to understand not only our Indian writers but the larger literary culture of which they are so vital a part as expressions of the essential unity of the diverse elements of American experience, we may finally resolve the old question of what the term *American* means and indeed may begin to realize our old dream of becoming brothers and sisters at last.[114]

It is a beautiful vision. The siren song of assimilation always is: rising "above the superficialities of race when we define the elements of *our* literature," understanding "*our* Indian writers" and "the larger literary culture of which they are so vital a part as expressions of the essential unity."[115] We are not in "denial," as Berner states. Critics who espouse American Indian Literary Nationalism are not struthious. As Womack writes, "The Native Americanist does not bury her head in the sand and pretend that European history and thought do not affect Native literature, nor does she ignore the fact that Native literature has quite distinctive features of its own that call for new forms of analyses."[116] Influences are *undeniable*, but influences alone do not define either inclusion or exclusion. The *auteurs* of the *nouvelle vague* were deeply influenced by American film noir, but no one would deny that they are still French cinema. Or, to stick to written literatures: in the past Krupat has argued that Indian literature should exclude "writing influenced in very substantial degree by the central forms and genres of Western, or first world literature." Would anyone be taken seriously if she or he claimed that Ngugi,

Mudrooroo, or Mishima were not, respectively, Kenyan, Aboriginal, or Japanese writers simply because they adopt Western literary forms? Conversely, Cherokee playwright Lynn Riggs, as I make clear in *Cherokee Night and Other Plays*, was profoundly affected by Shakespeare, but this makes him neither an Elizabethan dramatist nor a part of British literature.[117]

Or it may be simply the pluralist separatism to identify and write as Native without being chided or pressured to acknowledge our mixed-bloodedness and hybridity. As Daniel Justice writes, "We are a people of many shades and perspectives, many bloods mingled into shared senses of nationhood." Amer-European critics do not insist that African Americans embrace their hybridity. Simply because the late August Wilson had a white father, no one seriously argues that he must identify as anything other than African American. No one insisted that he must write in a voice like that of Barack Obama at the 2004 Democratic National Convention. Perhaps it is an unconscious remnant of the one-drop rule: if you are black, you are black. But contemporary, crossblood Natives are too often looked upon as inauthentic.

In *Red Matters*, Arnold Krupat tells the story of meeting a man in Minneapolis who identified himself as "Finndian" because "his father was Chippewa and his mother was Finnish, although now, as far as he is concerned, he is an Indian whose mother was Finnish." As Krupat intelligently analyzes the man's situation:

> Perhaps had he pursued the possibilities of Finndianness, one would have had to confront this as a truly hybrid, a new and emergent identity. An Indian with a Finnish mother is also something new, to be sure, for no Indians had Finnish mothers way back whenever. But given this man's sense of the matter—that he is an Indian, albeit of a different kind—it seems to me a mistake to emphasize the emergent hybridity of his identity rather than its changing sameness, its likeness to rather than its difference from the traditional. Thus, while not denying the hybridity of contemporary Indian identities in the fiction I know, I want to emphasize their Indianness.[118]

Similarly, John Moss says of Tomson Highway:

Tomson Highway is Cree, and, to use the word properly, a "native" to the land of his forebears, inseparable from the earth and its people. Tomson Highway is Canadian. These are not mutually exclusive. In fact, in his [work], he proves the absurdity of the hyphen. He is not Cree-Canadian or Canadian-Cree. To be Cree is to originate in the land, long before it became known as a continent or was named by invaders, long before northern Manitoba was measured by distance and direction from Greenwich in England and declared to be remote, or was measured by the culture of the settler contagion and found to be dangerous and also irrelevant. To be Canadian is more elusive, intrinsic to the experience of each generation in turn. As a Cree, Tomson Highway is telling our story and I am learning to be what I am.[119]

Moss is a Mohawk and, as he describes Highway, possesses a dual—not hyphenated—identity. Natives today often possess dual identities. At least enrolled members of federally recognized tribes in the United States are dual citizens, much like a dual citizen of the United States and the United Kingdom. Winston Churchill's mother was American. Yet his voluminous writings are not normally counted as part of American literature. As Krupat alludes, it is a question of emphasis and participation, and the resolution is not always transparent—certainly not to those in the dominant culture.

Finally, though affirmation of Native tribal nations is a necessary aspect of Native American Studies, American Indian Literary Nationalism can be either tribal-specific or "pan-Indian" (though I recognize the disrepute of such a term—I use it consciously). As Simon Ortiz says of the saint's day ceremonial at Acoma, "It is Acqumeh *and* Indian." I am not an "indigenist." I do not envision a category or canon of "indigenous literature." I use Smith, or Rob Nieuwenhuys, or whomever in my work because I see their utility, given the commonalties of colonial experience. But that does not make me an indigenist, any more than Robert Dale Parker is black simply because he employs Homi Bhabha, or Skip Gates, or bell hooks in his argumentation. Womack and Justice write in a tribally specific manner, for instance, while Warrior, Howard Adams, Craig Howe, and I, although equally "nationalistic," tend to take a more pan-Indian approach. As Ortiz concludes his ruminations, "And finally, it is the voice of countless, non-literary Indian women and men of this nation who live a daily life of struggle to achieve and maintain meaning which gives the most authentic character to a national Indian literature."[120]

III. Seeing Red, Reading Red

In *Muting White Noise*, James Cox "privileges Native sources in the reading of novels by Native authors as a critical lens through which to read the traditional and revised European American canon." Although the work deals primarily with Native authors, an important underlying current "is that the critical interpretation of works by European and European-American authors can and in some contexts should proceed primarily from Indian sources." Cox limns "red readings," a term he borrows from Jill Carter, an Anishinaabe graduate student at the University of Toronto. These "privilege a critical practice based on the work of Native creative writers and intellectuals and foreground the issues that they raise as important to Native people and communities." He provides a Red reading of *Moby-Dick* as a novel of Native absence.[121] This process in which Cox engages is the same one in which Natives are involved whenever they read any text, privileging Native experience and determining how the work in their hands addresses their daily lives and concerns. In this, they are little different than any reader.

Some years ago in my class on Native American Women Writers, I handed out, as an illustrative counter-text, a story from Herbert Schwarz's *Tales from the Smokehouse*, a collection of Native erotic stories. In the story, a Christian missionary enters the room of a young Native female convert, finding her naked on the stone floor, her arms outstretched, gazing at a crucifix on the wall. When he inquires as to her actions, she replies, "It is my desire to suffer, to be cold and hungry. . . . In that way, I feel closer to him." According to the account, the cleric, purporting to be moved by her example, removes his clothing, saying, "You have set me an example, and it is only right that I too should follow. And if you are suffering on that cold chilly floor, then I shall suffer likewise." Seeing the man's erection, the young girl inquires, "What is that pointed stick that stands out from your belly?" His Pauline response is: "My child . . . this stick is a thorn in my side, which causes me great pain and misery." The naïve catechist replies, "It grieves me to see you so. Although I am cold and hungry, my suffering is but small compared to yours. . . . I want you to torture me with that thorn of yours, and put it where it will hurt me most!" The story then progresses to its obvious, gruesome conclusion, made all the more disgusting because it implicitly says that Native women do not know their own bodies. Schwarz claimed that the story was factual, having been narrated to him in 1955 by the real "gentle Indian girl" involved in the incident.[122]

After the students had read the story, I asked for their reactions. A young woman, an Apache who had been born, raised, and educated on Mescalero, lifted her hand and said, "Isn't this a story from *The Decameron?*" Indeed, as I already knew, it was: the so-called "put the devil in hell" tale. I believe that Schwarz's "informant" was having a bit of fun at the expense of the amateur ethnographer, a not uncommon practice (though Italian Renaissance literature is not normally involved in the jape).[123] After the young woman's question, she and her fellow students deconstructed the offensive story along logical lines. The student had given both Bocaccio and the text in front of her Red readings.

Although Ortiz's countless, ordinary "non-literary Indian women and men" may not have read *The Decameron*, they are, thanks to the educational system of the United States, far more likely to have encountered *Huckleberry Finn* or *The House of the Seven Gables* than they are to have read *House Made of Dawn* or *Ceremony*. And out of their own experience they naturally give these Red readings, even if they, through operant conditioning, often keep such readings to themselves.

This chapter began with examples of first utterances. Belying the old saw that Americans are great on beginnings, alright on middles, and lousy on endings, if one examines American literature, there are only three great opening lines. Around the world, wonderful first lines abound—Dickens, Du Maurier, Waugh, Malraux, García Márquez, Carlo Levi, Lawrence Durrell, Tsitsi Dangarembga, and on and on. (My personal favorite is from *The Alley Cat* by Quebecois writer Yves

Beauchemin, which in translation runs, "One April morning around
eight o'clock, Médéric Duchêne was walking briskly past postal station
'C' at the corner of Ste-Catherine and Plessis Streets when one of the
bronze quotation marks from the inscription at the top of the old building fell onto his skull.") But poor, impoverished American literature has
only three: "Call me Ishmael"; "My mother is a fish"; and "We were
somewhere around Barstow on the edge of the desert when the drugs
began to take hold."[124] The first, of course, is Melville. The last is
Hunter S. Thompson from *Fear and Loathing in Las Vegas*. The one in
the middle is William Faulkner.

Technically, it isn't a first line at all. It doesn't even occur until a
third of the way through the novel, but it is the first sentence of a chapter. In fact, it is the only line *in* the chapter, and it is the line that gives
the book its resonance. It is from *As I Lay Dying*, one of the superlative
novels of the twentieth century.

When I was in college in France, we were told that the French were
only then discovering Faulkner. I first read Faulkner in France, a reading both out of time and out of place. *As I Lay Dying* had just been
translated. Its title in French was *Comme J'angoisse*. As I anguish. It is
certainly a cautionary tale for those in comparative literature and literature in translation. How does one translate Faulkner? "Ma mere est un
poisson" just does not have the same force. My mother is a fish.

Given that in more than 150 years of truly American literature, from
Hawthorne and Melville to the present, there are only, by my lights, three
great opening lines, it should be no great surprise that Native American
literature has yet to produce one—though "Abel was running" comes
close. Again, I know that it isn't a first sentence. It begins the second paragraph, but it is that which, no pun intended, sets the novel in motion.

In this section, I want to reverse the gaze and play a bit with a Red
reading of Faulkner, his place, his sense of place, and Indians. In the
process, I will say something about Native literature and the place of
American Indian Literary Nationalism as well.

No one could seriously dispute that Faulkner is one of the most
influential American writers of the past century. It is therefore only natural that be would have an impact on Native writers. Acknowledged or
unacknowledged, he has influenced two generations of Indian authors

as diverse as Scott Momaday, Louise Erdrich, Leslie Silko, and Geary Hobson, among others. I am not alone in hearing echoes of him in the work of Tomson Highway, Craig Womack, and LeAnne Howe. Perhaps more improbably, I also hear those notes at least faintly in writers like Gerald Vizenor and Thomas King.

To begin at the beginning, certainly not of Native literature, but of the so-called "Literary Renaissance," the influence of Faulkner on Scott Momaday has been well commented upon. Louis Owens, whose own creative work owes more than a passing debt to the Nobel laureate, notes the Faulknerian character of the German tank in Abel's nightmare in *House Made of Dawn*. And although Momaday himself likened the white man that Abel kills to the "intelligent malignity" of Moby Dick, the description of the stabbing is purely Faulknerian.[125] Compare the description of the killing in *House Made of Dawn* to the perceptions of the President and the Secretary of the Chickasaw chief in "Lo!" Both the albino and the chief are repulsive, objects of revulsion described in terms both human and inhuman. Both are grotesque and fat, and yet there is a repugnant (to Momaday and Faulkner) sexual ambiguity to each. The "white man's" flesh is described as "loose, and it rode on the bones of his jaws." His "face was huge." During the final struggle, his "white immensity of flesh lay over and smothered" Abel. He embraces Abel and blows in his ear and the Native can feel "the scales of the lips and the hot slippery point of the tongue." In "Lo!" the chief is depicted as a "bland, obese mongrel." At the parlay table (a duel of a different order), the President and the Secretary regard him:

> Immobile, they contemplated the soft, paunchy man
> facing them with his soft, bland, inscrutable face—the long,
> monk-like nose, the slumbrous lids, the flabby, *café-au-lait*-
> colored jowls above a froth of soiled lace of an elegance
> fifty years outmoded and vanished; the mouth was full,
> small, and very red. Yet somewhere behind the face's
> expression of flaccid and weary disillusion, as behind
> the bland voice and almost feminine mannerisms, there
> lurked something else: something willful, shrewd,
> unpredictable and despotic.

Similarly, in *Big Woods*, Moketubbe, Issetibbeha's successor, is described as "a creature so gross and fat." The crucial difference is that the animalistic-yet-intelligent malignancy attributed to the absolute Other in Momaday's novel is ascribed to the albino's whiteness, whereas for Faulkner it is marked by the Natives' darkness.

Matthias Schubnell, in his book *N. Scott Momaday: The Cultural and Literary Background*, published in 1985, traces the influence of Faulkner, as well as Isak Dinesen and D. H. Lawrence. Kenneth Lincoln makes similar claims in *Native American Renaissance*, two years earlier. The twin impacts of Faulkner and Lawrence are not coincidental, as we will see, but rather of a piece.[126]

Schubnell writes:

> Momaday's indebtedness to Faulkner is reflected in some of the technical aspects of his writings, particularly *House Made of Dawn*: the fragmented narrative perspective, the disjointed time scheme, the connection of surface meaning to underlying symbolic patterns, the use of different styles for different characters. Thematically the two writers resemble each other in the way they stress the importance of a functioning tradition for individual human existence. They see the acceptance of responsibility in the historical continuum as a prerequisite for survival. Faulkner's remark that "no man is himself, he's the sum of his past, and in a way... of his future, too" and Momaday's contention that "notions of the past and future are essentially notions of the present" are crucial for understanding their works. Faulkner's Joe Christmas and Abel... are characters who suffer because they have lost control over their pasts and, without the support of viable traditions, have lost their sense of self.[127]

The same could be said of Tayo in Silko's *Ceremony*. Both Schubnell and Lewis Dabney in his *The Indians of Yoknapatawpha* note that Francisco's pursuit of the bear in *House Made of Dawn*, published separately as the short story "The Bear and the Colt," owe much to Faulkner's story "The Bear."[128]

Momaday met Faulkner during the academic year 1956–57, when he was enrolled in a law program at the University of Virginia. In a 1973 interview, Momaday said, "I like Faulkner, and I've read a lot of Faulkner, and I want to write like Faulkner;...and I'm sure that I've tried to, but to what extent Faulkner is an influence on me, I really don't know." Sixteen years later, in the extended interviews with Charles Woodard, published as *Ancestral Voice*, he again acknowledged Faulkner on the issue of voice. A few pages later, however, Momaday seemingly retracts both the previous statements, saying:

> I think he often states the obvious. He becomes drunk with words. He frequently loses sight of his objective and becomes so deeply engrossed in his language that he becomes trapped in his own devices. Where he is best is in his mythic imagining. When he begins talking about the South and its romantic ideals, and when he writes about the bear, which is a mythic evocation of the South and the southern landscape, that's great.... But I don't think Faulkner is a man to emulate. I wouldn't want to try and write like Faulkner, though maybe I do in small ways because I have read him.[129]

Certainly there are those who might be forgiven for thinking that in some of those words Momaday could be talking about himself, as well.

Geary Hobson produces a very Faulknerian novel in his *The Last of the Ofos*, which tells the first person story of Thomas Darko, a member of the fictional Mosopelea (known as the Ofos to whites), from his birth in 1905 until old age, when he realizes that he is the last of his tribe. Certainly Thomas Darko's journey to this self-awareness mirrors the experience of Sam Fathers in "The Bear." Fathers is a person who, at least in Louisiana, would be pejoratively labeled a "Redbone," which is to say that he is of tri-racial ancestry, African American, Native, and white. His Native ancestry is Chickasaw, though he has been forced by the social order to live as black. When the last full-blood Chickasaw dies, he withdraws from society and goes to live in the woods.

Louise Erdrich is often compared to Faulkner in "her fictional terrain, a coherently populated geography" onto which she inscribes stories of survival. Faulkner is, in fact, reportedly one of her favorite authors, and, of all Native writers, she is perhaps the most deliberately, at times even mimetically, Faulknerian. Robert Silberman, writing in Vizenor's edited volume *Narrative Chance*, comments on this:

> Michael Wood once remarked that Faulkner was a key figure for many of the Latin American writers of the "Boom" (Vargas Llosa, Donoso and above all García Márquez) because he demonstrated that novels could be formally experimental works of modern art while not abandoning the traditional concern with social description. Faulkner after all wrote family sagas, historical novels portraying communal life from generation to generation. . . . Erdrich's *Love Medicine* has more than a passing resemblance to *As I Lay Dying, Absalom, Absalom* and *The Sound and the Fury*. Whether or not Erdrich was directly influenced by the Latin Americans [and thus by one more remove by Faulkner], and in particular, by García Márquez, her work uses some of the same methods and at times a similar tone. The constant shifting of point of view and chronological jumps in the narrative make divergent versions of a single event possible, introducing a modernist sense of relativism and discontinuity as well as a good deal of ironic humor.[130]

Though, in his postmodernist wordplay, Vizenor may seem far removed from Faulkner and his modernism, I would argue that it is in these same ways that he shows some kinship with him.

In his first novel, *Kiss of the Fur Queen*, Tomson Highway tells the story of two generations of a Cree family in northern Manitoba. Abraham Okimasis, a trapper and championship dogsled racer, becomes in 1951 the first Native to win the grueling Millington Cup race. When their first son is born a few months later, he and his wife name him Champion in honor of the achievement. Champion and his younger brother, Ooneemeetoo, born three years later, grow up living an idyllic traditional life until Champion reaches age six, when he is taken to Birch Lake Indian Residential School. With that plane flight to school, both boys' lives are changed forever. Ooneemeetoo follows a few years later.[131] The pair endure nightmarish residential school experiences: forbidden to speak their Native languages, renamed Jeremiah and Gabriel, sexually abused by Catholic priests. Later, as urban Indians in Winnipeg, they encounter the casual racism and disregard of Anglo-Canadians. Discussing the book, Moss writes, "Tomson Highway gives us a renewed sense of place with words as familiar once read as the environs of Yoknapatawpha, which is William Faulkner's great gift to the world. I have been to Eemanapiteepitat and I did not ever want to leave and live in a residential school run by the church that would work with the state to drown with their vaulting resources my small boy's mind and body, but from which I will emerge to breathe underwater and hear the music of the stars."[132]

Highway is first and foremost a dramatist. Tom King is primary a novelist. Yet both have demonstrated themselves capable of adroitly changing expressive forms. In *Other Words*, I also argue for a Faulknerian tone to some of King's work. In particular, his still unproduced play *Drums*, displays a Faulknerian sense of time and history. For King, no less than for Faulkner, the past isn't dead and gone; it isn't even past yet.[133] This, of course, is also a very Native view of time. (In Silko's *Almanac of the Dead*, an event that occurred seventy years ago still has ramifications because "seventy years was nothing—a mere heartbeat at Laguna.") I also believe, however, that in his use of space and his evocation of landscape in his highly underrated novel *Truth & Bright Water*, as Moss avers for *Kiss of the Fur Queen* and Highway, King demonstrates an affinity for Faulkner.

What is it that has drawn these, and many other Native writers, to William Faulkner, other than his indisputable artistry and mastery of language and fictional form? To be sure, it is not his portrayals of Native Americans. Though there are some (such as Sam Fathers), they are few and far between. Fenimore Cooper contended that he drew his depictions of Indians in *Leather-Stocking Tales* from personal knowledge but, in actuality, drew them from John Heckwelder's treatise and privately admitted that he never met an Indian. Similarly, Faulkner, when asked from where he derived his Indians, reportedly replied, "I made them up."[134] Cox contends that "[Willa] Cather makes some of her White characters Indians, while Faulkner either confines Native characters to the past of his fictional Yoknapatawpha County or has non-Native characters inherit their views and values. For example, Sam Fathers passes his knowledge of the natural world and even part of his Native language to Isaac 'Ike' McCaslin before he dies in *Go Down, Moses* (1942). Both Cather and Faulkner affirm colonial domination and enable its perpetuation by refusing to acknowledge a historical context of violent colonial invasions of Native land and by naturalizing contemporary indigenous absence." In sum, writes Cox, "Faulkner's Indians play a substantial role in the fictional history of Yoknapatawpha County, yet Faulkner is unable to imagine them in the narrative present or future of his short stories and novels."[135] As Laura Adams Weaver states concisely, "The only thing past for Faulkner is the Indian."[136]

Yoknapatawpha County was originally Chickasaw territory, though Faulkner is inconsistent, sometimes referring to Choctaws. The first Amer-European settlers came to the region between 1800 and 1811. It was ceded in 1814 by the Treaty of Fort Jackson, ending the Creek War—a land cession so large it makes up present-day Mississippi and Alabama. Subsequently, the Chickasaws agreed to Removal in 1832 by the Treaty of Pontitock Creek. Though some Chickasaw remained after Removal, by 1936, Faulkner gives the population of Yoknapatawpha as 6,298 whites and 9,313 blacks. From a Native standpoint, it is an ethnically cleansed landscape. The presence of "Redbones" like Sam Fathers only highlights this fact. In him and others one sees a descent from a racially pure past. Remember that when the last full-blood Chickasaw dies, Fathers retreats (indeed recedes) into the forest.

Faulkner also gives readers inconsistent stories about Ikkemotubbe, the Chickasaw chief whose territory once included Yoknapatawpha. He and Issetibbeha, described variously as his son and his uncle, appear in "A Courtship," "Red Leaves," "A Justice," *The Reivers, Absalom, Absalom!, Go Down, Moses, Requiem for a Nun, The Town,* and *The Sound and the Fury.* In the last of these, Ikkemotubbe is referred to as a "dispossessed American king" who "granted out of his vast lost domain a solid square mile of virgin North Mississippi dirt as truly angled as the four corners of a cardtable" to Jason Lycurgus Compson, the "grandson of a Scottish refugee who had lost his own birthright by casting his lot with a king who himself had been dispossessed." Ikkemotubbe is known by the English name David Callicoat, but he is also called Chief Doom.

This is said to be an anglicized corruption of the French "Du Homme," a recognition both of his position and his humanity, but the signification is unmistakable. Ikkemotubbe, like the other absent members of his people, is doomed, foreordained to vanish in the face of Amer-European civilization and its inexorable logic. As Louis Owens states, "Writers from Freneau and Cooper to Faulkner and LaFarge would stop here, with a crocodile tear for the dying noble savage."[137]

In Faulkner, more is at work than a simplistic "vanishing" of Native presence. In his writing, he reinscribes a narrative embedded deep within the psyche of white Mississippians, and indeed within the Southern Amer-European mind generally. Though it may have been inadvertent (the sloppy and casual result of writing disparate pieces over time), his contradictory genealogies of Ikkemotubbe and his kin reinforce an attitude that Natives are sexually loose: these are Indians, they are all related somehow, but ultimately it is inconsequential. It simply does not matter. Would Faulkner be so nonchalant about the genealogies and interrelationships of the Compsons or, for that matter, any of his white characters?

As noted above, Faulkner is also contradictory as to the tribal identity of Ikkemotubbe and his family. In "The Bear," he is referred to as "the Chickasaw chief." Sam Fathers recedes into the woods when he, like Hobson's Thomas Darko, is, at least figuratively, the last of his tribe, in his case the Chickasaw. Yet in "A Justice," Fathers describes his ancestor Ikkemotubbe ("the Man"/Du Homme) as "a Choctaw chief." This betrays a homogenized Indian identity in the American mind generally. Indians are Indians. Tribal distinctions, like family lineage, are without importance. Faulkner slips easily back and forth between references to Choctaws and Chickasaws in Yoknapatawpha County because, again, in the end, it is inconsequential. It is much the same as in Georgia, for instance. There, Mary Musgrove—known as Creek Mary—is a foundational/mediational figure cut from the same Amer-European–supplied cloth as Pocahontas. And the Cherokees are memorialized throughout the state, despite the historical fact that the Creeks and their Muscogean kin occupied more of the state geographically than they did (and forgetting entirely the Siouian Yuchi).

In the final analysis neither a muddled genealogy nor a confused tribal affiliation matters because, as obvious and banal as it is to point out, Indians for Faulkner are already vanished, erased in totality from the landscape. In *Big Woods*, Issetibbeha's Negro "body servant" realizes, as his master lays on his deathbed, "his true situation, how desperate, how irrevocable, how doomed [again a nice play upon Du Homme/ Chief Doom]," sharing the fate of the Native he served. In the introduction, entitled "Mississippi," Faulkner writes that "Choctaw and Chickasaw braves, in short-hair and overalls and armed with mule-whips in place of war-clubs and already packed up to move west to Oklahoma, watched steamboats furrowing even the shallowest and remotest wilderness streams." Even as whites flock in for settlement, the Natives are "already packed," seemingly willing, even eager, to surrender the land for an as yet non-existent place named Oklahoma ("Oklahoma" would not even be invented as a name until 1866).

In his complete erasure of Natives, Faulkner is merely repeating the white Mississippian origin myth of his time. In the February 18, 1845, edition of the *Vicksburg Sentinel*, a piece appeared proclaiming "Farewell to the Choctaws." In lachrymose prose, it stated:

> The last remnants of this once powerful race are now crossing
> our ferry on their way to their new home in the far West.
> To one who, like the writer, has been familiar to their bronze,
> inexpressive faces from infancy, it brings associations of
> peculiar sadness to see them bidding farewell to the old hills
> which gave birth, and are doubtless equally dear, to him and
> them alike. The first playmates of our infancy were the young
> Choctaw boys of the ten woods of Warren County. Their
> language was once scarcely less familiar to us than our mother
> English. We know, we think, the character of the Choctaw
> well. We knew many of their present stalwart braves in those
> days of early life when Indian and white alike forget to
> disguise, but, in the unchecked exuberance of youthful feeling,
> show the real character that policy and habit may afterward
> so much conceal; and we know that, under the stolid and stoic
> look he assumes, there is burning in the Indian's nature a
> heart of fire and feeling and an all observing keenness of
> apprehension that marks and remembers everything that

occurs and every insult he receives. Cunni-at-a-hah! "They are going away!" With a visible reluctance which nothing has ever overcome but the stern necessity which they feel impelling them, they have looked their last upon the graves of their sires—the scenes of their youth—and have taken up their slow toilsome march with their household gods among them to their new home in a strange land. They leave names to many of our rivers, towns and counties and, as long as our State remains, the Choctaws, who once owned most of her soil, will be remembered.[138]

The editorial is remarkable for a number of reasons and is deserving of a careful exegesis in its own right. Such a close reading is, however, beyond the scope of this study. For our purposes, I will discuss only two points.

The Choctaws were the first to capitulate to the perceived inevitability of Removal. The Treaty of Dancing Rabbit Creek was executed on September 27, 1830, a scant four months to the day from when Andrew Jackson signed the Removal Act into law. The bulk of Choctaw Removal was finished by 1834. The newspaper article is more than a decade later. To be sure, of those who remained—and that number was not insignificant—there were families who continued to self-remove after the initial, formal 1831–33 removals. These removals continued throughout the 1840s. The last census of Mississippi Choctaws occurred in 1855.[139] Here in 1845, the *Vicksburg Sentinel* proclaims the process complete. Choctaw absence is now total. It is, however, simply not true. More remained. As late as 1903, the Commission to the Five Civilized Tribes reported 264 "full-blood" Choctaws migrated from Mississippi to Indian Territory. And yet still more remained and remain there to the present day.[140]

Even as the editorial declares the Choctaws extinct in Mississippi, it proclaims that their presence remains. They will always be remembered because their names remain upon the land. Like Chauncey Yellow Robe's survival on celluloid thanks to the magic of the filmmakers, the sterile persistence of Choctaws in their homeland hinges upon the whims of settlers, land speculators, and cartographers. Faulkner closes the introduction to *Big Woods* describing the place of his nativity, "that Idea risen now, suspended like a balloon or portent or a thundercloud above what used to be wilderness, drawing, holding the eyes of all: Mississippi." Though the state unquestionably has Choctaw place-names, the irony is that "Mississippi" itself is not one of them. Even as "what used to be wilderness" is tamed by settlers' axes and plows, the land is rechristened with an Anishinaabe name meaning "big river," a name at once still Native and yet completely non-autochthonous.

Though Lewis Dabney acknowledges Choctaw continuance in Mississippi, he allows for no such survivance of the Chickasaws, writing, "the local Chickasaws had left only the place names and their Xs on the land patents." Yet, at the very least, crossbloods like Sam Fathers remain. In "A Justice," the narrator goes to Fathers's carpentry shop and listens to him. Asks Dabney, "Had the writer heard such a mixed blood holding forth on his Indian forebears?" Immediately preceding this question, he notes, "There were traces of 'the wild blood' in white men and black, lessening during his lifetime. In the appendix to *The Sound and the Fury* in 1945 it is 'seen only occasionally in the nose-shape of a Negro on a cotton-wagon or a white sawmill hand or trapper or locomotive fireman.'"[141] To take Faulkner's words at face value on this point leaves one fairly gobsmacked. It is a definitional extermination akin to that undergone by the native Tasmanians.

Faulkner's Indians do not vanish all at once. Rather they decay over time, disappearing gradually even before Removal. Or, perhaps more precisely, his Indians do vanish, leaving only their mixed-blood simulacra as reminders of their presence past. Ikkemotubbe degenerates from the princely youth of "A Courtship" and *Requiem for a Nun* to the despot who turns his tribe's land to his own personal possession in "A Justice."[142] Issetibbeha succeeds him, inheriting both his land and his slaves. In "Red Leaves," the latter travels to Paris on the proceeds of the slave trade and develops a taste for French frippery. He lives to be "so old that nothing more was required of him except to sit in the sun and criticize the degeneration of the People and the folly and rape of politicians." His son is the corpulent and repulsive Mokketubbe, who literally cannot fit into his father's shoes. Their degeneracy stems from their white blood and their embrace of their hybridity as exemplified by their acceptance of private property and chattel slavery, "because on the instant when Ikkemotubbe discovered, realised, that he could sell it [the land] for money, on that instant it ceased ever to have been his forever, father to father to father, and the man who bought it bought nothing." Of the line, only Sam Fathers is noble because his black blood frees him from the taint of either.

For Faulkner, the Indian's complicity in the twin sins of slavery and claims to private ownership of the land justify their removal. While this fits neatly with the writer's romantic ideology of decay from a pure Indian past and land as the common heritage of all, it nonetheless creates an ahistorical irony. The major reason for Removal was white covetousness of the land and Native refusal to surrender it and, with it, their communal notions of property. East of Mississippi, the Cherokees, for instance, during the height of the Removal crisis, passed a law making it a capital offense to alienate the land. And as Major Ridge, the author of that enactment, affixed his signature to the patently illegal Treaty of New Echota, he observed, "I have just signed my own death warrant," a statement that would prove prophetic.

Beyond his undeniable mastery of English letters, Faulkner attracts Native readers and writers through his deep-seated affinity for the land, as arriviste as the sentiment might be when compared to the autochthones whom he largely dismisses. Faulkner spins beguiling tales of Native absence, of vanishing and victimization. It is there that Native writers part company with Faulkner. Though there is often tragedy and anger (As Leslie Silko writes in *Almanac of the Dead*, "There were hundreds of years of blame that needed to be taken by somebody."), in general, they refuse to succumb to victimry and victimization. As Owens says of Vizenor's work, "In Vizenor's fictional world—a coherent and fully realized topography as complete as Faulkner's South or Garcia Marquez's Macondo—the tortured and torturing mixedblood represented so unforgettably in Mark Twain's 'Injun Joe' and Faulkner's 'Chief Doom' simply refuses to perish in the dark cave of the American psyche but instead soars to freedom in avian dreams and acrobatic outrage."[143] Though no one does exactly what Vizenor does—and certainly no one does it with the same *je ne sais quois*—something analogous could be said of many Native writers. In the main, they do not depict the "Vanishing Indian," and when they do, like Hobson in *The Last of the Ofos*, they do so with a purpose. They themselves refuse to vanish or to stifle their own voices or those for whom they write.

Schubnell, in writing about Momaday, has suggested that treatment of, and ties to, environment and land is another place where Faulkner and Native authors find, perhaps literally, "common ground."[144] While this may be superficially true, as I have just noted, it is once again a major divergence between Natives and the southern American writer and serves more to obscure than it does to illuminate.

Beginning his analysis of Louise Erdrich, Owens writes, "Central to Native American storytelling, as Momaday has shown so splendidly, is a construction of reality that begins, always with the land." Geary Hobson makes a similar point in his aptly named volume, *The Remembered Earth*. Land is, of course, an ordinate category for Native peoples. As I have previously written, "When Natives are removed from their traditional lands, they are robbed of more than territory; they are deprived of numinous landscapes that are central to their faith and their identity, lands populated by their relations, ancestors, animals, and beings both physical and mythological. A kind of psychic homicide is committed."[145]

According to Schubnell:

Faulkner contrasted this insensitivity toward the physical environment with a sense of place which grows out of a man's rootedness in the land. Central to this idea is the belief that individuals and cultures are molded by their homelands and that they must maintain a close relationship to them. One of Faulkner's characters spells out this notion of geographical determinism: "That's the trouble with this country: everything, weather, all, hangs on too long. Like our rivers, our land: opaque, slow, violent; shaping and creating the life of man in its implacable and brooding image." The idea reappears in *Light in August*, where Faulkner wrote about the fleeing Joe Christmas that "it is as though he desires to see his native earth in all its phases for the first and last time. He had grown to manhood in the country, where like the unswimming sailor his physical shape and his thought had been moulded by its compulsions without his learning anything about its actual shape and feel."[146]

In such a sentiment, one clearly recognizes the grace notes of Momaday's "Man Made of Words." Yet, at the same time, and not to the exclusion of the other, one hears Vine Deloria in his statement that "the white man knows that he is alien and that North America is Indian." Or Luther Standing Bear, almost fifty years earlier:

> The white man does not understand the Indian for the reason that he does not understand America. He is too far removed from its formative processes. The roots of the tree of his life have not yet grasped the rock and soil. The white man is still troubled with primitive fears; he still has in his consciousness the perils of this frontier continent, some of its fastnesses not yet having yielded to his questing footsteps and inquiring eyes. He shudders still with the memory of loss of his forefathers upon its scorching deserts and forbidding mountain-tops. The man from Europe is still a foreigner and an alien. And he still hates the man who questioned his path across the continent.

Amer-Europeans, not Sam Fathers, are still Faulkner's unswimming sailors in the ocean of North America.[147] As Faulkner himself stated in terms akin to D. H. Lawrence, "I think the ghost of that ravishment [Removal] lingers in the land, that the land is inimical to the white man because of the unjust way in which it was taken from Ikkemotubbe and his people."[148]

Thus, to be sure, Faulkner did critique the rapacity of Amer-European pioneers, "who desecrated the wilderness for utilitarian purposes." In "Big Woods," he wrote that "then came the Anglo-Saxon, the pioneer, ... turning the earth into a howling waste from which he would be the first to vanish ... because ... only the wilderness could feed and nourish him." Matthias Schubnell writes of Faulkner and Momaday, "For Faulkner nature was where man could learn the lesson of the wilderness and cultivate a code of honor. Through an appropriate relation to the natural world man could improve himself ethically and achieve the fullest realization of his humanity. Momaday's appeal for a return to a greater consciousness of and respect for man's physical environment not only suggests a similar land ethic but reflects a hope which Faulkner had lost. For him the wilderness was doomed and with it human integrity, which was severed from its source of nourishment."[149] Of course, for Natives, the natural environment was never "wilderness," a region untouched, uninhabited, unministered to by human beings and their other-than-human kin.

Ultimately, Faulkner's view of the American earth is that of Lawrence as limned in the latter's *Studies in Classic American Literature*, a foreign and haunted landscape, populated by grinning demons, where the Amer-European is doomed to contest desperately with himself and the ghosts he has created in an effort to prove that he belongs, to establish his own indigeneity. It is, to be sure, no accident that Sam Fathers retreats into the forest, into, as it were, the wilderness—that place beyond the polis that has been, since the first colonizers, a wild place, a dark and fearful place, an animalistic place, a Native space.

The center of Faulkner's fictional landscape, that place in which he sought rootedness, was Yoknapatawpha County. According to Faulkner, the name means "water flowing slow through the flatland." In *Flags in the Dust*, the name is given as Yocona, the name of an actual river in Lafayette County, Mississippi, the model for his fictional place. It may be from this fact that Faulkner derives his definition. Later he changes the name to Yoknapatawpha. But Yoknapatawpha is actually a compound of the Choctaw/Chickasaw words "yocona" and "petopha," earth and split. Yoknapatawpha is thus "split earth." Arthur Kinney, in *Go Down, Moses: The Miscegenation of Time*, suggests an additional meaning, positing that Faulkner might have consulted a 1915 Choctaw dictionary, from which one can parse "yakni patafa" as "plowed" or "cultivated" land. Perhaps reflecting an Amer-European view that, to be of worth, land must be tooled, the biblio-juridical position that cultivators of the soil had a greater claim to the land than hunters and gatherers—not that it did the Chickasaws (or any of the other agriculturalist tribes of the Southeast) any good when it came to the time of Removal.[150]

I want to suggest that Yoknapatawpha is a kind of metaphor, indeed a powerful one, for Native existence in general and Native literature in particular. Not only have Natives been split from their lands until, at the most extreme, they exist, in one vision of Vizenor in *Landfill Meditation*, in a world of pan-tribal urban emptiness where "people are severed like dandelions on suburban lawns, separated from the living places of the earth," but since the arrival of Europeans, the land itself has been split, not only by the conqueror's plow, but by the conqueror's law. What was once home and family is now mere property, a commodity to be owned and possessed, bought and sold. The land that was once wholly Natives' has been split from them. A physical, but also a psychical, fissure has cleaved Native land from non-Native land. Call it what you will: "civilized" from "savage," "technological" from "natural," "possession," from "home." D. H. Lawrence wrote, "America isn't a blood-home-land. For every American, the blood-home-land is Europe. The spirit-home-land is America."[151]

Yoknapatawpha, this split, however, is equally applicable to Native American literature. In *Red on Red*, Craig Womack talks about the "'translation problem' with its skepticism and emphasis on literary diminishment" that leads to a "pure versus tainted" split, a framework that infects so much of Native American Studies. In this binary opposition, as he reiterates herein, the perceived primitive purity of pre-Contact times, orature, Native languages, and Indian religion and culture are set against the "impure" forms of the post-Contact era, letters, translation, Native Christians, and Indian politics.[152]

I have already analyzed how for many non-Native scholars, literature ceases to be Indian when it employs the languages of the colonizer and adopts such Western forms as the novel, short story, or autobiography. Would not logic dictate that the same would be true about the use of European- or Amer-European–derived critical tools and forms? Womack writes:

> Some Native American writers have made inclusionary arguments, claiming that they do not wish to be considered "just an Indian writer." My problem is with the word "just," and my question is, why not? When we use this kind of language, admitting lesser roles for ourselves, to what degree are we internalizing dominant culture racism? What's wrong

with being an Indian writer? Why is that a diminished role among writers? Who made up these rules? Why should we want to adhere to them? Does a description of Faulkner as a southern writer make him less an important figure? Should his Nobel Prize be taken back because he was "just a southern writer"? Just what is there more important than Native authors testifying to surviving genocide and advocating sovereignty and survival? Here, I am endorsing Flannery O'Connor's well-known argument that the deeper an author delves into her home country, the more universal and powerful her writing becomes.[153]

Does the fact that Womack invokes Faulkner and Flannery O'Connor make his remarks "less Native"?[154]

Regardless of their intentions, non-Native scholars must understand, when they begin to divide Native literary production (implicitly labeling some "authentic" and some less so) or when they seem to dictate to Natives that they must acknowledge their hybridity and employ European theory, how this is heard by Native Americans. To the ears of many of us, such discussions sound not only paternalistic, but the strategies behind them seem to be part and parcel of continued attempts to define indigenes out of existence.

IV. Conclusion: Questing for the New Human Person

Near the end of her life, Australian Aborigine writer Daisy Utemorrah declared:

> Here's my words. You listen. I want people to hear them. Long long time ago, in the early-early days, our black people fought the white people with spears, they fought 'm with guns, you know? But these days we only fight with words. Fighting with spears and guns is no good for us black people anymore. It doesn't work. Our people fought with spears and guns and

they still lost the land. So that's why I'm a storyteller.
That's why I'm a writer. I fight with words for my people.
I'm gonna take back the land with words. Words are my gun
and my spear.

The government, they use words, too. They plenty good
using words just like they used to be plenty good at using guns.
They stopped using guns on us black people now. Now they
use words on us.[155]

Writing out of North American context, Kateri Akiwenzie Damm states,
"Through the power of words we can counteract negative images of
Indigenous peoples. We can fight words with words. Then, with the
weakening of colonial attitudes we can move together towards greater
cultural, artistic and creative forms of expression that reflect the changing faces of who we are." For my part, and not at all to negate the powerful visions just cited, in *That the People Might Live*, I write, "Though,
of necessity, Native writers, in their communitist commitments, are often
subversive, this is not meant to imply that such artists are somehow communitist commandos, employing the stylus rather than Sten guns or
word processors instead of plasticage. It does mean, however, that they
refuse to be colonialist minstrels in Redface on the dominant culture's
showboat. They resist the often nearly irresistible pull to remake Native
peoples in the image of White America."[156]

In advancing American Indian Literary Nationalism, we harbor no
illusions. As Smith writes, "In a decolonizing framework, deconstruction is part of a much larger intent. Taking apart a story, revealing underlying texts, and giving voice to things that are often known intuitively
does not help people improve their current conditions. It provides words,
perhaps, an insight that explains certain experiences—but it will not prevent someone from dying."[157] Nevertheless, very few of us would do
what we do unless we believed it could have some real world impact.[158]
To the extent that we don't perpetuate a discourse of assimilation and
imperialism, and to the extent that we can help people see contemporary Natives as Natives and tribes as sovereign nations, there is some
potential benefit in shaping minds, however indirect. Because "[t]o
acquiesce is to lose ourselves entirely and implicitly agree with all that

has been said about us. To resist is to retrench in the margins, retrieve what we were and remake ourselves. The past, our stories local and global, the present, our communities, cultures, languages and social practices—all may be spaces of marginalization, but they have also become spaces of resistance and hope."[159]

It seems to us that this is the nub of it. This is the essence of intellectual sovereignty. After more than five hundred years of ever-consolidating colonialism and conquest, the last thing Natives can be sure of sovereignty over is words, thoughts, compositional strategies. Yet even these abstractions are not without practical efficacy. Political philosopher Hannah Arendt taught us all that, in the final analysis, the only freedom is the freedom to discipline oneself. In other words, as Seneca elder John Mohawk said, "If you want to be sovereign, you have to act sovereign."[160] "Thinking sovereign" is a necessary precondition.

In his award-winning study, *Che Guevara: Economics and Politics in the Transition to Socialism*, economist Carlos Tablada discusses Guevara's 1965 article "Socialism and Man in Cuba." In that piece, the revolutionary wrote that if communism were to be achieved, it would be "necessary, simultaneous with the new material foundations to build the new man." According to Tablada, Che described the "ultimate objective" as "creating a social structure that will provide optimum conditions for the *type* of 'human nature' aspired to. The *new* man will emerge both as a result of revolutionary effort and as the product of conditions inherent to the structures created by the revolution. He will take hold of his own existence in order to dominate the forces that previously imposed their destiny upon him."[161]

None of the three of us advocates revolutionary socialism. And Guevara was writing out of the Latin machismo of the Cuban revolution. Neither are any of us interested in building "the new *man*." The Anishinaabe refer to animals—the beavers, the deer, the rest of the created order—as "other-than-human persons." Though not human, they are nonetheless persons. They too are part of the wider community. Perhaps we need to foster the birth of a "new human person." Literary criticism may not be able to prevent someone from dying, but it can participate in a process by which people think differently about indigenous peoples (as well as the wider community of other-than-human persons) and by which

Natives think differently about themselves. In other words, in helping reframe the narrative we believe there is genuine and estimable benefit. As Tablada wrote in the Cuban socialist context, this is not romanticism, "not a dream of a utopian paradise. It should be self-evident that the development of consciousness must be the strategic objective." It derives, he states, from an "understanding of how social being determines social consciousness, and how both elements can only be transformed jointly, through social practice."[162] To put it differently: if you want to be sovereign, you have to act sovereign, and before you can do that you have to think of yourself as sovereign. One has to be able to envision oneself in a sovereign manner. Though it may be efficacious only at the margins, literary criticism can aid in such thinking.

Tablada acknowledged that "the *new man* cannot be precisely defined," but said "it is nonetheless perfectly clear what we *do not want him to be*."[163] Similarly, I previously said that we cannot define precisely what the contours of American Indian Literary Nationalism will be; nor would we want to do so. Equally, we cannot say exactly what the new human person to whose formation we would contribute through such criticism will look like. Even at this preliminary juncture, however, we can, like Tablada, say what we do *not* want him or her to be.

We do not want the new human person to be one who pursues an individualistic agenda without commitment to Native people and the ongoing sovereignty of Native nations. From the *reducciones* of missionaries in "Latin America" to their counterparts in the North, from allotment to boarding schools, from the Curtis Act's abolition of tribal courts and governments to the twin-headed policy of Termination and Relocation, the consistent assimilationist goal of the dominant culture has been the individualization of Natives and the diminution of the rights of Native nations and their citizens.[164] Too often scholarship, either intentionally, by inadvertence, or sheer force of habit, has supported these same ends. The new human person must be empowered to think sovereign and act sovereign.

The new human person must not be a victim. As Alfred succinctly states, "We are entitled to lay blame, but not to make excuses." He concludes, "Native people can't cry their way to nationhood. Fulfilling the responsibility to reconstruct the nation means moving beyond the politics of pity. A sensitive pragmatism is needed to reinfuse our societies with the positive energy required to confront the continuing injustice, protect what remains, and build our own future."[165] As critics, we are more interested in examining our own histories and cultures than in simply cataloging the sins of both commission and omission of Amer-Europeans, no matter how multitudinous and multifarious.

This leads to the next quality we would wish absent from the new human person. In the affirmation of Native community and sovereignty, she or he must refrain from romanticizing some halcyon pre-Contact culture and existence. Alfred writes, "In lamenting the loss of a traditional frame of reference, we must be careful not to romanticize the past. Tradition is the spring from which we draw our healing water; but any decisions must take into account contemporary economic, social, and political concerns."[166] In advocating American Indian Literary Nationalism, we are not looking backward to some pure, idealized past. We are not thinking about how our great-grandparents lived; we are thinking about how our great-grandchildren will live.

Finally, though it may seem self-serving, we do not want the new human person to be anti-intellectual. Indigenous peoples around the world have a skepticism concerning research and theory. This is understandable given that, in many cases, these have been impositions upon Native existence and because both their methods and effects have been so damaging to communities and individuals. Alfred writes, "It is incumbent on this generation of Native people to heal the colonial sickness through the re-creation of sound communities, individual empowerment, and the re-establishment of relationships based on traditional values." Internally generated theories that grow out of the concerns of Native peoples and not those of others, and that advance sovereign thought are integral to this process. They can help Natives imagine and understand themselves *as Natives.* We agree with Smith when she writes:

> I am arguing that theory at its most simple level is important
> for indigenous peoples. At the very least it helps them make
> sense of reality. It enables us to make assumptions and
> predictions about the world in which we live. It contains
> within it a method or methods for selecting and arranging,

for prioritising and legitimating what we see and do. Theory enables us to deal with contradictions and uncertainties. Perhaps more significantly, it gives us space to plan, to strategize, to take greater control over our resistances. The language of a theory can also be used as a way of organising and determining action. It helps us to interpret what is being told to us, and to predict the consequences of what is being promised. Theory can also protect us because it contains within it a way of putting reality into perspective. If a theory is good it also allows for new ideas and ways of looking at things to be incorporated constantly without the need to search constantly for new theories.

This is a collective process.[167]

American Indian Literary Nationalism, which takes seriously Native sovereignty and survivance, has indigenous self-determination at its core and decolonization, survival, recovery, development, and transformation in its penumbra.[168] We see American Indian Literary Nationalism as an essential way of analyzing Native American literatures but not the only way. Just as Womack in *Red on Red* stated that his tribal-centric method was not the only way to understand such literatures, we also make no claim to exclusivity. To do so would be to merely substitute a new imperialism for the old. We do not want our identity defined for us or our theory and methodology dictated to us, and we would not presume to prescribe them to others.

Arnold Krupat says in *Red Matters*, the cosmopolitan critic needs the nationalist critic.[169] We do not see American Indian Literary Nationalism so much as erecting ramparts that must be defended as offering a permeable barrier, neither Veil nor Buckskin Curtain. As an approach that supports sovereignty, it is broad enough to encompass not only Warrior, Womack, and Weaver, but also scholars as disparate Elizabeth Cook-Lynn, Paula Gunn Allen, Gerald Vizenor, Geary Hobson, LeAnne Howe, Jack Forbes, and Daniel Justice, to name only a few. To be sure, we have our disagreements, but they are our own, and that's the point. It can also include sympathetic non-Natives like Elaine Jahner and James Cox, to single out only two. American Indian Literary Nationalism is a set of critical strategies, growing out of the concerns and issues of Natives themselves, that is equally as applicable to analysis of Cooper, Faulkner, and Rudy Wiebe as it is to Momaday, Silko, and Sherman Alexie.

American Indian Literary Nationalism is separatist, but it is a pluralist separatism. We are splitting the earth, not dividing up turf.

Several years ago, at a panel organized on Craig Womack's and my work at the American Literature Association, Womack was asked what he saw as the future of Native American literature. His reply was simply, "More and funkier." As we now move toward the third generation of Native writers since the beginning of the Renaissance, I would certainly agree, as themes of loss ebb but themes of place and community remain vital and strong. A. A. Carr's *Eye Killers* has an aged Navajo chasing European vampires. In *Shell Shaker*, LeAnne Howe gives us a novel of powerful Choctaw women, tribal corruption, the Mafia, and Irish Republican Army terrorists. Womack, in his novel *Drowning in Fire*, weaves a story of place, family, Creek history, Christianity, and jazz. What could be more Native than these? As we now enter the twenty-first century, more than five hundred years after Columbus and the events he set in motion, the three of us look forward to more and funkier stories that still remain nonetheless Native. We hope you share both our hope and our anticipation.

J. G. W.

○

Notes

1. From "I Lost My Talk" in *We Are the Dreamers: Recent and Early Poetry* (Wreck Cove, NS: Breton Books, 1999). Joe's poem details the loss of language at Shubenacadie, a Canadian residential school and what in the United States would have been called a boarding school.

2. Quoted in Elizabeth Seay, *Searching for Lost City: On the Trail of America's Native Languages* (Guilford, CT: Lyons Press, 2003), 88.

3. Howard Adams, *Tortured People: The Politics of Colonization*, rev. ed. (Penticton, BC: Theytus Books, 1999), 115.

4. Columbus indeed believed he reached Asia and never acknowledged anything else. When Amer-Europeans commemorate Columbus Day, they celebrate a man who didn't know where he was going, didn't know where he was when he was there, and died thinking he had been someplace else. He called those he found Indians because he thought he reached the Indies. A favorite Native joke is that it is a good thing the Admiral of the Ocean Sea didn't believe he'd arrived in Turkey. It should be noted that Columbus's departure also coincided with an order for the expulsion of Jews from the same territory. There were reportedly Jews among his crew.

5. This utterance is sometimes attributed to Samoset. I believe, however, that the better and more likely case to be made is for Squanto, and these attributions far outnumber those for his compatriot.

6. Besides Pocahontas, one could also mention Mary Musgrove, her Georgia counterpart, sometimes known as "Creek Mary."

7. Arnold Krupat, *Ethnocriticism: Ethnography, History, Literature* (Berkeley: University of California Press, 1992), 44, 186. Emphasis original.

8. Kimberley Blaeser, "Native Literature: Seeking a Critical Center," in *Looking at the Words of Our People: First Nations Analysis of Literature*, ed. Jeannette Armonstrong (Penticton, BC: Theytus Books, 1993), 53–54.

9. Adams, 114.

10. See Jace Weaver, *That the People Might Live: Native American Literatures and Native American Community* (New York: Oxford University Press, 1997), 69.

11. Susan Berry Brill de Ramirez, *Contemporary American Indian Literatures and the Oral Tradition* (Tucson: University of Arizona Press, 1999), 8. Krupat himself has, as any responsible scholar would, kept up with the field, as he demonstrated most recently in *Red Matters* in 2002. Linda Smith, in 1999, seemingly echoes these sentiments, writing, "The development of theories by indigenous scholars which attempt to explain our existence in contemporary society (as opposed to the 'traditional' society constructed under modernism) has only just begun" (*Decolonizing Methodologies: Research and Indigenous*

Peoples [London: Zed, 1999], 38). It should be remembered, however, that she is writing out of a social science context. She continues, "Not all these theories claim to be derived from some 'pure' sense of what it means to be indigenous, nor do they claim to be theories which have been developed in a vacuum separated from association with civil and human rights movements, other nationalist struggles or other theoretical approaches. What is claimed, however, is that new ways of theorizing by indigenous scholars are grounded in a real sense of, and sensitivity towards, what it means to be an indigenous person," ibid.

12. Sidner Larson, review of *Other Words: American Indian Literature, Law, and Culture, Studies in American Indian Literature. Studies in American Indian Literature* 15:2 (Summer 2003), 86–88.

13. Sidner Larson, *Captured in the Middle: Tradition and Experience in Contemporary Native American Writing* (Seattle: University of Washington Press, 2000), 56.

14. Ibid., 3, 5.

15. Jace Weaver, ed., *Native American Religious Identity: Unforgotten Gods* (Maryknoll, NY: Orbis Books, 1998), xi–xii.

16. Taiaiake Alfred, *Peace, Power, Righteousness: An Indigenous Manifesto* (Don Mills, ON: Oxford University Press, 1999), 84.

17. Smith, 28.

18. Julie Gough, "History, Representation, Globalisation and Indigenous Cultures: A Tasmanian Perspective," in *Indigenous Cultures in an Interconnected World*, ed. Claire Smith and Graeme K. Ward (Vancouver: University of British Columbia Press, 2000), 96–97.

19. P. K. Page, "Cook's Mountains," in *The Hidden Room* (Erin, Ontario: Porcupine's Quill, 1997).

20. W. H. New, *Grandchild of Empire: About Irony, Mainly in the Commonwealth* (Vancouver, BC: Ronsdale Press, 2003), 17–18.

21. Robert Dale Parker, *The Invention of Native American Literature* (Ithaca, NY: Cornell University Press, 2003), 196.

22. Daniel Justice, "Our Fire Survives the Storm," "Introduction," unpublished manuscript, 8–9. "Intellectual sovereignty" is, of course, the concept of Robert Warrior, coauthor of this book, first put forth in his book *Tribal Secrets*.

23. Parker, 15.

24. Arthur J. Ray, *I Have Lived Here Since the World Began: An Illustrated History of Canada's Native People* (Toronto, ON: Lester Publishing/Key Porter Books, 1996), 143–45; Alan D. McMillan, *Native Peoples and Cultures Canada*, 2d rev. and enl. ed. (Vancouver: Douglas & McIntyre, 1995), 49.

25. W. H. New, "Learning to Listen," in *Native Writers and Canadian Writing* (Vancouver: University of British Columbia Press, 1990), 4–5.

26. Terry Goldie, *Fear and Temptation: The Image of the Indigene in Canadian, Australian, and New Zealand Literatures* (Kingston: McGill-Queen's University Press, 1989), 157.

27. H. P. Carver, dir., *The Silent Enemy* (1930).

28. New, "Learning to Listen," 5.

29. Bill Ashcroft, Gareth Griffiths, and Helen Tiffin, *The Empire Writes Back: Theory and Practice in Post-Colonial Literatures* (London: Routledge, 1989), 145.

30. Weaver, *That the People Might Live*, 23.

31. See Adrian C. Louis, *Wild Indians and Other Creatures* (Reno: University of Nevada Press, 1996), 101–9.

32. New, *Grandchild*, 32.

33. Alfred, 29. Though Alfred is a political scientist, not a literary critic, his observation remains valid in this context. He is a social critic and an advocate of "an ideology of Native nationalism" (ibid., xvii). Similarly, Maori educator Linda Tuhiwai Smith writes from a social science perspective, yet has relevance for literary criticism. Her book, though about Maoris and not North American indigenes, is one of the most influential books in Native American Studies in the last half dozen years. It is a mark of the growing maturity of Native American Studies as its own discipline that it draws together scholarship and perspectives as diverse as these into a single discourse.

34. New, "Learning to Listen" 4.

35. Chadwick Allen, *Blood Narrative: Indigenous Identity in American Indian and Maori Literary and Activist Texts* (Durham, NC: Duke University Press, 2002), 30.

36. Ibid., 30–31.

37. Elvira Pulitano, *Toward a Native American Critical Theory* (Lincoln: University of Nebraska Press, 2003), 7, 1, 191.

38. Though the critics analyzed by Pulitano have been unquestionably important in the development of Native American criticism, others are curiously absent. She does not include Elizabeth Cook-Lynn, an arguably equally important nationalist voice, though she does allow the Dakota critic a couple of comments. Though she critiques the concept of "sovereignty," she makes no mention of Gerald Taiaiake Alfred, who raises similar questions. I am dismissed in a footnote as adding "very little to a discourse on Native American critical theory that is attempting to generate rhetorical strategies of its own," presumably because, unlike what she claims about Allen, Warrior, and Womack, I engage and critique Western theory while maintaining a nationalist position, thus undercutting much of her argument.

39. See Pulitano, 66.

40. Pulitano, 193.

41. Ibid., 81.

42. Alfred notes that "pure self-identification and acting the part, however diligent the research or skilful the act" is not enough (85).

43. Janet Gray, *Race and Time* (Iowa City: University of Iowa Press, 2004), 6.

44. Henry Louis Gates, *Loose Canons*, quoted at http://islandia.law.yale.edu/ayers/stanford.disc.pdf.

45. Gray, 13–14.

46. Weaver, *That the People Might Live*, 4.

47. Krupat, *Red Matters: Native American Studies* (Philadelphia: University of Pennsylvania Press, 2002), 112.

48. "Tight-shoe night" was Saturday night when country folk put on their best clothes, including tight, hard shoes and went into town to party. See Carol K. Rachlin, "Tight Shoe Night: Oklahoma Indians Today," in *The American Indian Today*, ed. Stuart Levine and Nancy O. Lurie, rev. and exp. ed. (Baltimore: Penguin Books, 1968), 160. To demonstrate how whacky and chaotic (and thus rich) the environment remains in criticism of Native American literature, Vizenor is one of the principal exemplars of her "dialogic" approach. Yet curiously Sid Larson terms him one of the Native critics "most resistant to dialogue." Larson, "*Other Words*," op. cit.

49. Brill, 1–2.

50. Parker, 4.

51. Brill, 203.

52. Ibid., 7, 9–10.

53. I am indebted for this insight and phrase to my wife, Choctaw scholar Laura Adams Weaver.

54. Brill, 35–36.

55. Ibid., 1, 203.

56. J. M. Bridgeman, review of *Granchild of Empire: About Irony, Mainly in the Commonwealth*, March 1, 2005, (http://www.prairiefire.ca/reviews.html, 2).

57. W. W. Penn, *The Absence of Angels* (Sag Harbor, NY: Permanent, 1994), 6.

58. Smith, 35.

59. Jace Weaver, *Turtle Goes to War: Of Military Commissions, the Constitution and American Indian Memory* (New Haven, CT: Trylon and Perisphere Press, 2002), xii.

60. Brill, 7.

61. Stokely Carmichael, "Power and Racism," in *The Black Power Revolt*, ed. Floyd B. Barbour (Boston: Porter Sargent Publishers, 1968), 71. See also Stokely Carmichael and Charles V. Hamilton, *Black Power: The Politics of Liberation in America* (New York: Random House, 1967), 58–84.

62. Krupat, *Red Matters*, 23.

63. Alfred, 70.

64. Cox, "Muting White Noise," unpublished manuscript (2005), 1–2.

65. New, *Grandchild*, 28.

66. Blaeser, 55–56.

67. Smith, 29.

68. Cox, 1–2.

69. Alfred, xi, xv.

70. Smith, 7.

71. Gough, 93.

72. Rolf Boldrewood [T.A. Browne], *Old Melbourne Memories* (Sydney, AU: George Robertson, 1884), 98; Goldie, 153.

73. Goldie, 154; Smith, 72–73.

74. See, e.g., Freda McDonald, "No Longer an Indian," in Weaver, *Native American Religious Identity*, 69–73, and Bradford W. Morse, ed., *Aboriginal Peoples and the Law: Indians, Metis and Inuit Rights in Canada*, rev. 1st ed. (Ottawa, ON: Carleton University Press, 1991), 429–31.

75. Isabelle Knockwood, *Out of the Depths* (Lockport, NS: Roseway Publishing, 1992), 98. The poster child for hybridity and mixed-bloodedness is golfer Tiger Woods, who rather than identify himself as African American calls himself "cablanasian" (Caucasian, Black, Native American, and Asian), an appellation that, if not actually unique to Woods's hereditary makeup, applies to only a very small group. See Henry Yu, "How Tiger Woods Lost His Stripes," in *Popular Culture: A Reader*, ed. Raiford A. Guins and Omayra Cruz (London: Sage Publications, 2005), 198–99; see also, generally, Henry Yu, *Thinking Orientals: Migration, Contact, and Exoticism in Modern America* (New York: Oxford University Press, 2001).

76. Smith, 38.

77. Alfred, 28.

78. Adams, 113.

79. Weaver, *That the People Might Live*, 24; Goldie, 217.

80. John Moss, "The Opposite of Prayer: An Introduction to Tomson Highway," in *Comparing Mythologies*, Tomson Highway (Ottawa, ON: University of Ottawa Press, 2002), 8–10.

81. For Warrior, "the rhetoric of ancientness and novelty" is the tendency to proclaim—repeatedly—any work by a Native author as the "first" of its type, regardless of how spurious such a claim might be (e.g., the announcement at the time of its publication that *House Made of Dawn* was the first Indian novel, despite several previous examples, stretching back to the nineteenth century).

82. Ortiz, 7–8, 10. Ortiz writes, "Throughout the difficult experience of colonization to the present, Indian women and men have struggled to create meaning in their lives in very definite and systematic ways. The ways or methods have been important, but they are important only because of the reason for the struggle. And it is that reason—the struggle against colonialism—which has given substance to what is authentic" (9).

83. New, *Grandchild*, 64.

84. Ortiz, 8.

85. Krupat, *Ethnocriticism*, 186.

86. New, *Native Writers*, 5. Emphasis original.

87. Or a Cherokee act, depending on how one looks at it. It is not hard to imagine John Ross himself with a copy of Thucydides on his own mantel.

88. Kathie Irwin, "Towards Theories of Maori Feminisms," in *Feminist Voices: Women's Studies Texts for Aotearoa/New Zealand*, ed. Rosemary du Plessis (Auckland, NZ: Oxford University Press, 1993), 5; Smith, 38.

89. Quoted in Jace Weaver, *Then to the Rock Let Me Fly: Luther Bohanon and Judicial Activism* (Norman: University of Oklahoma Press, 1993), 146. The case dealt with the right of terminally ill cancer patients to choose their course of treatment.

90. Blaeser, 61.

91. Harold Cardinal, *The Unjust Society* (Edmonton, AB: M.G. Hurtig, 1969), 1; Jonathan Scott Holloway, *Confronting the Veil: Abram Harris Jr., E. Franklin Frazier, and Ralph Bunche, 1919–1941* (Chapel Hill: University of North Carolina Press, 2002), 1.

92. Weaver, *Native American Religious Identity*, xi–xii.

93. Allen, 1; Weaver, *Native American Religious Identity*, 15.

94. Smith, 14. I have, I must confess, participated in discussions with postcoloniality, if only to argue for its problematic nature. See, "From I-Hermeneutics to We-Hermeneutics: Native Americans and the Post-colonial," in Weaver, *Native American Religious Identity*, 1–25, revised and reprinted in Jace Weaver, *Other Words: American Indian Literature, Law, and Culture* (Norman: University of Oklahoma, 2001), 280–304; and Jace Weaver, "Indigenous and Indigeneity," in *A Companion to Post-Colonial Studies*, ed. Henry Schwarz and Sangeeta Ray (Oxford: Blackwell Publishers, 2000), 221–35.

95. See Gerald Vizenor, *Manifest Manners: Postindian Warriors of Survivance* (Hanover, NH: Wesleyan University Press/University Press of New England, 1994), 105. I am indebted for the word "pericolonialism" to the suggestion of my wife, Choctaw literary scholar Laura Adams Weaver.

96. Allen, 30.

97. Womack is consistent on this point both in *Red on Red* and, as quoted, in his chapter herein.

98. Tim Schouls, *Shifting Boundaries: Aboriginal Identity, Pluralist Theory, and the Politics of Self-Government* (Vancouver: University of British Columbia Press, 2003), 3.

99. James (Sákéj) Youngblood Henderson, "Postcolonial Ghost Dancing: Diagnosing European Colonialism," in *Reclaiming Indigenous Voice and Vision*, ed. Marie Battiste (Vancouver: University of British Columbia Press, 2000), 63–64; Krupat, *Ethnocriticism*, 180.

100. Ortiz, 12.

101. Smith, 6.

102. Weaver, *Turtle*, 168, xiv.

103. See e.g., Vine Deloria, Jr. and Clifford Lytle, *The Nations Within: The Past and Future of American Indian Sovereignty* (New York: Pantheon Books, 1984).

104. Alfred, xiv, 25, 65–66.

105. Justice, Ch. 1, 6.

106. In Alfred's monograph, this point is graphically driven home when the author interviews another Mohawk and queries him about the word "sovereignty." The response is, "'Sovereignty' is a word I use a lot, traditional people use it a lot." The interviewee acknowledges that "in the European system the Crown is sovereign. In our system the people are sovereign. Their concept of sovereignty is very different from ours historically." The interview subject, Atsenhaienton, equates sovereignty and self-determination. Alfred, 109–10.

107. Justice, Ch. 1, 6. Alfred, of course, is writing primarily about Canada, where, I acknowledge, the legal context is different from that in the United States.

108. Ibid., 7; Alfred, 54.

109. A retronym is a word that loses it meaning because of appropriation or use in a different context and now requires an adjectival modifier to convey the correct sense. An example is "chauvinism," once meaning an excessive nationalistic patriotism. The obscure term was so successfully appropriated by the Women's Movement that without an adjective, "male chauvinism" is most likely to come to mind.

Other examples "black-and-white television" (once all TVs were black-and-white) and "silent movie" (redundant until the advent of talkies). I have suggested that we must really think of "multiple sovereignties" and specify which we mean (e.g., economic sovereignty, political sovereignty, intellectual sovereignty).

110. See Harold Cardinal, *The Rebirth of Canada's Indians* (Edmonton, AB: Hurtig Publishers, 1977); Justice, Introduction, 7; Ch. 1, 7. Emphasis original.

111. Weaver, *Turtle*, xiv–xv.

112. Schouls, x.

113. Weaver, *Turtle*, xiv–xv; see also, A. T. Anderson, *Nations Within a Nation: The American Indian and the Government of the United States* (Chappaqua, NY: Privately printed, 1976); Deloria, Jr., and Lytle, *The Nations Within*; Augie Fleras and Jean Leonard Elliott, *The "Nations Within": Aboriginal-State Relations in Canada, the United States, and New Zealand* (Toronto, ON: Oxford University Press, 1992). I am aware once again that the situation is different in Canada, where Natives have "citizenship-plus" status or are considered "Citizens Plus," and where they have been able to use the constitutional negotiation process and the courts to gain increased self-determination. See, Alan C. Cairns, *Citizens Plus: Aboriginal Peoples and the Canadian State* (Vancouver: University of British Columbia Press, 2000). I am also aware that this immediate discussion does not take into account state-recognized tribes and individuals other than enrolled members of federally recognized tribes— those A. T. Anderson termed "the uncounted," 75. (I brought this small book by Anderson, who was a special assistant to the American Indian Policy Review Commission, back into print in Jace Weaver, *American Journey: The Native American Experience* [Woodbridge, CT: Research Publications, 1998; book on CD-ROM].)

I am indebted once again to Laura Adams Weaver for the concept of "constitutional others." Blacks, of course, were othered by counting them as $3/5$ of a person, and Indian tribes were singled out as the exclusive purview of Congress.

114. Robert Berner, "What Is an American Indian Writer?" in *Native American Values: Survival and Renewal*, ed. Thomas E. Schirer and Susan M. Branster (Sault Ste. Marie, MI: Lake Superior State University Press, 1993), 133–34. Emphasis original.

115. Emphasis mine.

116. Berner, 132; see Womack, Ch. 2, herein.

117. Jace Weaver, "Foreword," in *Cherokee Night and Other Plays*, Lynn Riggs (Norman: University of Oklahoma Press, 2003), xiv.

118. Krupat, *Red Matters*, 111.

119. Moss, 15–16.

120. Ortiz, 8, 12. Emphasis mine. In 1991, Craig Howe, then at the University of Michigan, delivered a paper at the Third Annual Native American Studies Conference at Lake Superior State University in which he described developing a course in Native American literature that "focuses on nationality rather than ethnicity." He avers that "there is a body of identifiable literature that is 'Native American'" as opposed to merely tribal specific. The course he describes follows two prongs, one pertaining to "Native Americans collectively" and the other "entails in-depth analyses of the literature of five cultural groups, from creation stories to contemporary novels. Instead of conducting a superficial survey of 'Indian' literature, this organization exposes us to selected Native American genres plus enables us to study them in-depth within specific Native nations." Craig Howe, "Working with Words: Teaching (in progress) Native American Literature," in Schirer and Branstner, 438–39.

121. Cox, 2, 9, 19.

122. Henry T. Schwarz, *Tales from the Smokehouse* (Edmonton, AB: Hurtig Publishers, 1974), 65–68, 102.

123. Richard Erdoes and Alfonso Ortiz reproduce a remarkably similar story in *American Indian Myths and Legends*. In their version, a cross-dressing trickster Iktome fools "an ignorant girl" into the same act in the like manner. The provenance of the story states, "Told in Pine Ridge, South Dakota, and recorded by Richard Erdoes." Richard Erdoes and Alfonso Ortiz, eds., *American Indian Myths and Legends* (New York: Pantheon Books, 1984), 358–59. Unlike other stories recorded by Erdoes in the volume, this one offers no teller's name. One cannot help but suspect that some Lakotas were having one off at the expense of the Indian enthusiast and would-be ethnographer in the same way Schwarz was taken advantage of. At least there is no implication here that the story is actually factual.

124. There are, to be sure, numerous runners up. My current favorite is the opening line of Philip Roth's stunning alternate history, *The Plot Against America*: "Fear presides over these memories, a perpetual fear."

125. Louis Owens, *Other Destinies: Understanding the American Indian Novel* (Norman: University of Oklahoma Press, 1992), 100, 102.

126. Matthias Schubnell, *N. Scott Momaday: The Cultural and Literary Background* (Norman: University of Oklahoma Press, 1985), 68; Kenneth Lincoln, *Native American Renaissance* (Berkeley; University of California Press, 1983), 117.

127. Schubnell, 68–69.

128. Ibid., 70; Lewis Dabney, *The Indians of Yoknapatawpha* (Baton Rouge: Louisiana State University Press, 1974), 156.

129. Schubnell, 21; Charles L. Woodard, *Ancestral Voice: Conversations with N. Scott Momaday* (Lincoln: University of Nebraska Press, 1989), 133–35.

130. Robert Silberman, "Opening the Text: *Love Medicine* and the Return of the Native American Woman," in *Narrative Chance: Postmodern Discourse on Native American Literatures*, ed. Gerald Vizenor (Norman: University of Oklahoma Press, 1993), 105–6.

131. One cannot miss the play of the names here: Champion and Ooneemeetoo. Champion the older and his younger sibling "Oh, no, me too!"

132. Moss, 11.

133. Weaver, *Other Words*, 63.

134. Jace Weaver, "An Early Frontier Depiction of Native Americans," in Weaver, *American Journey*; Faulkner quoted in Jason Corley, *The Unvanquished: Yoknapatawpha County, Mississippi*, 2120, http://www.nprime.net/aeonsociety/trinity/setting/settooo4.html (1999; 3/5/06).

135. Cox, 262, 10.

136. Laura Adams Weaver, conversation with author (Sept. 15, 2004).

137. Owens, 53.

138. "Farewell to the Choctaws," *Vicksburg Sentinel* (February 18, 1845).

139. See Clara Sue Kidwell, *Choctaws and Missionaries in Mississippi, 1818–1919* (Norman: University of Oklahoma Press, 1995), 171–72.

140. Dabney, 31. Of course, it was not only whites who accepted the myth of Native absence. Even historian Muriel Wright, herself a Choctaw and the granddaughter of Chief Allen Wright, who coined the name "Oklahoma," demonstrated that she was capable of falling victim to it. Though she recorded the song those who remained sang for their departing kinfolk: "Hinaushi pisali, Bok Chito onali, yayali (I saw the trail to the big river and then I cried)" [Muriel H. Wright, "A Chieftain's 'Farewell Letter' to the American People," *American Indian* 1 (December 1926), 7, 12], in her 1929 history of Oklahoma, she not only includes "Farewell to the Choctaws" in the documentary appendix, but she writes, "Small, self-immigrating parties continued to arrive during the first part of 1834, but owing to their tardiness, many failed to receive the benefits of commutation from the Government. The number of Choctaws who had come to live in Indian Territory now amounted to about 12,500, between 5,000 and 6,000 still remaining in Mississippi in 1834. All these people or their descendants—with the exception of 1,200 who live in Mississippi today, 1928—came to Indian Territory throughout the succeeding years, some of them as late as 1902." All of them came—with the exception of those who remained. Even the figure of 1,200 is low. Joseph B. Thoburn and Muriel H. Wright, *Oklahoma: A History of the State and Its People*, vol. 1 (New York: Lewis Historical Publishing Company, 1929), 170.

141. Dabney, 25–26.

142. See ibid., 142.

143. Owens, 225.

144. Schubnell, 70.

145. Weaver, *That the People Might Live*, 38.

146. Schubnell, 69–70.

147. Vine Deloria, Jr., "Foreword: American Fantasy," in *The Pretend Indians: Images of Native Americans in the Movies*, ed. Gretchen Bataille and Charles L. Silet (Ames: Iowa State University Press, 1980), xvi; Luther Standing Bear, *Land of the Spotted Eagle* (1933; Lincoln: University of Nebraska Press, 1978), 248.

148. Dabney, 21.

149. Schubnell, 70.

150. See Dabney, 24.

151. D. H. Lawrence, *Studies in Classic American Literature* (1923; New York: Penguin Books, 1977), 120.

152. Craig Womack, *Red on Red: Native American Literary Separatism* (Minneapolis: University of Minnesota Press, 1999), 65.

153. Ibid., 7.

154. To follow the logic of those who would maintain that literature ceases to be Native when it employs Western forms, Gerald Vizenor would cease to be not only a Native American writer but also an American writer when he writes in haiku, a Japanese form. To put it differently, Thomas Alva Edison arguably invented both the phonograph and the motion picture camera. Is everyone who has ever made a movie or cut a record involved in a cosmopolitan collaboration that puts them beyond or outside their national cinema or music? The answer is no. The camera and the phonograph are technologies. Literary genres and forms are simply kinds of technology. To argue otherwise smacks of the gymnastics of authenticity, again.

155. Harvey Arden, *Dreamkeepers: A Spirit-Journey into Aboriginal Australia* (New York: HarperCollins, 1994), 19–20.

156. Kateri Damm, "Dispelling and Telling: Speaking Native Realities in Maria Campbell's *Halfbreed* and Beatrice Culleton's *In Search of April Raintree*," in *Looking at the Words of Our People: First Nations Analysis of Literature*, ed. Jeannette C. Armstrong (Penticton, BC: Theytus Books, 1993), 24; Weaver, *That the People Might Live*, 163.

157. Smith, 3.

158. In her book, Pulitano queries whether those who take nationalist stances can maintain them despite the fact they speak from the privileged position of the academy and publish with university presses. She writes, "Does the fact that Womack holds a professorship at the University of Lethbridge (in Alberta) change the way he speaks to his own community? . . . *Red on Red* remains . . . a sophisticated work of literary criticism and, as such, inaccessible to those members of a Native audience who cannot approach it from a similarly privileged position." Pulitano, 92. These are important lines of questions, and they are ones with which most Native scholars continually interrogate themselves. The true danger comes when one stops asking oneself such questions. Pulitano's inquiries ignore, for instance, Warrior's long-standing

participation in the I'n-Lon-Schka, or Womack's move from Canada
to Oklahoma to be closer to the stomp grounds, or the fact that he
donates the royalties from *Red on Red* to the Muskogee Nation
Language Preservation Program, or Joy Harjo's work with the
Muscogee community and her constant questioning of herself as
to how her work is heard by folks at home, or my own work with
Native Christians in Oklahoma and across the country. In declaring
the absolute inaccessibility of our writing to people on the ground,
she also ignores the number of ordinary Osages, Creeks, or Cherokees,
or whatever, including elders, who have read *Tribal Secrets*, *Red on
Red*, the poetry of Harjo, or any of our other work and think they
have gotten something from them. Are these people simply deluded?

159. Smith, 4.

160. Russell Means, "Foreword," in *Defending Mother Earth: Native
American Perspectives on Environmental Justice*, ed. Jace Weaver
(Maryknoll, NY: Orbis Books, 1996), xii. See also, generally, John
Mohawk, *Utopian Legacies: A History of Conquest and Oppression
in the Western World* (Santa Fe: Clear Light Publishers, 2000).

161. Carlos Tablada, *Che Guevara: Economics and Politics in the
Transition to Socialism* (Sydney, AU: Pathfinder/Pacific and Asia,
1989), 136, 77. Emphasis original.

162. Ibid., 86.

163. Ibid. Emphasis original.

164. As a lawyer and legal scholar, I am aware that counter examples can
be cited, but these are most often eddies and backwaters in policy
and jurisprudence, not the main channel of the river. Even in those
examples that seem the most affirmative of Native sovereignty, such as
the Indian New Deal and our current policy era of Self-Determination,
the sovereignty that is advocated is what, in legal terms, is known as a
"clipped sovereignty," subject to the superior, paternalistic sovereignty
of the United States. It is a continuation of a Marshallian conception
of "domestic dependent nations."

165. Alfred, 35, 36.

166. Ibid., 28.

167. Ibid., 35; Smith, 38.

168. See, Smith, 117. I owe this image to Smith and her figure illustrating "The Indigenous Research Agenda." "Survivance," of course, is a concept of Gerald Vizenor, who gives the "actual" word new meaning. In *Captured in the Middle*, Larson writes, "Vizenor's work suggests it is time to investigate the implications of the future to balance considerations of the past, and he perceives a postmodern form of oral tradition as a necessary element. This emphasis on older forms also suggest that 'survivance' means survival in the most basic sense. If we can accept that the increasingly common ethnic warfare is a glimpse of our own future, we can begin to understand how technology and theory may soon have to take a backseat to 'survivance' and its conflation of survival and existence in a tribal-style 'we'" (45–46). He thus misconstrues Vizenor's notion. "The end of living and the beginning of survival" is sense for Larson. No. "Survivance" is not "survival" and "existence." If it were, even the spelling would be wrong. For Vizenor "survivance" is survival + endurance, much like my communitism. Survivance counters "the manifest manner of domination." Vizenor, *Manifest Manners*, 4. In *Fugitive Poses*, Vizenor writes: "survivance, in the sense of native survivance, is more than survival, more than endurance or mere response; the stories of survivance are an active presence.... The native stories of survivance are successive and natural estates; survivance is an active repudiation of dominance, tragedy, and victimry." Gerald Vizenor, *Fugitive Poses: Native American Indian Scenes of Absence and Presence* (Lincoln: University of Nebraska Press, 1998), 15. So the term is linked not only to endurance but to resistance.

169. Krupat, *Red Matters*, 1.

Chapter Two

The Integrity of
American Indian Claims

(Or, How I Learned to
Stop Worrying and Love My Hybridity)

> Responsibly, one cannot just say anything
> one pleases and in whichever way one may
> wish to say it.
>
> —Edward W. Said,
> *Humanism and Democratic Criticism*

A primary motivation for writing this chapter is to encourage young Native critics who I would like to speak to for a moment. You can work through issues of hybridity and essentialism rather than simply remaining in the back of the seminar room, so to speak, because you are not alone and people who care would like you to join the conversation. You need to have some savvy about the quality of that talk, however, because it varies, and, inevitably, you must make choices. Our field, like other endeavors, is dominated by books both popular and palatable, including some of those authored by Native literary scholars. Native authorship does not guarantee astute Indian literary criticism. Thinking through critical issues is hard work, and most will opt for the already familiar in theoretical analysis.

Native literary critics face the problem of intellectual laziness as much as non-Native critics writing about Native literature. There is room, and encouragement, however, for the young Native critic who wishes to ask the difficult questions rather than answer the easy ones addressed time and again at the latest conference, the most recent journal issue, and even in some university press books that continue to carry forward the same assumptions about Native literature into perpetuity.

The way our field is currently configured may not always be encouraging to young Native scholars in terms of the kind of theory that has been the most available and the most recognized. In spite of a sometimes discouraging criticism and the troubling prominence of work that should have received more vigorous scrutiny, I remain optimistic. I ask young Native critics not to give up on us.

Let me offer some hope about what we do. One of the things that constantly amazes me is the fact that while I worked five years in Canada, supported by Canadian tax dollars, I was allowed to write, almost exclusively, about Muskogee Creek people in the present-day state of Oklahoma, and I was granted tenure for it. If we were honest with ourselves, many of us who are Native critics would have to admit we have unprecedented opportunities to write and teach almost anything we want to in the academy. Few endeavors anywhere provide so much freedom. Simply whining about the ways the university fails to acknowledge or appreciate indigenous knowledge often overlooks the fact that it gives us virtually free reign in producing it ourselves. So let us begin, and let us continue, to produce it. We can either remain in a state of constant lamentation, bemoaning all the different ways from kindergarten to graduate school we are told about our intellectual deficits as Native people, or we can do something about it. Most critics will choose lamentation because creating indigenous knowledge is more difficult than bemoaning white hegemony.

To turn to the critical task before me now in this chapter, I hope to carefully examine the charges against my book *Red on Red: Native American Literary Separatism* in Elvira Pulitano's *Toward a Native American Critical Theory*, her recent 2003 University of Nebraska Press publication. In some ways, I feel like my goal, to use Lisa Brooks's language from the Afterword, is to gather ideas back together after the diaspora of them that occurs because of the Pulitano book. Simply put, I want to clarify some things and hope for restoration in an environment of confusion.

Two possible objections might arise in relation to writing back to one of my critics. Some might ask "Why provide Elvira Pulitano all this space, this attention?" suggesting I should ignore her rather than giving voice to her opinions. Pulitano's book must be addressed because the philosophical issues that underpin her skepticism will have some role in shaping future creative and critical works. If we, as literary critics, hope to have a role in facilitating the work of Indian writers who are innovative, subversive, deviant, critically accomplished, or who embody any number of other traits we deem valuable, then we will have to at least say what those criteria are, why they are meaningful, and what makes them Indian if we're going to claim the existence of a Native literature and a Native criticism. We cannot do that by walking away from the Pulitano book and ignoring it.

A second objection I have heard is that Pulitano may take all the attention as a compliment. And she very well may. Stranger things have happened. This is not about a single critic; however, it is about creating an environment where Native literature can flourish and critics can help, rather than hinder it. I think of potentially exciting work like LeAnne Howe's forthcoming novel on baseball, the *Miko Kings*, published by Aunt Lute. While I know that LeAnne would have written this novel with our without the help of critics, I would like to think that a critical environment could exist that would lend support by establishing strong philosophical foundations capable of explaining, for example, what is Indian about baseball. We need to take on such issues.

My aim is to give a single chapter of Pulitano's book the kind of close reading she fails to give anyone who is the subject of her study. Pulitano, an assistant professor of English, teaches at the University of Geneva in Switzerland. The central theme of her book is that the intersection of Native and non-Native worlds makes it impossible to claim a Native perspective without acknowledging the inevitable European underpinnings of any Indian claim. In her introduction she says, "any attempt to recover a 'pure' or 'authentic' form of Native discourse, one rigidly based on a Native perspective, is simply not possible since Native American narratives are by their very nature heavily heteroglot and hybridized."[1] Variations of this statement, which borrows strongly from Arnold Krupat's earlier work, are chanted like a mantra scores, possibly hundreds, of times throughout the book.

My greatest fear in tackling this critical chore is the very real possibility that instead of clarifying the incredible confusion the Pulitano book creates, I will simply add to it. For this reason, I want to begin with a clearly stated thesis that I hope will permeate this chapter from beginning to end: One means (not the only means but an important one) of evaluating literary theory is scrutinizing how accurately it describes the social world it references. This need not be a naive realism that assumes a one-to-one relationship between writing and reality that negates imagination—somewhat similar to unwieldy accusations regarding the authenticity of Indian characters in fiction who are not "real enough," where the critic assumes that Native people act like essays about Indians rather than individuals with the capacity to surprise and delight.

Yet when literary critics make claims about social realities in the context of their criticism, they have a responsibility to those they are choosing to represent in print. In practical terms, I claim that reality checks are a good thing. In more theoretical terms, I claim that old-fashioned realism still has some relevance in today's world, especially with respect to a Native activism that is more interested in issues of redress rather than digress. The power of Lisa Brooks's Afterword is that it constitutes a process analysis of exactly what is at stake: the way we view words, and the theories built from them, creates definitions of history that may determine whether a group of people even exists in the minds of majority culture—with effects that are so concrete, the linguistically and theoretically erased indigenous nation may no longer be able to fish a river they have depended on for thousands of years.

Given the central role of interpretations of history in relation to Native survival, a major criticism of the Pulitano book will be the ahistorical mode in which she makes universal claims, thus engaging in an essentialism that she is keen on observing in everyone except herself. I myself may be guilty of not living up to the lofty goal expressed by

Edward W. Said in the opening epigraph, yet I suggest it as a benchmark for ethical criticism and make no bones about the fact that I feel Pulitano has failed to speak responsibly. If I am guilty of the same, I hope others will point this out, and we can learn from each other to do better. My email address can be located easily enough on the University of Oklahoma web page. I have tried to the best of my ability to avoid statements that are personal rather than ideological and to provide philosophical justifications for my claims, sticking close to the texts that are the subject of my study. No doubt I have responded strongly and with reason: Pulitano's book is no polite celebration of the work of Womack, Warrior, and Allen.

When a critic chooses to describe Native Americanists as reinscribing colonialism and argues for a criticism that makes the work we do impossible, our response is not a lamb's bleat. A responsible and compassionate criticism need not be a wimpy one. Toward that end, this chapter will put forward some forceful arguments. Both Indian and non-Indian critics have been throwing the cliché around for years that we are "word warriors," so perhaps we should not act surprised when we live up to the phrase.

Beginning with the most basic structural device of *Toward a Native American Critical Theory*, Pulitano creates a hierarchy of Native literary criticism based on which critics, in her view, most successfully challenge Eurocentric hegemony, a hierarchy in which she deems Chippewa writer Gerald Vizenor the most convincingly subversive; Greg Sarris (Pomo) and Louis Owens (Choctaw-Cherokee) just on Vizenor's heels for challenging and engaging Eurocentric discourse; and myself (Creek), fellow contributor to this volume Robert Warrior (Osage), and Paula Gunn Allen (Laguna) running almost neck-to-neck, Allen a nose behind, for dead last, having supposedly rejected any possibilities for dialogue outside the Indian world at all; thus, it would seem, not subverting anything. In Pulitano's conclusion she says,

> More forcefully and more provocatively than the other theorists I have discussed, Vizenor combines revolutionary content and revolutionary style, presenting a significant alternative to Western hermeneutics. Rejecting any form

of separatism and essentialism as far as Indian identity is concerned, he celebrates a discourse that is communal and comic. Like Sarris and Owens, Vizenor embraces a cross-cultural approach, one merging Native epistemology with Western literary forms. His approach, however, is more revolutionary than theirs, attempting as it does to fuse, at every level of discourse, the tribal with the nontribal, the old with the new, the oral with the written.[2]

First of all, I would argue, it is not fruitful to consider Vizenor's work as a kind of Indian exceptionalism in relation to completely avoiding essentialism. No one can write, or say anything about the world, without ever using generalizations. Lynn Lewis, one of the graduate students in a seminar I taught at OU, pointed out that Vizenor's work abounds with statements that either imply or directly say "the Indian is . . ." and "the Indian is not . . ." even if the definitions seem to opt for a more liberated Indian. Essentialism can be mediated; none of us can escape and "reject" it in "any form." There is good reason to wonder why we should want to.

[Monolithic treatments can be tempered by citing historical and cultural particulars, emphasizing differences, deviances, and individualities as often as similarities.] To escape essentialism entirely one would have to quit writing and speaking. This is one of the reasons why naming essentialists sometimes feels more like a witch hunt than a scholarly endeavor—to point out an essentialist will always require having four fingers pointed back at oneself.

Lisa Brooks, in her Afterword, suggests a compassionate reading strategy that begins with "strive[ing] to comprehend what the author is trying to communicate or argue first, before deciding what you wish to agree with or critique." Given an optimistic reading, Pulitano's aim seems to be a critique of monolithic treatments, a serious interrogation of jargon that reduces the worldviews of indigenous people in the Americas, and sometimes worldwide, to a single cliché that covers all cultures and time periods. She examines the manifestation of these manners, to borrow Vizenor's phrase, in claims of purity and isolation. As such an endeavor the Pulitano book cannot be entirely dismissed.

In this chapter, however, I will argue that it matters *how* one resists essentialism and try to pay attention to the *way* claims are made as well as the claims themselves. I will admit that reading Pulitano's book caused me to return to my own work and think through things more clearly and, certainly, to try to articulate those thoughts here. For this, I am grateful. Without Pulitano this chapter would not have been written, or not in the same way, obviously.

In this volume Robert Warrior remarks on a disturbing trend in which Native Studies may be moving away from the intellectual tradition of critique. Some researchers have gone as far as to suggest that the "Indian" thing to do is to allow tribes to have final approval of what is published about them. This is interesting in light of a recent historic Oklahoma Cherokee Nation decision that deemed the Indian thing to do was to make the tribal newspaper independent of tribal government, thus establishing a landmark principle in regard to freedom of the press. Interestingly, this issue also boils down to certain essentialisms—if there is only one true Indian answer vested in a particular group of Indian authorities—tribal council, ceremonialists, clan leaders, whoever—then arguments can be made about granting that group final authority given their transparent relationship to knowledge. It also assumes, of course, this particular group is of a uniform opinion and that they will always act in the tribe's best interest. Anyone who has actually lived and worked in Indian Country—or anywhere else come to think of it—might be worried about these assumptions.

Well, Pulitano certainly gives us critique, and we most definitely need some way of approaching Native literary critics' work as something other than a manifestation of our own sacred cows. We are asking for no more than an application of intellectual traditions that have to do with justifying warrants, as well as paying attention to issues of ethos. These so-called "western" strategies seem quite useful to me if a person wants to co-exist in a responsible world. I believe this is what Edward Said means in the statement that opens this chapter.

There is an interesting contradiction in Pulitano's diction with her phrasing of the word "fusing" when Vizenor "fuse[s]" the "tribal with the non-tribal," which means there is, in fact, a tribal. This contradicts much of the book that maintains "tribal" can only be claimed as hybridity. In proposing the second- and third-string critics Pulitano says,

"Unlike Allen, Womack, and Warrior, who take separatist approaches to a Native discourse, Sarris and Owens insist on the necessity of displacing the margin-center opposition, not by remaining outside in the margin and pointing an accusing finger at the center, but by implicating themselves in that center and sensing the politics that makes it marginal."[3] The phrases "unlike Allen, Warrior, and Womack, Vizenor instead . . ." or "Sarris instead . . ." or "Owens instead" occur dozens of times throughout the book, as does their converse "unlike Vizenor, Owens, and Sarris, Womack instead . . ." or "Warrior instead . . ." or "Allen instead . . ." or various combinations of the three of us in cahoots as the opening to any statement that describes something Pulitano does not like. Pulitano's oppositional hierarchy is even built into the most basic structures of her book. She begins with the "worst" critic, Paula Gunn Allen, and works her way up to the "best" in a final chapter on Gerald Vizenor.

I hope to argue convincingly in this chapter that dumping me into a reductive category with my colleagues Robert Warrior and Paula Gunn Allen makes no more sense than opposing me to my colleagues Greg Sarris, Louis Owens, and Gerald Vizenor. Lisa Brooks contributes an interesting observation in the Afterword when she contrasts the way Jace Weaver puts Native critical voices in dialogue with each other in the Introduction to *That the People Might Live* and the way Pulitano pits one group of critics (Warrior, Womack, and Allen) against another (Vizenor, Owens, and Sarris). Pulitano's oppositional approach of separating one critic from another seems strange in a book whose central argument is that the separatists do not allow their criticism to rub up against other kinds of literary theories.

Pulitano's hierarchy unfolds something like Ruby Turpin's vision of the races in Flannery O'Connor's short story "Revelation." In my years of knowing Vizenor, Owens, and Sarris, I never heard any of them describe Native literary criticism as a hierarchy in which their work surpassed everyone else's and most epitomized subversion, all other Native authors falling "short of the glory of God," nor have I read any such statement in their writings. If Pulitano wants to describe with great frequency the ways in which the three critically unenlightened writers reinscribe colonialism, then she needs to choose a better rhetorical strategy than divide and conquer.

The hierarchy is interesting given the book's constant references to the "lower" critics' putative sin of reinforcing European power structures. (Please note, when I use terms like "lower critics" and variations on this theme, these sarcastic word choices are mine, not Pulitano's). Pulitano levies frequent charges of essentialism, and many other faults, against the "minor" critics whom she believes insist on right and wrong ways to do Native literary criticism, as in the following example: "At the 'Translating Native Cultures' conference, held at Yale University in February 1998, the Santee Sioux writer and critic Elizabeth Cook-Lynn delivered a passionate keynote address significantly drawing a line between those whom she described as being on the right and the wrong sides of American Indian Studies."[4]

Pulitano, however, in her prescriptive, rather than descriptive, demands for American Indian critics to challenge Eurocentric discourse as their number one priority employs the same critical strategy as the one she criticizes Cook-Lynn for. Vizenor, Sarris, and Owens, she states explicitly and frequently, are doing theory the right way; Womack, Allen, and Warrior the wrong way.

In relation to challenging Eurocentrism, Pulitano says, "my critique of Allen's ethnographic stance aims at showing the limitations of such a methodology in the context of a Native American theoretical discourse whose main goal is to challenge the analytic tools of Eurocentric theory while dismantling romantic definitions of Indians . . ."[5] Please note the phrase "main goal," which suggests that addressing the non-Indian world is the first and foremost responsibility of the Indian critic.

She also says of another critic doomed to the lower echelons of her hierarchy, "One might ask how Warrior justifies the fact that, in his ideal erasing of binaries, *Tribal Secrets*, does not engage in any significant way with the critical discourse of Western tradition, not even to mount a forceful critique."[6] This seems to contradict the earlier quote we just examined that told us the "third-string" critics had an accusing finger pointed at the center.

Pulitano cites a passage from Warrior's 1992 *Wicazo-sa* "Intellectual Sovereignty and the Struggle for an American Indian Future." In the passage she quotes on page seventy-seven of her book, Warrior expresses concerns for the way in which French theory's most prominent poststructuralist critics sometimes illuminate theory rather than praxis. Pulitano follows this quote that expresses one aspect of Warrior's theoretical concerns with the claim, "what is significant in these statements of Warrior's is his suspicious attitude toward any form of Western critical discourse."[7]

Evidently, reservations about poststructuralism indicate a rejection of all knowledge associated with the West! If this is the case there are a good number of people "suspicious...toward any form of Western critical discourse," many of them poststructuralist critics who have had some time to further think through the implications of their theorizing. Terry Eagleton's book *After Theory* (2003), for example, is a work in which a theorist questions some of French theory's lack of concern with material realities and speculates about what might come next in a world that is, on the one hand, threatened by various fundamentalisms and in need of less fixed definitions, and, on the other, facing catastrophes that need to be named concretely and demand a physical, material response.

Hitting closer to home, in my case, Pulitano says, "More forcefully than Warrior, Womack insists on a Native consciousness and a Native viewpoint out of which a Native American critical theory should originate. Unlike Warrior, he does not envision any moment of dialogue with Western critical discourse..."[8] If readers are not scratching their heads yet they should be, since on the previous page, as I have just demonstrated, we are told Warrior is "suspicious...toward any form of Western critical discourse," but now I am the one who does not envision any such moment and Warrior does.[9]

Before tackling the issue of exactly how Pulitano has overlooked the ways in which our studies might challenge the West, I simply want to ask who made up these rules anyway? Did the Creator issue an edict I missed, a worldwide ruling that every Indian critic is born for the express purpose of challenging Eurocentric discourse? How come She told this to Pulitano and not me? What is this if not a line in the sand about the right and wrong way to do Native criticism? What if someone like me comes along, too dumb to know about the universal law that all Indian critics must challenge Eurocentric discourse, and I decide I want to do something else like try to get Creek people excited about Creek literature or participate in a discussion about how literature might play some role in community building at home? If I am not speaking about the non-Indian world does that mean I am not saying anything? Can Native scholarship become something other than a defensive presentation geared toward non-Indians? Can one also assume the need to challenge *Indians* and *Indian* discourse, to question commonly held assumptions in the Indian world?

One might wonder just who Pulitano's audience is. Sometimes Pulitano seems to be addressing a non-Indian audience, patting them on the back for the ways in which they are the actual originators of Indians, and, at other times, scolding Native critics for their failure to achieve this same understanding. In the latter case, she seems to be laying out the rules for some kind of training camp for Indian critics. This makes the book especially strange given her own positionality. She fails to consider the issue of just *who* she can most effectively speak to and *how* she might be convincing to that particular audience, and this lack of critical attention to these key issues is fatal in terms of communicating something meaningful. My prediction is the book will not be received well by either Native or non-Native readers.

Can Pulitano's theories help someone like me who is developing a Muskogee Creek literature course at the University of Oklahoma in cooperation with Creek language efforts and courses that are ongoing at our campus, someone who dreams of Muskogee literature classes offered as electives in Eastern Oklahoma high schools with large numbers of Creek, and non-Indian, students who might be interested in the classes as well? I envision someplace like Bacone (a hypothetical example) with a historic relationship to the Creek Nation becoming a center for Muskogee Creek studies.[10] Can I advocate for such programs by arguing there is no such thing as a Creek perspective? Without a dream, the people perish. Give me a theory that at least lets me dream.

Hoping to encourage Creek people to continue writing, and consider evaluating, Creek literature, as a part of tribal life that might be as relevant as housing, health, economic, and land issues, is not an essentialist project. Arguing that literature is an aspect of culture and a people's idea of themselves does not rely on a naive insistence on cultural purity. (The subject of another essay I have written for a forthcoming collection of Native-authored criticism argues that not all essentialisms are bad, anyway. Some are quite useful. The point is, if I am an essentialist, Pulitano's analysis seems incapable of explaining why. I am not the kind of essentialist she says I am. Essentialism, like other areas of inquiry, suffers when it is given a monolithic treatment.)

Charges of essentialism have become far too easy in critical debates these days. Given the way essentialism is often defined as making universal claims in ahistorical modes, it is ironic that accusations of essentialism have often become a substitute for historical work and philosophical scrutiny, instead simply labeling people with an abstraction, one might even say with an essentialism. One might wonder, for example, about the following footnote in Robert Dale Parker's *The Invention of Native American Literature*, published in 2003 by Cornell:

> For an effort to build a pro-essentialist argument, see Womack. Womack bases his portrayal of contemporary critical theory on ideas that had a brief vogue in the high deconstructionist moment of the late seventies and that virtually no one has advocated since then, although the rumor of their dominance has persisted, especially among right-wing pundits who would be anathema to Womack's anti-capitalism. Just as I don't find Womack's arguments for essentialism convincing or well-informed about the critical debate around essentialism, so I can't abide his implication that non-Native critics cannot contribute helpfully to the discussion of Native American literature. On the other hand, the often ugly history of white-produced writing about Indian peoples gives us reason to take Womack's point of view seriously. I also applaud his encouragement for the study of particular tribal literatures and the example he offers for a study of tribal literature that joins—as a work of writing—in the literature it studies.[11]

The footnote is certainly intriguing in all its suggestiveness about me lining up with some outmoded deconstuctionists, whoever these folks might be and whatever their claims might have been. I mean is this Deep Throat, some secret source? Why not just say? Who are these people, and in what ways do my views intersect with theirs? What caused their mysterious disappearance, and how did I manage to stubbornly persist?!

If Parker is going to claim that I am an essentialist, does he not at least owe his readers some kind of example from my work that illustrates his point? If my essentialism, as he says, is unconvincing, OK, I am game, what is unconvincing about it?

Essentialist hunting is a little bit like Salem: the proof of someone's essentialism is whenever someone says he is an essentialist. Along somewhat similar lines the proof that essentialism is an untenable philosophy is asserted by accusing someone of essentialism. Far too frequently philosophy seems to be a moot point in relation to these charges.

Especially puzzling is what follows, the statement about my position on non-Native critics, given that I have never said non-Indian critics cannot or should not participate in the criticism of Native literature—no such statement appears in a book or publication of mine, and I have never suggested anything like this in public or even in private. If these are indeed, "Womack's arguments," to use Parker's exact phrase, shouldn't Parker locate them in Womack's work or Womack's statements? Specifically, should he not be able to cite something that backs up these claims, or should he only be required to chant *Red on Red* or Womack as if these terms themselves embody the very essence of essentialism? Mostly Parker's assessment of my writing in other parts of the book is an appreciative one, and I think he makes a concerted effort throughout his text to present what I do in its best light—but the footnote is certainly perplexing, a dark moment in a strong book, and, to my way of thinking, an interesting example in terms of illustrating the way essentialism often gets discussed: by not discussing it, only levying it as an accusation. In fairness to him, it is a footnote and thus given a brief treatment, but it illustrates a fascinating set of problems in the field at large.

Getting back to Pulitano, in terms of this "one size fits all" critical vocation she has laid out for us that demands we must subvert Eurocentric discourse, whatever happened to individuality? To artistry? To vision? To deviance? To innovation? To Indians deciding for themselves?

More disturbing are Pulitano's statements that are errors of fact rather than interpretation. She says, "Womack categorically dismisses any kind of cross-cultural communication with the academy."[12] Elsewhere she repeats, "Womack categorically dismisses any possibility of dialogue with the Western Academy and forcefully endorses the necessity of a 'Native

American Literary Separatism' (as he subtitles *Red on Red*)."[13] This statement assumes that separatism equates to a rejection of dialogue with the Western Academy, a problematic claim in and of itself given the rather diverse history of various forms of separatism that resist such a monolithic treatment. I have already quoted in fuller form the statement "Unlike Warrior, he does not envision any moment of dialogue with Western critical discourse . . . "[14] In a similar vein she says that in my work, I "hope to recover a precolonial purity, thereby creating some kind of national consciousness entirely independent of the European colonial enterprise."[15] In regard to my analysis of Joy Harjo's poetry, Pulitano writes, "Creekness and pan-tribalism legitimate, for Womack, a Native American literary separatism that categorically excludes any possibility of encounter at the cultural crossroads."[16] One might wonder here how pan-tribalism, by virtue of the definition of the term, could "exclude any possibility of encounter at the cultural crossroads."

More to the point, Pulitano provides no page citations where I say anything about categorically dismissing dialogue with the West and for good reason—there are no such statements in *Red on Red*. Since Pulitano fails to provide citations to my book about this categorical dismissal, let me offer some. *Red on Red* includes references to the following non-Indian novelists, poets, playwrights, short story writers, artists, musicians, actors, critics, historians, anthropologists, activists, and thinkers: James Adair (28, 297), Bossu (51), John Swanton (57, 59, 61, 78, 86–87, 89, 93–94, 95, 98–99, 161, 164), Phyliss Braunlich (272, 272, 284, 285, 286, 290, 296, 299), Alfred Hitchcock (263–69), Robert Burns (139, 141, 178, 179), Witter Bynner (272, 277, 278, 284, 285, 287, 295, 299), Raymond Carver (263), John Collier (40), David H. Corkran (28, 33, 53), Joan Crawford (281), Michael D. Green (228), Bette Davis (281, 287), Angie Debo (28, 29, 30, 36, 43, 149, 190, 283), Charles Dickens (109), Ralph Ellison (8), William Faulkner (7, 136), Grant Foreman (34), Gabriel García Marquez (64), Enrique Gasque-Molina (or Ramon Naya) (72, 281, 283), Farley Granger (264), Thomas Pynchon (252, 253), Eric Havelock (96), Harry Hays (300), Ernest Hemingway (166–67), Charles Hudson (30, 43, 240, 244–45), Langston Hughes (135, 136), Dell Hymes (63, 66), Pam Innes (77, 79, 80, 86), Washington Irving (166), Alexia Kosmider (134, 136–37, 137–38, 139, 141, 148), David Michael Lambeth (54–55), George

Lankford (54), Craig Lesley (247), Albert Lord (96), Joel Martin (12, 51, 52, 240), Arthur Miller (271), James Mooney (230), Theda Perdue (57–58), Jim Nicklin (256), Flannery O'Connor (7, 195), Eugene O'Neil (271), Walter Ong (63, 96, 166), Paul Radin (89), Anne Rice (275), Jerome Rothenberg (63, 65, 66), LaVonne Ruoff (107, 111, 115, 116, 126), Edward Said (59), John Scarry (223–24), William Shakespeare (109, 141, 154, 178, 179, 185), Amy Tan (8), Dennis Tedlock (63, 66), Dylan Thomas (247), Henry David Thoreau (141, 179), W. O. Tuggle (57, 59, 61, 78, 93, 94, 95, 96), Mark Twain (185), Tennessee Williams (271), Bob Wills (74, 305), James Wright (252), and Kirk Zebolsky (16–17).[17]

This is not a complete list, but I think readers will get the general idea. Anticipating Pulitano's line of attack, I want to say that in citing this large and varied group of non-Indian thinkers I did not merely put them in the book in order to attack them as anyone can tell by simply reading *Red on Red*. In addition to this list there are also some forty-nine or so non-Creek Native American authors cited in the book. Some more reasonable readers than Pulitano might think this constitutes a pretty large body of multicultural work.

In trying to defend myself, there is a difficulty in producing evidence as arguments against Pulitano's claims. Because of the ever changing philosophical basis of her book, anything one mounts in his or her own defense can be used for or against him or her based on Pulitano's whims. In fact, in lieu of the evidence in Warrior's work of his recognition of the cross-cultural aspects of the literature he studies in *Tribal Secrets*, Pulitano argues that somehow he is still a multiculturalist in denial, and this allegedly proves that no Indian perspective can exist apart from its inevitable cross-cultural foundation.

One wonders how Warrior can be in denial when he acknowledges the cross-cultural nature of his project, but this seems to be part of Pulitano's damned if you do and damned if you don't reasoning that she reserves for the "lower level" critics in her hierarchy. In fact, what is essentialism in Allen becomes Greg Sarris's strongest virtue as seen by this quote in the Sarris chapter: *"Unlike a Western articulation* of a philosophy that depends on linear, sequential reasoning, crucial within the *Native worldview (a worldview common, I would suggest, to most tribal people in North America, despite cultural and historical diversity)* is the notion of interconnectedness leading toward a holistic conception of the universe. Such a view makes the *Western idea* of cataloging and dissecting chunks of information almost meaningless" (my emphasis).[18] Pulitano goes on to say: "In the context of a Native American discourse whose main goal is to articulate a critical voice deeply grounded in an *indigenous rhetoric*, Sarris's storytelling strategy becomes a feasible technique through which to convey a *Naive epistemology* not traditionally articulated in conventional academic discourse" (my emphasis).[19]

Pulitano can do her "unlike a Western articulation" to her heart's content, and celebrate it in the work of her favorite authors and critics, but here is what happens when Paula Gunn Allen insists on differences between Native and Western viewpoints:

> Allen's separatist solution raises even more troubling questions as far as a definition of *Indianness* is concerned. With the expression *to my Indian eyes* Allen seems to revert to the essentialist position conveyed in *The Sacred Hoop*, in which she argues that "Indians never think like whites" and goes on to assert: "Whatever I read about Indians I check out with my inner self."[20]

Allen's claims for a distinguishable Native perspective is essentialism; however, among the Chosen, Pulitano's favorite critics, the same strategy is liberatory and anti-foundational. In all the chapters that precede the Sarris discussion, which kicks off the "best for last" turn to her critical Elect, Pulitano has posited that any claim for an "indigenous rhetoric" or a "Native epistemology" is hopelessly naive without recognizing its inevitable European influences. In these earlier chapters Pulitano insists an Indian worldview is an impossibility when it claims distinguishing characteristics from the West. The only reason such claims are no longer essentialist in this case, it would seem, is because this statement occurs in a chapter on Greg Sarris, who exists on a higher level of the hierarchy. The same qualities celebrated in Vizenor, Owens, and Sarris are held against Womack, Warrior, and Allen.

A major problem in the book is the epistemological shift that occurs in the second part when the discussion turns to Pulitano's favorite critics and all the former vices become virtues in her first-string Native writers; thus, in the second half one reads a statement such as the following which was totally undermined in all the earlier chapters: "Owens's reference to the ideology of mapping is indicative of the radically different cosmographies held by the Natives and the Europeans."[21] In celebrating Vizenor, Pulitano lays claim to an essentialized Native worldview that could be lifted straight from those passages she is most critical of in Allen's *The Sacred Hoop*. Once again, for clarity's sake, this is Pulitano speaking, not Allen: "There is in Native epistemologies no separation among the various realms of existence, the universe being conceived of as a balanced equilibrium of forces. A tribal perspective thus views things very differently than a Western scientific perspective."[22]

In order to catalogue all these inconsistencies I would have to write a book on Pulitano's book, but I will try to pick some "highlights." Pulitano says,

> In the light of Mathews's and Deloria's cosmopolitanism, a position that Warrior himself has ironically emphasized, readers of *Tribal Secrets* may find it problematic to consider these authors as ideal subjects for a constructive engagement with an authentic tradition of Indian intellectualism. The same readers might, then, on considering Mathews's and Deloria's autoethnographic writing, also wonder about Warrior's rhetorical strategies and how effectively they produce a response or challenge to the idiom of mainstream discourse.[23]

Separatists are to be faulted for being too separatist and insufficiently cosmopolitan unless they become cosmopolitan—as here when Warrior fully acknowledges the cosmopolitanism of Mathews and Deloria—in which case they are to be faulted for not being separatist enough. One wonders, ultimately, what Pulitano's criticism of the lower critics is other than not liking them given her indefensible positions. The next sentence after this quote reads, "When compared with the discursive approaches taken by Allen, Womack, Sarris, Owens, and Vizenor, Warrior's methodology appears to be more visibly grounded in the Western rhetorical pattern of the classical critical tradition *rather than in a Native epistemological orientation*" (my emphasis).²⁴ Why in this, and only in this, instance I get to play with the big boys I have no idea. What I do know is this statement occurs in a book whose central argument is no "rather than" exists, that a "Native epistemological orientation" is inextricably bound up in a "classical critical tradition." Here Warrior is too cosmopolitan and not separatist enough!

On the same page Pulitano claims, "instead of arguing how works of criticism (including his own) can pragmatically convey the idea of tradition in new written forms, Warrior proceeds to analyze the poetry of Jimmy Durham and Wendy Rose, thus reinforcing the idea that poetry remains the primary choice in promoting the kind of intellectual sovereignty that he has been theorizing throughout his work."²⁵ This statement, in addition to ignoring Warrior's concentration on two major nonfiction works, *Talking to the Moon* and *God Is Red*, as well as a novel, *Sundown*, all of which take up the great bulk of Warrior's discussion, opposes criticism and poetry as if poetry cannot suggest critical strategies.

Does poetry contribute to theoretical formulations? I surely hope so for the sake of both theorists and poets, one group that challenges itself to be more lyrical (theorists) and another whose work deepens when it is philosophical (poets). Further, one might note here some literary history: Walter Benjamin on Baudelaire, Geoffrey Hartman on Wordsworth, Harold Bloom on Stevens, and any other number of possibilities that are a matter of literary public knowledge.

In my own case, Pulitano cites passages in which I acknowledge the relevance of Western theory: "Translating trickster's ideology into his own theoretical discourse, Womack strives for balance between Native American viewpoints and postmodernism, thus contradicting his previous assertions."²⁶ I am quite curious to know what those previous assertions of mine are and why they are contradictory given that I never claim attempting a Creek analysis necessitates rejecting a Western one, nor that such a rejection is inherent in Creek projects. The next of Pulitano's sentences on pages ninety-five to ninety-six reads,

> He [Womack] writes that contemporary theory should not be abandoned, only "examined critically as to its values in illuminating Native cultures" (242). Later on he claims

"The Muskogee world is not the opposite of the Western world, it is a world that must be judged by its own merits, in its own terms . . . Native literatures deserve to be judged by their own criteria, in their own terms, not merely in agreement with, or reaction against, European literature or theory. The Native Americanist does not bury her head in the sand and pretend that European history and thought do not affect Native literature, nor does she ignore the fact that Native literature has quite distinctive features of its own that call for new forms of analyses [sic]."[27]

After this quote from *Red on Red* Pulitano concludes, "In the light of the literary separatism that Womack has advocated throughout *Red on Red,* such a position appears, indeed, contradictory."[28]

At this point, Warrior, Allen, and myself might well ask what does this person want from us? How to read all of this is anyone's guess. In Cherokee critic Jace Weaver's study, *That the People Might Live: Native American Literature and Native American Community* (1997), Weaver includes a broad array of non-Native sources, yet Pulitano dismisses Weaver as unworthy of her attention in a footnote. She calls Warrior to task for his emphasis on Indian source material in a statement he makes about the number of Indian authors in his bibliography, an observation Pulitano regards as a separatist act that is theoretically unjustifiable.[29] Because of the international experiences of the subject of his study, Mathews and Deloria, they cannot represent any pure Indian viewpoint, nor can any of the Indian thinkers Warrior includes in the bibliography of *Tribal Secrets* according to Pulitano.

Yet in her own introduction she claims, "In contrast to numerous articles and essay collections that rely on Western critical discourse in interpreting Native American texts, I argue that Native American authors themselves have produced (and keep producing) discursive strategies that might and should be taken into consideration in a discussion of Native American literature and culture" and Pulitano precedes to unfold a study that focuses on six Native authors![30] Can someone explain to me how this works?

Pulitano tries to distinguish herself from Arnold Krupat by pointing out that Native critics have not simply divorced themselves from theory but produced works with strong theoretical implications.[31] In most other matters, however, she mimics Krupat's hybridist views, repeating old ideas from earlier works that it seems like Krupat may even be revising. A major flaw in hybridist reasoning that Pulitano carries forward from earlier hybridist criticism is the attribution to Warrior and myself a model whose primary criteria for intellectual history, sovereignty, and nationhood is authenticity and/or cultural purity. Pulitano writes, "On an ideological level, Warrior's and Womack's position regarding the nature and content of a Native American literary theory converge in significant ways. Both insist, for example, on authentic traditions of Indian intellectualism."[32]

This is simply untrue—we insist on the relevance of Indian intellectual traditions, period, not "authentic" traditions. I will admit that it is not exactly in the nature of most educators to search for inauthentic traditions to emulate; teachers have a tendency to work more by positive examples than negative ones. Nonetheless, I have often heard Warrior present papers on Native intellectuals—one example is a presentation at Yale in 1998 on Elias Boudinot—whose life and work is not altogether exemplary, a point Warrior made very strongly. In *Tribal Secrets*, Warrior makes it clear that John Joseph Mathews had his detractors among the Osages in his own time and now. Anyone who reads the "Wynema" chapter of *Red on Red* cannot possibly miss the fact that I argue that Alice Callahan was an insider who was often less than insightful in regard to Creek matters. It is incorrect for Pulitano to conflate a particular appreciation of Indian intellectual history with a universal assumption of Indian intellectual authenticity. Warrior and I, simply, are not that stupid. We are not, after all, Luddites.

Further, it is philosophically untenable to argue that the act of analyzing Indian intellectual history inherently carries with it a naive belief in the guaranteed wisdom of any Indian who might be described as an intellectual. Who would possibly define "intellectual" as "flawless?" It would be impossible to teach the courses that both Warrior and I have developed at the University of Oklahoma on nineteenth- and early twentieth-century or even contemporary authors by arguing that these intellectuals were some kind of ideal Indians. Like competent scholars in many disciplines, we understand that the word "critical" is one-half of the phrases "critical thinking" and "cultural criticism." In Warrior's own writings he has talked about the applicability of Kwame Anthony Appiah's critique of the Nativist who only sees his or her culture in celebratory terms. Both of us have argued vigorously, and in various ways, that Native intellectual traditions should be subject to harder scrutiny than they have been in the past, given the tendency to regard Native intellectuals as sacred icons rather than humans asserting opinions. We want the field to be more smart, not less, and we should be given credit for our considerable efforts toward that very goal.

Pulitano repeats the old hybridist saw about our naiveté in regard to cultural purity and isolationism when she says, "Again and again, Womack appeals to issues of authenticity and nationhood to legitimate space for a Native American critical theory that is defined by internal, or tribal, rather than by external sources."[33] As with many of her arguments, Pulitano includes no page citations because none can be found. There is no claim in *Red on Red* that nationhood is pure, purely Indian or purely anything, or authentic. The book, instead, concerns itself with how sovereignty might be relevant to modern Indian life. Once again, it is philosophically untenable to assume sovereignty constitutes an inherent demand for purity, isolation, and authenticity. Since sovereignty, by definition, has to do with government-to-government relations, it has everything to do with intersections and exchanges between inside and outside worlds. Instead of having a conniption fit every time the word sovereignty is uttered, one would think that the concept would have some appeal to the hybridists and to Pulitano. The beauty of sovereignty is that it liberates tribes from anthropologically based cultural definitions by recognizing them as legally defined political entities, thus providing an alternative to the problem of ahistorical essentialist modes of analysis. A tribe is more than a culture; it is a government (and, of course, I understand the interdependency, rather than the oppositional nature, of culture and government). The point is that the government part of the equation is often missing from hybridist analysis other than arguing for its irrelevance.

To be a citizen of a modern nation-state, a person does not have to prove authenticity or her degree of purity either racially or culturally.

Because I taught in southern Alberta, I ended up becoming a Canadian citizen. When I took the citizenship test in Canada, there were no questions about my race or whether I had exposed myself to un-Canadian influences. Neither was I given a task (such as curling, god forbid, or worse yet, eating *poutine*, a mixture of french fries, cottage cheese, and brown gravy!) where I had to prove myself culturally Canadian. I did have to swear allegiance to the Queen, so I dealt with this by simply swearing allegiance to all queens and afterward felt pretty good, like I had made a stand on behalf of my people. The point is that citizenship is not an exclusively racial, or even cultural, status. It is defined—in some pretty significant ways—legally as well. Pulitano never addresses the legal ramifications of tribal identities as she is always bogged down in an anthropological search for cultural traces, whether white or red, or, most often, blurred. There are no instances anywhere in her book where Pulitano refers to federal Indian law, court decisions, tribal constitutions, or other forms of tribal law. Based on the dearth of political and historical analysis in her work, one fears that Pulitano might lack conviction as to whether tribes can exist in any legitimate sense whatever her real beliefs might actually be.

Pulitano relies on recent Native criticism of sovereignty to corroborate her arguments, claims that sovereignty is of European rather than Indian origins.[34] Here, we are back at square one, the anthropological insistence on a search for origins rather than the validity of a concept like sovereignty in the modern Indian world. While sovereignty may inherit certain problematic legacies badly in need of revision whether they come from Europe or Native North America, it cannot be simply dismissed because of possible European origins unless one adheres to the notion that Europe is inherently evil and all things that can be traced in any way to the continent should be destroyed.

Start burning those Mozart records!

Pulitano's claim is that given the inherent hybridity of sovereignty, such a concept contradicts Warrior's supposed separatist schema, which she says naively insists on Indian intellectual authenticity. The key issue, of course, is that Warrior has never linked intellectual history or nationhood with authenticity, and there is nothing inherent in the meaning of either concept that makes them an inevitable claim for authenticity.

In relation to my own work Pulitano says,

> At the beginning of his discussion, Womack argues that, as
> an intellectual idea, sovereignty is inherent in Native cultures
> and that, as a political practice, it predates European contact.
> Creeks, for example, had local representations in autonomous
> towns, and, more important, Creek storytelling articulated
> concepts of nationhood and politics (*Red on Red* 51).
> The Creek's creation story itself "combines," according to
> Womack, "emergence with Creek national concerns" (54).
> Whereas Warrior, Deloria, and the other critics mentioned
> earlier acknowledge the European theological and political
> origin of the term *sovereignty*, arguing that it has little to
> do with the original status of indigenous American realities,
> Womack goes back to the time before European treaty
> relationships with Native nations in order to claim sovereignty
> as a possession of Native communities. As does Allen in taking
> a gynocentric perspective, Womack appeals to a supposedly
> authentic past in terms of one shared culture, a sort of collec-
> tive one true self to reinforce the idea of nationhood. While his
> intent is to demystify the notion of oral tradition as an ethno-
> graphic artifact and illustrate the crucial role of stories within
> the political life of a tribal culture, his position raises many
> doubts about the concept of tradition and cultural identity.[35]

I strongly reject the argument that describing Creek forms of government, past or present, is by default an appeal to a return to a precolonial past of one shared culture. To study history is an insistence on a
return to the pre-Contact era? What is disingenuous about this statement is the fact that Pulitano never mentions in this passage or elsewhere
I have an entire chapter on modern Creek government that historicizes
its evolution and changes up to its present-day 56,000 membership, its
jurisdiction over eleven east central Oklahoma counties, and the latest
forms the government has taken since the adoption of its 1979 constitution: the first chapter in the book entitled, "The Creek Nation." Since
Creek membership is always growing, the government continues to grow

likewise, and I relied a bit too much on a dated source when writing *Red on Red*. I would like to direct those interested to the Muskogee Creek web page at *http://www.muscogeenation-nsn.gov* where, among many other things, readers can find the Creek Constitution.

Given that no other work of Native literary criticism besides *Red on Red* contains a chapter analyzing a modern tribal government, this is an amazing oversight on Pulitano's part—especially since she has so much to say about my flawed understanding of sovereignty and my fixation with the pre-Contact era in relation to nationhood. I am accused of misrepresenting Creek government, fixing it in the past, using Muskogee political history to essentialize sovereignty, and in order to make this argument she skips my chapter on Creek government.

It is not just Warrior's or my own explorations of sovereignty, however, that are problematized in Pulitano's book. Any search for an Indian viewpoint is seen as separatist, nostalgic, a reenactment of colonialism, a quixotic search for authenticity, a naive return to the pre-Contact era (unless, of course, Pulitano or one of the prioritized critics are asserting such a claim). Given the prevalence of this idea throughout the book, one wonders if the title is a mean joke. Should it not be called *The Impossibility of a Native American Critical Theory*? Pulitano writes,

> As I argued at the beginning of this chapter, the term *Native perspective* is itself problematic and contradictory. Once the oral tradition enters into dialogue with the rhetorical systems of the Western tradition, once it forcefully enters a book such as *Red on Red*, a product of the conjunction of cultural practices and hybridized discursive modes, an authentic Native perspective, such as the one promoted by Womack, becomes an ironic contradiction. To insist, as Womack does, that seeking out a Native perspective is "a worthwhile endeavor" (*Red on Red* 4) amounts to a dismissal of the mutual inter-dependencies that more than five hundred years of history have thrust on the American continent. More significantly, it means turning Native identity into a textual commodity that continues to perpetuate fabricated versions of Indianness.[36]

Claiming that seeking out a Native perspective is a worthwhile endeavor automatically equates to a dismissal of inter-dependencies? How does such a claim do that? I said Native perspectives are *worthwhile* endeavors, not *pristine* perspectives. The two ideas cannot be equated.

I have always admitted from the outset that a Native perspective is simply, as the term indicates, the perspectives of Native people—not flawless perspectives, isolated perspectives, pure perspectives, perspectives in a vacuum. I am wondering if, as an alternative, Pulitano recommends *not* seeking out Native perspectives? Because if that is what she advocates, we have already had five hundred years of that. Further, in this statement Pulitano assumes that on the Native side of the hybrid mix will be the Native oral, which will come into contact with the Western written, and this will produce the cultural conjunction that makes the Native perspective impossible because it is not one hundred percent Native.

This argument uses the reductive categories Pulitano is always criticizing, since Natives will make the oral contributions and Europeans the written ones. A major claim in Warrior's *Tribal Secrets* is that an under-examined body of Native *written* tradition exists that might shed light on Native letters. There is nothing essentialist about saying a body of literature is under-examined.

One wonders how Warrior becomes the essentialist when Pulitano is the one who holds the following views that claim orality and writing as inherent oppositions: "Clearly [Kimberly] Blaeser is correct to point out that the story [Vizenor's "Almost Browne"] 'comments on the origin and existence of the words outside *the static written tradition, on the authenticity of the oral,* on the presence and power of sound and language, on the "almost" quality of mere words'" (my emphasis).[37] Pulitano goes on to say, "Vizenor's interest in a *living oral as opposed to a static written tradition* is also one of the primary motifs in *Bearheart*" (my emphasis) and "the name of the Bioavaricious Word Hospital clearly reflects Vizenor's feelings about the *inability of the written word to liberate our imagination*" (my emphasis).[38] If Vizenor really believes, most creed-like, in the terminality of writing, as Pulitano claims, this would certainly be a strange position for a novelist, poet, journalist, and literary critic. Throughout the book Pulitano prioritizes orality and claims Native criticism that is the most "oral" is also somehow the most effective (while also claiming that my work *Red on Red*, unlike that of her favored critics, does not use stories to comment on criticism, a puzzling reading of the book in light of the central role of the dialect letters).

Pulitano treats a Native perspective like a blood quantum, a CDIP card, certificate of degree of Indian perspective, in this case anything short of one hundred percent turning its bearer into a hybrid instead of an Indian. At this point why do we not just give up and call it Hybrid American literature instead of Native American literature? A disturbing question is whether or not Pulitano actually believes in the existence of Native people, and, especially, tribes, given that her racial binary seems to only allow for non-Indians and hybrids. One wonders how, if at all, Native hybrids can be distinguished from any other American hybrid of various racial and cultural backgrounds. These are vanishing traps that we try to teach students to avoid in introductory Native Studies courses by emphasizing the role of Native governments rather than depending exclusively on romanticized racial and cultural notions.

Pulitano's failure to discuss the meaning of critics' work in relation to their tribal affiliations further underscores the important issue of whether or not she believes in the existence of tribal governments or, instead, ubiquitous "hybrid" individuals. Overall, the book demonstrates something that has concerned me for many years given the obsession in Native literary studies with the slippery shape-shifting characteristics of trickster as a model for language and identity. These very qualities, carried to extremes, are not liberatory, and the traditional stories are full of examples of the carnage left in tricksters' wake. The trickster model is sorely in need of some careful reexamination. One of the things I learned up in Blackfoot country was that "Napi" means "foolish one." Somehow, as a literary trope, we seem to have instead mistaken him or her for role model, ignoring some of the more oppressive characteristics of this figure (look at the rapes, for example, that are sometimes part of trickster stories).

Pulitano has more to say about a Native perspective:

> Defining a Creek or Native perspective is, indeed, problematic; even more problematic, I argue, is insisting on an essentially Creek or Native perspective in novels when the novel itself is,

Owens reminds us, a "foreign (though infinitely flexible) and intensely egocentric genre" (*Other Destinies* 10), a genre rising out of social conditions antithetical to whatever we might consider "traditional" Native American oral cultures. Critical of positions that legitimate authenticity and nationalism, Owens indicates that, "for the Indian author, writing within consciousness of the contextual background of a non-literate culture, every word written in English represents a collaboration of sorts as well as a reorientation (conscious or unconscious) from the paradigmatic world of oral tradition to the syntagmatic reality of written language" (6). Borrowing the vocabulary of Ashcroft et al. (in *The Empire Writes Back*) as well as from that of Mikhail Bakhtin, Owens explains how the dilemma of a privileged discourse already "charged" with "value" and "alien" is the primary concern for Native American fiction writers and significantly "adds complexity to the overarching questions of cultural identity" (7).[39]

There are all kinds of problems here in both Pulitano's and Owens's analysis. The first is the assumption that the novel is a foreign genre to Indians. Why would the novel be any more foreign to Indians than to Colombians, Israelis, Africans, the French, British, or Japanese? If the novel is that foreign, why are so many Indians writing them? Once again we are back to square one with the point of origin analysis: the novel did not originate in the Americas; therefore, it must be foreign. Here is the theoretical error: by making the novel foreign to Indians, Pulitano claims both hybridity and incommensurability at the same time. One minute the Indian novel is an intensely cross-cultural production between Native and non-Native, the next it is something foreign to Indians because it is so European.

The second problem is when the novel is said to be antithetical to traditional cultures, especially in light of all the claims, one just quoted, that the oral comes into contact with the written and creates the hybrid mix Pulitano is so fond of. Beyond that I would like to know just what it is that creates a natural disjuncture between the novel and Native traditionalism?

The third problem is when Owens, amazingly, claims that Native authors are "writing within consciousness of the contextual background of a non-literate culture." It has been a very long time since Choctaws were a "non-literate culture." How did Owens write all his books if not for the fact that he was incredibly literate (and, sadly, no longer with us to share his remarkable gifts)? Could he only accomplish this feat by distancing himself from his "Choctawness?" How does he explain the history of his own tribe, its unique relationship to literacy similar to the other southeastern tribes, the tribally run schools before Oklahoma statehood teaching students Latin, Greek, and British authors, a literacy rate that, per capita, sometimes exceeded that of whites in neighboring states, and modern Choctaw writers such as LeAnne Howe, Scott Morrison, Don Birchfield, and many others? There was a faction of Choctaw traditionalists who could not speak or read English for some time after the turn of the century in Oklahoma, and there continue to be Choctaws whose first language is Choctaw at the reservation in Philadelphia, Mississippi (most of whom also speak English). This is not the tribal faction, however, by Owens's own admission, that constitutes his background.

This goes back to a fundamental theoretical error in *Other Destinies* that has to do with Owens's application of Bakhtin throughout the book. Statements abound in Owens's study that pit Indians versus English and Indians versus the novel; in each case the second part of the binary is alien because of its European origins. Did Europe invent language and literature? When Owens makes English and novels alien, an authoritative discourse, and Indian languages and tribal values internally persuasive, Owens takes Bakhtinian theory in a direction in which it was never intended.

In Bakhtin's schema *all* languages are value-laden and enter into a tension-filled heteroglossic environment of diverse speech and ideologies. This would be equally true if Owens was writing in Choctaw, at least if we are to take Bakhtin at his word. Choctaw would have various forms of speech, different kinds of speakers, a multiplicity of ideas, internally persuasive discourse, authoritative discourse; again various forms of heteroglossia. This has to do with the fact that Choctaw, like other languages, is dialogic. It is communal, a shared, passed-on phenomenon. Given it is used by human beings, it is value-laden. It incorporates various perspectives. Bakhtin did not, for example, pit an internally persuasive Russian against an authoritative English.

This, however, is exactly the direction Owens takes Bakhtin by opposing Indians against English and novels. This is the error that allows Owens to view English as a foreign language, a strange position that does not even square up with his own primary language or the primary language of the great majority of Indian writers and Indian people. The answer to this conundrum would have been for Owens to value Native literature for its intrinsic merit rather than the ways in which it can be opposed to an alien Other. This is one of the reasons why my own work has hinged on tribally specific approaches: I want to explore what is valuable about Creek literature rather than how it is victimized by English. Loving Creek literature always seemed to me a better proposition than hating English.

For all we know, Indians may have even contributed something to the rise of the novel rather than simply becoming victims of the novel. Here I am thinking of the fact that *Don Quixote*, usually cited as the first novel, was published a century after the "discovery" of the "New" World. It is not impossible that exploration had an effect on the rise of the European novel. No one talks about the way Indians influenced French philosophy, either, in spite of Rousseau who spent a good deal of time thinking and writing about Native people in North America. While these are indirect influences, they could be influences nonetheless. Rousseau could not have written about Indians, one presumes, if Indians did not exist. Native people had an effect on the larger world outside of the Americas; in short they influenced European cultures. Whether or not Native people actually influenced the novel, certainly orality did, and Owens's constant assertions that the conditions and values of orality are incompatible with modern novels is deeply problematic. One might even argue that some Native people versed in orality might be *predisposed* to novel writing or the reading of them rather than alienated by them. This seems to be the case, at the very least, for a number of American Indian authors.

We know that Marx and Engels, to use another example of interrelationality in order to question these oppositions, quoted extensively from Lewis Henry Morgan's 1877 book about Iroquoian culture entitled *Ancient Society*. Given the huge influences of Marxism on continental literary theory, it is not impossible to imagine Native people having some bearing on the theoretical outpouring of the last four decades.

I might also mention historical examples of Indian literacy such as the pre-Contact mesoamerican writers producing books in southern Mexico and Guatemala in Mayan and Aztec and the rich body of colonial period and nineteenth-century Native writing in English that suggests something other than the nonliterate cultures Owens claims rather broadly for indigenous peoples. Pulitano's endorsement of Owens here is another retreat to point-of-origin analysis, the etymological approach to Native Studies. Who is it, again, who is trying to return to a romanticized pre-Contact past?

The fourth problem is when Owens claims "every word written in English represents a collaboration." This statement only holds up if English is a non-Indian language. English is an Indian language. I know a lot of Indians—been around them all my life—and every one of them speaks English. In some cases they also speak a tribal language. As evidence of this I offer the staggering numbers of U.S. Indians who speak English as their first language. I cannot cite a statistic, but I would be willing to guess it is well over 90 percent, probably closer to one hundred. (In Canada, I might note, this statistic would be different, as it would be in Latin America. The statistic, obviously, would vary in the United States if one compared, for example, residents on the Navajo reservation to sons and daughters of relocatees in Oakland, California.) I wonder who all these people are "collaborating" with when they speak English if not themselves, their communities, and whatever other worlds their speech acts intersect with.

Further, when English landed in the New World, it picked up Indian tribal words in the Americas and African tribal words in the Caribbean and along the routes of the slave trade. English may have been as affected by tribal people as tribal people were affected by English. English could not remain a solely authoritative language, an enemy's language, a patriarch's language, an oppressor's language, and so on and so forth, once it got to the Americas. The English lost control of their English. Viewing English as a threatening Other, as incommensurable with tribal languages, as an authoritarian discourse, even as an enemy's language that needs "reinventing" is dubious unless the "enemy" is Indian people themselves, since they have a vested interest in the English language. Native people are not mere victims of English.

The failure to consider Native words in English is emblematic of a larger problem. This is where it gets really interesting because by making assimilation a one-way street where only Indians are assimilated by non-Indian culture instead of non-Indian culture also being influenced by Native culture (the English language with its Indian influences being one of many examples), Pulitano constructs a "white purity" and fails to confess her hybridity like she wants everyone else to. Presuming the purity of whiteness and, ironically, an attendant privileged vantage point that allows her to understand the underlying true hybrid nature of all things, she then asserts herself into the vacuum where no Indians are left, only hybrids, and becomes the final arbiter of whatever postmodern traces of Indianness remain.[40]

By the time Mohegan author Samson Occom penned his autobiography in English in 1768, often claimed as the first published Native work, several thousand New England Indians had learned to read and write as evidenced by many letters and journals still available for scholarly analysis. Not all of these writers were the victims of literacy, forced by missionaries to take up the pen. Some of them viewed writing enthusiastically, as Indians, and all humans, have viewed new opportunities from time immemorial. Viewing English, novels, or Native literary criticism as "alien" to Native culture is dubious and, further, inconsistent with Pulitano's own analysis since it makes hybridity unlikely if Indians are this threatened by all things European. It may be true that certain forms of literary criticism are of little interest to many Indians, especially the kind authored by Pulitano that argues for Indian non-existence and appoints hybrids to take their place, but this does not mean that Indian culture constitutes some kind of inherent aversion to literacy or that Native people can never be interested in criticism.

Given the confusion these arguments create, I want to return to the issue I raised at the beginning of this essay. One way to measure the efficacy of theories is by gauging how well they describe the social world they make claims about. When I used to walk into the classroom at the University of Lethbridge and stand face-to-face with a large number of Native students, about 50 percent of the class, many of them Blackfoot and from very traditional families who still spoke the language and were often ceremonialists, I was in no position to proclaim to these students the death of the Native perspective. Similarly, now at the University of Oklahoma, where I also teach classes with around 30 to 50 percent Native students in Indian literature courses and significant numbers of Creek students in my Muskogee literature course, I cannot announce the death of a Creek or Native perspective (though I certainly can, and do, discuss at great length how Indian perspectives can be opened up to multiple rather than singular viewpoints). This is the difference—and what a difference it is—between teaching in Lethbridge, Alberta, or Norman, Oklahoma, in comparison to Geneva, Switzerland, where Pulitano is a professor.

This is not mere sarcasm. I claim that reality matters and that Indian experience means something. In *Reclaiming Identity: Realist Theory and the Predicament of Postmodernism*, published in 2000 by the University of California Press and edited by Paula Moya and Michael Hames-Garcia, the book's contributors weigh in against the radical skepticism that has problematized normative truth claims in today's theoretical environment. These theorists, referring to themselves as "post-positive realists," claim experience as a way of both generating and evaluating theory, making strong arguments as to how insider's claims can have validity. It is strange that Pulitano did not include this book in her study, a major statement from some very well-known theorists, many from Stanford and Cornell and other prominent universities, especially given its bearing on so much of what Pulitano has to say regarding authenticity and insider viewpoints.

This book constitutes a major challenge to Pulitano's claims. While I have my own set of issues with the postpositive realists because I think their staunch anti-foundationalsim often forces them simply to reinvent postmodernism with a slightly altered critical jargon rather than break through to a new understanding, this group of theorists is interested in evaluating theory in light of social realities, which makes them of interest to me. Of all the books Pulitano might have skipped, this is a strange oversight in light of her arguments. She quotes one of the contributors to *Reclaiming Identity*, Satya Mohanty, on other matters from an essay outside of this particular book or its issues, so it seems even more suspicious that she makes no reference to his, and others, realist claims given his prominence in the realist movement. There is a general pattern in Pulitano's book of skipping anything and everything that might contradict her arguments. She cites interviews she conducted with Vizenor and Owens but none with Warrior, Allen, or myself, whose quotes would have been detrimental to her position. We were not contacted.

Getting back to my reality check, when I walk into a classroom of Indian students I have to give them something better than telling them that their own viewpoints are either impossible or hopelessly naive unless they are willing to confess all of the ways in which they are "implicated" in Western discourse. What one might suspect as a lack of experience around Native people seems to be confirmed by Pulitano's own statements in the book. Pulitano admits that her only experience of Indians is textual. In the Sarris chapter she says, "unlike Jenny's [a friend of Greg Sarris's whose reactions to Mabel McKay's stories are discussed in *Keeping Slug Woman Alive*] experience with the oral tradition, mine has never been immediate, face-to-face with a storyteller; it has, instead, been intermediate, mediated by written texts, texts, moreover, that, despite a heavy reliance on the oral tradition, are still modeled after traditional Western genres."[41] If Pulitano taught Indian literature on a campus with large numbers of Native students, writing a book such as hers might have been a near impossibility—at least if she wanted any relevance in the classroom.

I hope that my dialogue with students in Indian Country forms the basis for some of my own philosophies. When discussing authenticity most critics simply throw up a theoretical wall and back away, claiming the topic as impossible. In conversations with classrooms full of Native students, however, I have learned that while a definition that *fixes* a notion of authenticity in a static, timeless vacuum is impossible; nonetheless, the *process* of thinking through issues of Native authenticity and even searching for forms of viable Native nationalisms are unavoidable in Indian Country—even if we can never provide an absolute definition and end up in discussions fraught with theoretical problems. We need a critical space where Indians can imagine forms of Indianism. In this sense, advocating "authentic" tribal literatures, promoting Native voices, and other such efforts are worthwhile, and I believe this is what Warrior means when he talks about process-oriented intellectual sovereignty in *Tribal Secrets*. At some point we cannot avoid, and should not avoid, the question, "What is acceptable to Indian people in relation to the study of their own cultures?" And this is the way in which we will never be able to simply dismiss ourselves from the authenticity issue. Classrooms with large number of Indian students are not the only place where discussions of Native literature take place; nonetheless, it is an important location in real time and space that shapes those of us who are there year after year.

I think Pulitano's idea of confession is one of the most fascinating topics in her book. Pulitano never actually uses the word "confess"; instead we must "acknowledge" our hybridity if we claim a tribal identity. (Somehow non-Indians need not worry about confessing anything.) With words like "complicity" and "implicated" thrown in so frequently to describe our relationship to Western discourse, and the way in which acknowledgment is demanded rather than described, it is little wonder that it feels like a confession.

The sin of the Indian separatist is not that he or she is a hybrid, since we are told all Indians are hybrids, as are their literatures and ideas. Like the concept of original sin, our lot is one of original hybridity. The separatists' problem is that, unlike our "superiors," we do not talk about our hybridity enough: "Unlike Allen, [Gayatri] Spivak acknowledges her complicity."[42]

Hello, I'm Gayatri, and I'm a hybrid.

Pulitano argues that confession is our first act before we proceed with anything else, confession before communion: "Any form of discourse involving notions of tradition, sovereignty, and commitment to communities should at first acknowledge the level of complicity between Native intellectuals (regardless of the kind of community in which they operate) and the dominant academic discourse."[43] In my own case I need special treatment, interrogation, because I should be the subject of an investigation: "Interrogating only his investigating tools when he should also be interrogating his position as a critic and subject of investigation, Womack voices simulations of tribal identity..."[44]

While all this tool interrogation is interesting in a campy, phallic kind of way (might I have to confess something for that as well?), I wonder about Pulitano's assumed position of authority here. Having never seen Pulitano at a Creek Baptist or Methodist church, a Creek stomp dance, a Creek family reunion, a Creek casino, bingo hall, or travel plaza, the national council house, the tribal headquarters, anywhere within the state of Oklahoma, or even as much as at a Native literature conference as far as I know, having only met two people who have claimed to have seen her *anywhere*, I might wonder how she could possibly comprehend the difference between my supposed simulations of Creek, and other, tribal identities, and her supposed intimate knowledge of the real thing. She goes on to say "Womack conveniently dismisses the fact that he is utilizing language and tools borrowed from the colonizer and that, by wishing to attach these instruments to some form of nationalism, he inevitably ends up exoticizing them."[45] The problem is that Pulitano cannot suggest *any* language or tools that I *can* use if I want to write as an Indian.

The book seems to boil down to the advice "just write like Vizenor." I think writing like Vizenor is a truly marvelous thing.

For Gerald Vizenor.

The difference between those of us bringing up the rear on Pulitano's critical Great Chain of Being and the more highly evolved Vizenor, Owens, and Sarris is our denial. We do not say it enough. We are complicitous . . . We are complicitous . . . We are complicitous. Our books are complicitous. Our criticism is complicitous. Our ideas are complicitous . . . Our people are complicitous . . . only thirty-nine lashes to go. Consider the separatists of our field. We don't acknowledge; neither do we interrogate.

Why do I feel like this demand for me to confess is some kind of inverted dance for the tourists: "Can I get my picture took with an *unreal* Indian?" My criticism of confession is not to detract from the rather substantial way in which Greg Sarris has illuminated stories by telling his own in his critical texts, analyzing his positionality and situating himself in his writings. We might note that *Keeping Slug Woman Alive*, one of the most important books on tribal literature, ethnography, and reader response theory in many people's estimation, including my own, an appreciation I have shared with Sarris personally, also focuses on the literature of a single tribe, yet Pulitano does not regard Sarris's Pomo perspective with equal suspicion, something she never explains in her book. There is an important point here. In order to illuminate his critical texts, Sarris tells concrete stories rooted in a particular place and time. Character, setting, and plot, standard narrative devices, are essential. Sarris connects his theory to various social realities, his own and others. This is a much different project than the ahistorical blather about the need for confession, rooted in abstraction and disconnected from reality.

The word "complicity" has to do with sharing the blame for something. I would like to know what I am being blamed for before I confess. What will be the punishment? Will Pulitano be administering it? What acts of contrition does she have in mind? Will there be any tool interrogation? Can I pick who will interrogate mine?

I have to trust my own subjectivity here, my "internally persuasive discourse," if you will, and say this simply does not feel right. The demand for confessions creates a very strange platform from which to launch accusations that Warrior and myself have become agents of colonialism: "Even though objections could be made as to the applicability of such a term to Warrior and Womack's critical perspectives, I will argue that their cultural separatism eventually leads to the hopeless project of recovering a Native essence, a project that, ironically, embraces another sort of colonial invention."[46] Well, she is right about one thing: I plan to raise objections.

Does confessing hybridity necessarily challenge hegemony? I know when sinners confess to priests the result is not an inversion of power. Pulitano needs to explain how "acknowledgment" affects power balances, if she can.

I feel that a book that takes up Muskogee literature as its central focus is as least as subversive as confessing hybridity and complicity. *Red on Red* challenges a methodology as institutionalized in power systems as "Native Literature" and asks questions about what happens when such a term is used in the face of mind-boggling tribal diversity, as well as questions about the kind of criticism that might emerge by focusing on the output of a single tribe.

In Lisa Brooks's Afterword, a practical consideration is named: none of us can become experts on every single tribal nation, and we can use the help of tribal members who have expertise in their own communities. I think it would be premature to proclaim the "Death of the Indian" by claiming the superiority of the tribally specific, and I dislike criticism that claims to supplant what came before it, so I appreciate what Brooks offers instead: possibilities for tribally specific works to be placed in dialogue with other tribally specific works, with regional histories, even with materials focused on the ever-popular discussion of popular representations of Indians.

In terms of my own book, by arguing that one little corner of the world, the Muskogee Creek Nation, with its eleven-county jurisdiction in east central Oklahoma and 56,000 citizens, can constitute a nation of people whose concerns are central to their own lives, even if of little interest to anyone else, the very notion of power itself is challenged, especially the idea of power as a quantifiable verity invested most significantly in whatever or whoever is biggest, which might be a challenge to an especially virulent American form of Eurocentrism.

Given the concerns with globalization these days, U.S. Indian tribes present some of the most interesting living studies of what constitutes the modern nation-state because of the challenging questions they raise about the role of geography, political structures, and population as part of a matrix that constitutes nationhood. How much is enough to be a nation, which factors are significant, and what weight do they have in relation to the others? Tribes are case studies for these issues, and sovereignty has cutting-edge potential in Native literary studies if critics are willing to examine it with any kind of depth that exceeds simply dismissing it with accusations about the naiveté of its proponents. U.S. Indian sovereignty has worldwide implications and the potential to lift Native literary studies out of a stagnant morass that keeps it bound up in static cultural definitions. Rather than being a parochial field with a tiny minority constituency as Native Studies is often perceived, it has ramifications outside Indian Country in terms of relations across national and international borders.

Tribal literary nationalism, contrary to the stereotype, is not defined by isolation but by the way a microcosmic view of the world can lead to macrocosmic understandings and relations. Why is this so strange to postmodernists? Their reactions to essentialism have often focused on historicizing particulars rather than assuming ahistorical universals. I think there are a number of ways of illustrating how tribal literary nationalism can help further understandings, but one I will briefly mention is the important contribution Robert Warrior makes in his reading of John Joseph Mathews's novel *Sundown* in Warrior's book *Tribal Secrets*. There Warrior argues that many Native literary studies have focused on personal identity issues, but by turning to ideas about sovereignty, and communal viewpoints rather than first or third person ones, a new set of questions can be opened up—in the case of *Sundown*, the progress of the Osage Nation throughout the novel rather than simply Chal's personal development. I believe that chapter has changed the way many of us read Native literature.

As Pulitano would have it, a study like *Red on Red* that argues Muskogee Creeks have legitimate national interests within their own territory, within the United States, and within the world, in no way challenges Eurocentric hegemony or discourse? It is instead a pawn, sometimes even an agent, of colonialism? If prioritizing one tribe's literary output in a study is inappropriate, one wonders how demands to acknowledge the centrality of Europe improves on the schema.

If Pulitano was to turn her skepticism about identity and perspectives on to the terms of her own theory, she might ask, just who are these Europeans? What is Eurocentric discourse? How can it be distinguished from non-Eurocentric discourse? These phrases are so impossibly broad that her demands to subvert the Eurocentric center become meaningless. Just who should we start subverting? Are our targets identified by genetics, skin color, race, national boundaries, world views, philosophies? Who should we go after first?

If Pulitano were to tell me I should start speaking out against America's immoral and incredibly stupid colonial invasion of Iraq and protesting the discourse of George Bush and Donald Rumsfeld by comparing their speeches to sermons preached by nineteenth-century religious leaders using Christian theology to justify manifest destiny, well, then, I would have something I could sink my teeth into because of the way in which historical context creates an identifiable course of action. When she tells me my main job is to subvert or challenge Eurocentric discourse, however, she might as well say I should fly to the moon on a piece of green cheese. If a claim for Indian discourse is impossible without acknowledging its inevitable hybridity, how can I be expected to mount an attack against a monolithic, pure, cohesive Eurocentric discourse? Am I the only one with hybridity problems?

The point I want to make, and it is a pivotal one, is that Pulitano works in an ahistorical mode that makes concepts like resisting Eurocentric discourse impossible to substantiate. There are almost no references to historical events in her work; yet she aggressively lays claims to a staunch anti-essentialism. In her only reference to a historical date, she is off by nearly a century: "Vizenor's journey into the various simulations of Indianness begins with him invoking, as Lee points out, 'a two way exchange of journeys'. . . . Meriwether Lewis and Captain William Clark's expedition westward, in 1804–5, and Luther Standing Bear's step eastward in 1789. Whereas Lewis and Clark hoped to be seen by tribal people, Luther Standing Bear, the first enrollee in the Federal Indian School at Carlyle, Pennsylvania, would have seen whites."[47] The Carlisle Indian Industrial School, of course, did not exist in 1789 and was not ever called the Federal Indian School. The reference is off by ninety years. Most likely the error in the historical date is a typo. In spite of the fact that it is probably a typo, the glitch may have some symbolic value for readers who are put off by the utter lack of historical grounding in the text.

Pulitano presents theory apart from history, universalizing her arguments rather than historicizing them. When she criticizes Paula Gunn Allen's problematic claims to a universalized "Indian mind," Pulitano, in all actuality, might be staring in the mirror, seeing her own reflection, projecting, if one wishes to use psychoanalytic terms. So much of the confusion in the book stems from the fact that her study so deeply embodies all the strategies she detests. Without historical specificity, Eurocentrism can never be resisted because it is impossible to define what it is. By avoiding history Pulitano is stuck inside a model where she can only duplicate what she criticizes in others. Over and over again she will scour texts for their Indian essences. Sure, they might seem like a little bit different kind of essences since she is looking for Indian traits that can dialogue, challenge, and resist Western theory, as well as characteristics that synthesize Native and Western viewpoints. She searches, nonetheless, for inherent characteristics of orality, nonlinearity, multiple viewpoints, and so on, that can be traced back to an Indian world (its oral tradition) and that can be selected for an engagement with Western theory.

This is exactly why *Red on Red* turns to history and specificity in order to qualify universal claims. An interesting experiment is to consider two of the authors accused of essentialism, Warrior and myself, and note the number of historical references in our work in relation to Pulitano's book. Given that essentialism is often defined as making universalist claims in ahistorical modes, one wonders how Pulitano wriggles free of the charges of essentialism she directs at the rest of us. Warrior and I frequently reference public policy in our books. We include dates. Warrior's chapter titles are organized around specific time periods. Another writer charged with essentialism (advocating a right and wrong way to do Indian studies as quoted earlier) is Elizabeth Cook-Lynn.

In Elizabeth Cook-Lynn's latest book of essays, *Indian Hating in Modern America: A Voice from Tatekeya's Earth*, her working vocabulary includes frequent references to the *Oliphant* case, *Yankton Sioux Tribe v. South Dakota*, the Black Hills case, the Winters Doctrine, *Hagen v. Utah*, and continuous discussion about the relationship between history and the claims that can be made about Native literature. In comparison, Pulitano, the essentialist hunter, does not refer to a single legal case or federal policy and almost no date when anything occurred.

Further, we might expect Pulitano to at least know something about hybridity theory since it is the central theme of her book. Pulitano never renders the history of hybridity, its invention as Foucault might say—its relationship to the rise of cultural studies in Britain in the 1950s, the United States in the 1990s, and the effect on French theory that was written in the late 1970s and early 1980s and translated into English for U.S. publication in the 1980s, significantly affecting the aims of cultural studies and the hybridity notions that would come out of these various schools of thought. Instead Pulitano presents hybridity theory as ahistorical and universal, an a priori foundation. In the beginning was Hybridity.

In her demands for the less evolved writers to confess their hybridity, Pulitano might have considered for herself the possibility of occasionally crossing over to the Indian world and confessing something Indian. Or are these confessions only a one-way street? Maybe she could consider implicating herself in Indianness for a change of pace. She could at least historicize her own theoretical position.

Pulitano queries, "At what point does Warrior's Native intellectual come out of his Native community to embrace a dialogue with outside communities? These are some of the questions that Warrior's study tends to overlook, causing his overall argument to be trapped in ironic contradiction."[48] I would like to ask, "at what point does Pulitano come into *ours*?" Her accusation is an odd one for someone living and teaching in Geneva, Switzerland.

My motivation for writing *Red on Red* was a conviction that exploring Indian realities (whatever their degree of purity or impurity) was just as legitimate as confessing European influences. I never assumed, and the study does not suggest, that one world cancels out the other. In relation to Warrior, Pulitano writes, "Given the richly hybridized nature of Mathews's and Deloria's cultural backgrounds, and given the privileged discourse within which they inevitably speak, a reader might question what makes them the internal historical voices and major intellectual sources out of which, according to Warrior, an American Indian discourse, a mature Native cultural and literary criticism, should originate."[49]

The reason a Native perspective can emerge from these two thinkers is because they are two Native guys with perspectives. Does this mean their perspectives are guaranteed to be good ones or authentic ones? I think it is offensive for Pulitano to claim on our behalf that we answer the question in the affirmative. The role of the Native American Studies (NAS) practitioner is to scrutinize various perspectives that Native people articulate and try to determine their value, or lack of value, in relation to the Indian world and other worlds Indians coexist in. Further, Warrior states explicitly in some of the very quotes Pulitano reproduces in her book that these two men's cross-cultural experiences enrich rather than diminish their Native perspectives. As far as Warrior's right to use them as "internal historical voices," at least he has some. After finishing Pulitano's text, an uninformed reader might assume Native literature did not exist before Gerald Vizenor. There is no reference whatsoever to the body of literature before the contemporary writings that some critics have called the "Native American literary renaissance," referring to the writings of the last three and a half decades. Pulitano writes as if nineteenth-century Native literature, or even early twentieth century, never existed.

Pulitano quotes African writer Kwame Anthony Appiah to corroborate her arguments about the impossibility of a Native perspective:

"If there is a lesson in the broad shape of this circulation of culture, it is surely that we are all already contaminated by each other, that there is no longer a fully autochthonous *echt*-African culture awaiting salvage by our artists (just as there is, of course, no American culture without African roots). And there is a real sense in some postcolonial writing that the postulation of a unitary Africa over against a monolithic West—the binarism of Self and Other—is the last shibboleths of the modernizers that we must learn to live without" (155).[50]

When Appiah insists, however, on the inextricably bound destinies of Africa and the West, this is a much different thing than saying African writers cannot articulate African perspectives. The reason why African writers can articulate African perspectives is because of the existence of Africa—see a map—no matter how heteroglot those perspectives may be. Most agree that Africa exists as a geographically defined continent and that critics from there can and do assert various opinions. Can anyone really say there is no such thing as African literary perspectives because African novels contain references and influences from outside Africa? If any critic claims to have THE African perspective, this is a problem. The impossibility of a singular, monolithic African perspective, however, does not cancel out the possibility of various African perspectives, nor the need and incredible importance of Africans speaking for themselves and African critics responding to what they have to say. The right of a people to speak their mind, and the right of their communities to respond, is a far cry from a naive insistence on cultural purity.

Pulitano argues that a critic claiming any kind of Native perspective that fails to confess its European complicities sets him or herself up as some kind of authentic Indian informant doling out truth from a privileged knowledge. Pulitano writes, "Even more problematic are Allen's supposed knowledge of 'what is true about American Indians' and her definition of *Indian* itself. Is Allen's Indianness a guarantee of authentic knowledge, a position that makes her a representative 'Native informant,' to use Spivak's term, whose claims and observations are evidence of infallible truth?"[51] While I am as skeptical as the next guy of the latest Indian guru, does any author really want to set him or herself up as an *inauthentic* informant? With the exception, possibly, of the unreliable narrator in fiction, part of the ethos of writing is an attempt to establish one's credibility—one wants readers to believe the story one narrates.

In considering the possibilities and limitations of insider status, crucial here is a definition of experience—which we never get from Pulitano. While experience does not guarantee insight, this does not mean that insight from experience is impossible or even unlikely. Indian experience, thoughtfully considered and intelligently articulated, is, in fact, meaningful in relation to things Indian. Lest I am not making myself clear, let me be specific here: I think there are a helluva lot of Creek people who know much more about Creek perspectives than does Elvira Pulitano. There are a lot more Creek people who know more about them than I do as well. How can Pulitano claim that we are the ones insisting on insider privilege when she herself, knowing next to nothing about Muskogee people, goes to great lengths to define what a Creek perspective can and cannot do?

One wonders about the implications of all this for research. If Indian experience is an ironic illusion fostered by Indians on themselves, why would any researcher, Native or not, need to check his or her claims against oral, written, and other community sources? Why would the researcher need to be in a lived relationship with those he or she writes about? The researcher is "freed" from contact with humans, and her involvement need only be textual. The last couple of decades, marked by an insistence that those writing Native history consider a broader range of sources than the usual suspects by including community knowledge, have been a waste of time. Pulitano's own claim that Vizenor, Sarris, and Owens revolutionize their work by drawing on a Native oral tradition is meaningless. Pulitano, as well as some Native critics, need to carefully think through their commitments to poststructuralism.

While no doubt my critical position has flaws, as all do, I hope for an intellectual environment someday in which critics might be more willing to do their homework in order to understand my arguments. I am a long-standing member of Tallahassee Wakokiye Creek Ceremonial grounds. Creek grounds have never served an exclusively religious function; they have been at the heart of a vibrant Creek nationalism that, among other things, resisted the imposition of Oklahoma statehood on tribes and the dissolution of tribal government after the Dawes and Curtis Acts. As a theorist from Tallahassee Wakokiye, Creek nationalism is part of my inheritance, a perspective that inevitably influences the way I approach theory. My work, like all critical work, is subject to critique but please try to understand something about the historical environment that contextualizes what I do. Whatever the nature of the hybrid matrix that affects my philosophical commitments, Tallahassee Wakokiye is not simply erased from the equation, and I must disagree with critics who say that it is rather than sit idly by while someone demands that I confess the irrelevance of the nationalism that is part of my personal and communal history.

Pulitano's radical skepticism in relation to Native perspectives gets so ridiculous that at one point she even puts the word Native in quote marks: "Like Warrior, Womack appeals to concepts such as *autonomy, sovereignty,* and *self-determination* in order to theorize a 'Native' perspective that allows Indian people to speak for themselves."[52] Where are we in this discipline if even the word Native needs quote marks because we are unsure of the existence of Indians or their perspectives?

The danger here is real, not imaginary. In Scott Michaelson's 1999 University of Minnesota Press publication *The Limits of Multiculturalism: Interrogating the Origins of American Anthropology*, he argues that the writings of nineteenth-century Native authors have no distinguishing characteristics that differentiate them from nineteenth-century non-Indian ethnographers who also wrote books about Indians. Michaelson expands on this idea to argue that the very category of Indian itself is improbable, and not in an ironic Vizenorian kind of way that has to do with Columbus taking a wrong left-hand turn, but because Indians do not exist in any real sense. All the characteristics that define Indian differences from non-Indians, this is to say, are socially constructed. An argument for the nonexistence of Indians might not be the strongest legal strategy in a land, water, or jurisdiction case, and we can only hope judges and legislators do not start reading the likes of Michaelson. There is some real cause for concern here.

Further, in terms of Native Studies history in the academy, much of Pulitano's analysis of Paula Gunn Allen fails to consider the historical moment Allen wrote out of in the 1980s in terms of movements in feminism, the contributions of women of color, and a point in time when many NAS academic units were simply trying to establish themselves as programs or departments staffed with faculty to teach courses—probably not a good time to bring up the point that Indians might not exist. Allen's essentialism, problematic as it might be in *The Sacred Hoop*, comes out of this particular historical moment. In addition to critiquing her essentialism, Allen should be credited for the gifted way in which she helped pioneer a space for Native women to speak and for Native Studies to exist. As critical faults go, I will take critics like Paula Gunn Allen who say that an Indian voice is possible over the critics who say an Indian voice is impossible any day of the week, and this is not merely a matter of a feeble intellectual capacity on my part. It is smart, and it is the right thing to do.

I am in the middle of a collaborative project with a community of Native critics, almost all of them junior faculty and graduate students, who are putting together an anthology of all-Native literary criticism. A major goal has been creating a theory-friendly book that looks at theory as something else besides a threatening Other. I wonder how many of my colleagues and friends working on this project will find their theory phobias alleviated by reading Pulitano's book? Is not part of our job encouraging young Native critics to *find* their voices rather than telling them their voices are, best-case scenario, problematic—and more likely impossible? As Lisa Brooks reminds us in her Afterword, shouldn't we be gathering them back around the table, her metaphor for the exchange of ideas between Native people, rather than turning them away by telling them the table itself is illusory? "We know you are starving, but the food here is only pretend." Or must we tell them that they can have a perspective as long as they write like Vizenor, Owens, or Sarris? I am no more comfortable with that than demanding that they write like Womack, Warrior, or Allen. Should we tell them they are allowed to express Native perspectives only to the degree they are willing to constantly call attention to their un-Indianness? Little wonder Native critics have regarded theory with a certain amount of suspicion.

I am concerned about the emergence of a class of critical gatekeepers who are resistant to new forms of Native literary expression all the while claiming their, or select Indian writer's, viewpoints are on a higher plane than other Indian writers. As subversive as Vizenor may actually be, his work becomes something less than revolutionary when critics place it in a context that argues it is the only legitimate form of Native expression or the most subversive form in a community of his lessers. In this case Vizenor's work becomes canonical and institutionalized in the most conservative of senses. I would like to see young Native writers encouraged to venture *away from* the modes of Vizenor, Sarris, Owens, Womack, Warrior, and Allen rather than given a rigid dictate of "this is the way, walk ye in it." How can artistic and critical production flourish in a schema like Pulitano's with its stringent demand for uniformity?

Another need for a reality check might be Pulitano's endorsement of Gloria Anzaldua's well-known borderlands philosophy. Pulitano claims Allen's writings have improved somewhat in her more recent book *Off the Reservation* because she finally acknowledges her hybridity. Pulitano quotes an Anzaldua passage that begins "I am a border woman." Then Pulitano goes on to say, "[b]oth in form and content, *Off the Reservation* parallels Anzaldua's hybrid text with the intent to inscribe the author's threshold identity into her creative and critical writings while challenging the dominant culture's sociopolitical inscriptions, those labels that tend to define each person according to gender, ethnicity, sexuality, class, and other systems of difference."[53]

I am not entirely comfortable assuming that Anzaldua's take on Mestiza issues apply to all American Indians. While I am sure a number of Native people will relate to Anzaldua's borderlands position, what about the Indian mixed-bloods we see so frequently in Oklahoma—and many other places in Indian Country—who, in spite of their various cultural and genetic inheritances, identify as Indians rather than hybrids, socializing with Indian people and viewing themselves in the center, rather than at the periphery, of Indian worlds? Who will speak for these people, a rather substantial group in Indian Country? Should we send Pulitano among them so she can talk them into confessing their complicity? They have already had missionaries. Should they be told their ideas of themselves are delusional? While many Native writers and critics have emphasized marginality, this has not always matched Indian people's vision of themselves, a gap between literary and social worlds that deserves some attention. In all my years in Oklahoma I have yet to meet an Indian who introduced him or herself to me as a "hybrid." Maybe someone should wonder why a word that used to reference seed corn and cattle is now the term of choice for critics describing people of color. Certainly this 1842 article title from a "scientific" journal might give present day hybridists pause: "The Mulatto a Hybrid—Probable Extermination of the Two Races if the Whites and Blacks Are Allowed to Intermarry."[54]

In relation to applying hybridity theory to particular texts in terms of analyzing their cross-cultural characteristics, it may be worth noting that some books may be, in a sense, less mediated than others. Jack and Anna Kilpatrick's English translations of Cherokee incantations may be less of a cross-cultural production than Gerald Vizenor's trickster novels, for example, even though quantifying the different levels of mediation between the two works or prioritizing one form of discourse over another is theoretically untenable. (And, obviously, I understand the concept that translating something into English is a cross-cultural project.) Pulitano's hybridity analysis might more effectively explicate the Vizenor novels than the Kilpatricks' Cherokee work.

Some might argue that original language literature comprises such a small proportion of the body of Native literature that it is insignificant. We might note, however, that Ella Deloria translated over a thousand pages from Dakota into English for her work *Dakota Texts*. I understand there is a large body of untranslated pages in Cherokee that is part of the Kilpatricks' collection sitting in the Beinecke Library at Yale just waiting for the right scholar who has sufficient Cherokee background to work with them. Alan Kilpatrick, their son, has already produced a significant work from these materials entitled *The Night Has a Naked Soul*, dealing with the "darker" Cherokee incantations, and I understand he is working on a second volume at the time of this writing. For all we know, the next Indian literary masterwork may reside in these materials.

I would argue that one such poetic masterpiece already exists, almost completely ignored in Native literature in spite of its easy availability and skillful English translation, the Kilpatricks' *Walk in Your Soul: Love Incantations of the Oklahoma Cherokee*. The poetry in that volume is first-rate. Read it and see. Recently, Margaret Mauldin, a Creek language professor at OU, and Jack Martin, have translated and edited a Muskogee masterpiece, *The Creek Stories of Earnest Gouge*, which has the potential to significantly challenge earlier southeastern ethnography. The book reproduces both the Creek originals and Margaret Mauldin's English translations, so they will be of great relevance to Creek language classes as well as literature courses.

I wonder how well Pulitano's theories would fare if applied to these texts. If the approach was to scour them for their hybridity, one would end up reenacting the debate that already happened a century ago when James Mooney and the ethnographers fought over whether or not some Cherokee stories had European or African-American influences. The problem is once one determines they do, then what? How does this help explicate Cherokee stories? (Of course, there could be rich culturally and historically specific comparative studies of these external influences, which seems to me a much different chore than going on about hybridity.) What does one do with one's hybridity other than confessing it? It is rather like getting one's appendix out and the doctor hands it over, floating in a jar. Where does one put it? What is it good for?

In terms of the stories in original tribal languages, I am doubtful as to whether Pulitano's theories will encourage people to do work in these areas, ones that might uncover incredibly rich literatures if anyone would explore them. The very reason almost no one teaches *Walk in Your Soul* as Native poetry may have something to do with multicultural theories that tend to overlook these kinds of works.

In her defense, no single work can do everything, and this is as true of Pulitano's book as much as it is of mine, Warrior's, and Allen's. Even in terms of analyzing her favorite study, Vizenor, whose novelistic works and criticism are quite different in comparison to translations of traditional materials, Pulitano seems to pay little attention to the profound level of "Ojibwayness" in Vizenor's texts: his references to specific Chippewa geographies, language, songs, chants, ceremonial traditions, even aspects of the Midewiwin practices. Vizenor is very carefully read in the ethnographic record, and it is obvious he has studied Ojibway language, as well as amended this research with contact with living Ojibway tribal members. Vizenor is not simply writing in the oral tradition; in very important ways he is writing in an *Ojibway* tradition (as well as a poststructuralist tradition and other traditions).

Further, if one considers Vizenor's oeuvre in light of Ojibway written literary history, the shape of his work takes on a much different character, especially given that all the early and mid-nineteenth-century Ojibway writers were Christian preachers. This provides a foundation for comparison that is as interesting in terms of contrast as its similarities.

In addition to the Christian Ojibway writers, there is a whole body of Canadian and U.S. contemporary Anishinaabe authorship that surely must have some bearing on Vizenor's work—if for no other reason than Vizenor is part of the Ojibway community, as were these other Ojibway writers, and, as such, individuals are part of a larger whole.

Ojibway traditions, and Ojibway literary history, when taken into consideration, significantly alter the categorization of Vizenor as a hybrid. If he is a hybrid, that hybridity has a specific history, a history that Pulitano fails to account for.

All of this is to say that Pulitano's book, just like *Red on Red*, does not have universal applicability. She accuses *Red on Red*, however, of advocating a one-size-fits-all criticism: "Despite its Creekcentrism, *Red on Red* is envisioned by Womack as a theoretical approach that all tribal groups should imitate."[55] Evidently, Pulitano's copy of my book was missing the following sentences that were in everyone else's, significantly, on the very second page: "Just as there are a number of realities that constitute Indian identity—rez, urban, full-blood, mixed-blood, language speakers, nonspeakers, gay, straight, and many other possibilities—there are also a number of legitimate approaches to analyzing Native literary production. Some of them, I will argue, are more effective than others; nonetheless, *Red on Red* is merely a point on the spectrum, not the spectrum itself. I do not believe in a critical approach that preempts or cancels out all those that came before it."[56] No wonder Pulitano so frequently, and conveniently, fails to provide quotations and page references. They work against her.

Red on Red, obviously, is not the template for all Native literatures. An example that comes immediately to mind is those tribes who have yet to produce a written body of literature, though works could still be written about their oral traditions. *Red on Red* admittedly, focuses more on Creek references than cross-cultural ones, yet this is not a denial that such influences exist, and, if as Pulitano constantly insists, those influences are inherent and inevitable, why do I need to discuss them in a study that looks for Creek contexts if the cross-cultural influences already go without saying?

Claiming Creeks, or Native writers, or virtually any group on the planet, are influenced by other cultures is like claiming "humans breathe" as a new revelation. It is amazing that the hybridists have built entire careers out of so little. Pulitano bases a discussion of tradition on negation. As soon as it can be established that any given tradition originated outside a community or was influenced by external factors, it can no longer be claimed as anything but hybrid. This, of course, makes tradition virtually impossible for any culture since all cultural traditions exist in relation to their surrounding environments. Only hybridity is possible. A more astute model for tradition would acknowledge its meanings in a community rather than expending so much energy on point of origin. It would acknowledge other possibilities than hybridity by recognizing traditions that are fluid yet still retain some kind of continuity with the community that claims them and perceives them as part of its own culture.

This is not to say outside influences should not be studied; it is a comment on prioritizing hybridity as an abstraction and making it the main point of Native literary studies. Illuminating a particular historical non-Native influence on a Creek text could be quite interesting. A recent example is an article by Siobahn Senier in *American Indian Quarterly* 24.3 (2000) entitled "Allotment Protest and Tribal Discourse: Reading *Wynema*'s Successes and Shortcomings." Senier argues that I fail to consider the way in which the novel *Wynema* represents various perspectives concurrent to its production that have to do with the so-called beneficent "Friends of the Indians," or white reformer groups of Callahan's own time. This makes sense, and it provides a convincing reading of the novel that can flesh out areas I failed to consider in the particular Creek contexts I focused on.

Turning cross-cultural influences into abstraction about hybridity, as Krupat and others have done, however, should have only been of the briefest interest in Native Studies, rather than becoming the major trope to take over our discipline. The historical and contextual studies that Krupat provides are quite useful; the obsessive hybridity mantra is not. How many more times do we need Krupat to tell us Indians are hybrids? While the work of Krupat deserves attention of its own, especially since Pulitano draws so heavily on it, that will have to serve as the subject of another essay. Especially important is the issue of whether or not his recent book *Red Matters: Native American Studies* (2002) involves a new turn toward acknowledging the interdependency of various kinds of literary approaches within the field, an issue I will not try to scrutinize here. (Readers interested in an assessment of how Krupat's internationalist views may accommodate tribal sovereignty should examine Cherokee critic Sean Teuton's "A Question of Relationship: Internationalism and Assimilation in Recent American Indian Studies"[*American Literary History* 18.1 (2006)].

As if our complicity with European discourse and a Native perspective that can only proceed by virtue of constant confession of its hybridity are not enough troubles, Pulitano draws on Owens's essay "As If an Indian Were Really an Indian" to argue that Native authors and critics are a very privileged lot whose education and academic positions distance them from their tribal communities, one more thing we need to be confessing. Owens says, "As a group, published Native authors have an impressively high rate of education, most possessing not merely a university degree but at least some graduate work if not an advanced degree . . . we are inescapably both institutionally privileged by access to Euramerican education and distinctly migrant in the sense that we possess a mobility denied to our less privileged relations."[57]

Yet one wonders about both Owens's and Pulitano's position on these matters given that a Choctaw tradition, one might easily argue, is sending people to universities. Further, since Pulitano's book deals with Warrior's study of John Joseph Mathews, one might even say that an Osage tradition includes graduating Rhodes scholars. Indeed, if a person attends Osage doings in Oklahoma or actually knows a few Osages, he or she might be struck by the number of Osages with university degrees, as well as families who have gone to college for several generations. In terms of the diminished mobility of our less privileged relations, I do not really like looking at my relatives as handicapped, but, more to the point, I might argue that a study of Choctaw history would reveal an amazing mobility both before and after contact and continuing in recent times.

While it may not be the case in my particular family since I was the first person to attend a university, much less get a PhD, viewing the Creek community as my "less privileged relations" might present a problem given the Muskogees' historic proactive role in public education since the early 1800s. Owens and Pulitano would do well to historicize their claims as a way of grounding them. In applying the notion of privilege to *Red on Red* Pulitano queries,

> Can Womack's work still maintain, as the product of the University of Minnesota Press, its professed Creekcentrism? Does the fact that Womack holds a professorship at the University of Lethbridge (in Alberta) change the way in which he speaks to his own community? Can a book written, as *Red on Red* is, in response to the charge that only whites can "do theory" speak to Native communities in their own terms? Can Womack justify grounding his study in a notion of Creekcentrism when that study must, as it does, inevitably engage Western literary theory (even if only to attack it)?
>
> Ultimately, Womack is writing from a privileged position within the academy, his audience largely other academics, not Native communities. *Red on Red* remains, therefore, a sophisticated work of literary criticism and, as such, inaccessible to those members of a Native audience who cannot approach it from a similarly privileged position.[58]

I would like to know what is particularly un-Creek about a University of Minnesota Press publication? Once again, please remind me who it is here that is romanticizing the pre-Contact world. Let me pose a parallel question to Pulitano's "Can Womack's work still maintain, as the product of the University of Minnesota Press, its professed Creekcentrism?" My question is this: "Can the Muskogee Creek Nation, with its constitutionally based government, still retain a sense of its own Creekness?" The answer to both questions is of course they can! Further, when she says my audience is largely other academics, not Native communities, if she is talking about Native academics, how can it be that they do not constitute a Native community? If she is saying I have only non-Indian academics for readers, she is simply wrong.

With astounding frequency Pulitano succumbs to the very romanticisms she accuses everyone else of. The sentence that follows the university press statement assumes a theoretical book cannot speak to a theory-less community. How could Pulitano possibly know anything about the conceptual mind of the Creek community? This hearkens back to the criticism against Allen in regard to generalizations about "the Indian mind." If, in fact, Pulitano has never been around Creeks (I do not take this as a given, but I do not know anyone who has ever met her), how does Pulitano know they do not do theory? What if my community already does theory? How can she summarize these things?

Where does she come up with her claims about the inaccessibility of *Red on Red* to the average, "unprivileged" Creek? I have emails, letters, and memories of phone calls and conversations with Creeks from various walks of life who have read the book and shared ideas about it, a range of people from students, pastors, educators, stomp grounds members from my own grounds and from other grounds, and others. There are 56,000 Creek citizens; it is pretty safe to assume a few of them can read and think—and not just the privileged!

A critic who may have never stepped foot in Oklahoma has determined that only a privileged few Creeks can read my book. While I do not use my own work in classes I teach, I have Muskogee students in virtually every Indian literature course and, of course, significant numbers of them in the Muskogee literature course that is offered every fall. This, too, constitutes a Creek audience.

On various writing panels I have been on, someone invariably asks, "Who do you write for?" This is the equivalent of the musician who gets asked to play "Stairway to Heaven" at every gig. Other Native writers invariably answer, "I write for everyone." I do not write for everyone. I write for Muskogee Creek people. I am not naive enough to believe that only Creek people read my work, nor am I disappointed at having a larger audience. Writers want to be read. The point is even if I did not have one single Muskogee reader, which clearly is not the case, the act of *imagining* a Creek audience makes all the difference in the world in the literary outcome of such a vision. *Red on Red* would have been a very different book had I imagined a non-Creek audience or even imagined writing "for everyone"—the stories I tell and the way I tell them would be totally different. Imagining a Creek audience is a means of inspiration that reminds me of particularities, of places, of voices, of historical events, of my Aunt Barbara Coachman's mannerism of repeating the end of a joke three or four times, of the sounds of insects, stomp dance songs, and the gray just before dawn when I wonder if I can keep dancing.

Further, when Pulitano says my audience is "*largely* other academics, not Native communities," (my emphasis) what is this, a "size matters" issue? Maybe this is what happens when a person becomes obsessed with tool interrogation. Let us say I "only" have twenty Creek readers who are not academics. Does that mean this group of twenty people is unimportant? Surely, Pulitano can do better than this bigger is better analysis.

I do not doubt that I have privileges that other Native people do not have and other Creek people do not have. I am aware of the legacy of colonialism and the conditions that it has created. In these regards I can only humbly acknowledge my privilege, and, more importantly, do as much as I can to help Indian people avail themselves of the same opportunities I have had. That is why I am an educator after all. I know this much—my privilege will not become any less problematic if I preach to Native people the futility of their own perspectives. This will not alter positions of power, my own privilege, nor increase their likelihood to succeed.

Calling me privileged does not tell the whole story. This label erases my concentrated effort to deal with forms of privilege within *Red on Red*. I very self-consciously crafted a text that deals with the issue of searching for an appropriate language that might speak to tribal people. I am proud of this. In writing the book I had my family in mind. My brother, who did not graduate from high school, says he read my book and understands it. My mom, who also did not graduate, read it as well. No matter what Pulitano might say, as the old swing standard puts it, "You can't take that away from me." I felt a terrible burden writing the book—that if I produced a work that took up Muskogee people as a subject but failed to interest Muskogee people as readers, this constituted an unacceptable ethic. In *Red on Red* I was very strongly committed to a language that I hoped would clarify matters rather than obfuscate them and remain accessible to audiences outside the academy. This is a rather tall order, and I do not claim to have entirely succeeded, but if one compares the language of *Red on Red* to the kind of jargon in many works of literary theory, I think it is evident that I had accessibility in mind.

Nowhere is my attempt to deal with the elitism of academic discourse more apparent than the dialect letters that follow the chapters of conventional criticism. These letters raise complex questions about the issue of privilege, yet Pulitano only mentions them, in a handful of sentences, in order to dismiss them with this conclusion: "They [the characters in the dialect letters] created a 'different,' even funny book, one that argues for a Native perspective, 'untainted' by the 'malaise' of Western philosophical thinking. Jim and Hotgun might not be aware, however, that, by celebrating an authentic Native difference, they ultimately end up perpetuating further versions of colonialism, colonialisms in which the Native is once again significantly Othered."[59]

I want to warn Pulitano that Jim and Hotgun are a lot smarter than she thinks, and they are really pissed off. They are so very angry because of the dishonesty of this statement when *Red on Red* clearly shows that she has mischaracterized them. They played a complex role in a book that at every juncture challenges notions of cultural purity, as in the following statement:

> I want to point out some new ways to look at Native
> Studies. The problem with the "translation problem," with
> its skepticism and emphasis on literary diminishment, is
> that it places us within a "pure versus tainted" framework
> that so much of Native Studies gets cast in:
>
> | *Pure* | *Tainted* |
> |---|---|
> | oral tradition | writing |
> | performance | print |
> | original language | translation |
> | pre-Contact | post-Contact |
> | Indian religion | Indian Christians |
> | Indian culture | Indian politics |

We could go on and on with out short list here, but the problem is pretty obvious—this locks Native Studies into a system that does not allow the discipline to evolve; it is the way in which we have inherited the vanishing mentality.[60]

Once again Pulitano fails to cite *Red on Red*, a book that says something very different than the book Pulitano has written on my behalf.

She repeats her errors in an extremely misleading analysis of my chapter on the novel *Wynema*, in which Pulitano says I fault Alice Callahan for writing an assimilationist novel with Christian themes.[61] Yet a reading of *Red on Red* will reveal that I fault Callahan for writing a novel that presents itself as a Creek work yet fails to deal with Creek realities, including Creek assimilation and Creek Christianity, and I remark on the irony of this given the Callahan family's central role in the "progressive" faction of the tribe, including her father's political offices and support of other assimilated candidates like himself. I argue that Callahan fails to even depict Creek Methodism in any convincing fashion and I discuss, in detail, the history of Christianity in Creek country as well as direct readers to a more convincing book than Callahan's on Indian Methodism, Choctaw pastor Homer Noley's *First White Frost*.[62]

Pulitano leaves out other pivotal statements of mine, omissions that may have something to do with her aversion to history. A reading of *Wynema*, and all the Creek texts I consider, is profoundly related to this statement about Muskogee diversity, which provides solid evidence against what Pulitano claims as my monolithic and static approach to culture. This is what I actually say in *Red on Red*:

> The character of this [Creek] national culture at the turn
> of the century varied from Creek full-bloods taking medicine
> at the stomp grounds to Creek Baptist and Methodist
> preachers explicating the gospel in Creek, reading out of
> Creek Bibles, and singing out of Creek hymnals; from
> merchants and cattle ranchers to subsistence farmers
> practicing Creek agriculture; from those who didn't speak
> English (a large portion of the tribe during Posey's time)
> to those, like Posey himself, who had gone to Bacone and
> studied classical literature; from medicine men (*hilis heyya*)
> and town chiefs (*miccos*) to tribal judges who worked for
> the nation; and a whole slew of other nuances of Creek
> life too numerous to mention here. Rather than argue for
> Posey's biculturalism, I would argue that he was thoroughly
> immersed in a Creek world, and that Creek world, *like other*
> *nations*, was a complex one that cannot be simply analyzed

inversely to its relationship to the pristine; that is to say, its cultural power does not diminish to the degree it evolves.[63]

One wonders how Pulitano justifies leaving this statement out of her study given the claims she makes about me.

Under Pulitano's gaze, I suffer from what my dad calls the "caint win for losing" syndrome. Reading my analysis of Lynn Riggs's work on pages ninety six to ninety nine, Pulitano faults me for inconsistently using queer theory, which, because of its emphasis on destabilized identity, contradicts my study. Yet in the quotes she uses to back up her assertions, any reader can see that the two words "queer theory" do not appear anywhere in them. The word "queer" does, in fact, appear in the quotes. Even a cursory reading in the field illuminates the difference between a gay and lesbian studies approach and a queer theory approach. While gay and lesbian studies uses the word "queer," its proponents do not adhere to the radical skepticism of queer theory in which identity categories are questioned at every turn to a degree that is probably the most extreme of the movements within poststructuralism. *Red on Red* makes very clear that I think tricksterish identity shape-shifting needs to be challenged much more vigorously than it has been rather than assumed as some kind of normative model for Native literature.

In summing up my evaluation of Linda Alexander's Turtle story, Pulitano's catalogue of my rather impressive list of sins includes, "work[ing] in the same ethnographic mode, albeit with the terms reversed," "becom[ing] the insider claiming to present the correct meaning of the story merely on the basis of an authentic Native perspective," not looking at my tools enough, which I have already quoted, claiming a "quintessential Creek literary form . . . that of the persona," "fix[ing] . . . [the] tradition as a cultural artifact," "defin[ing] Creekness . . . as a universal and transcendental category inside people on which history has made no fundamental mark," "dismissing the fact that . . . [I am] utilizing language and tools borrowed from the colonizer," and last but not least, "at best . . . repeating the errors pointed out by Fanon and other Third World intellectuals and at worst of turning into a reductionist Nativism."[64]

First, and most importantly, I never claim, and I defy Pulitano to show me where I do, to have the most authentic reading of the turtle story.

To take a traditional story that belongs to an oral community and claim to have the only correct or most correct or most authentic reading would be a most un-Creek thing to do. I would be a fool to make such a claim. Such a claim cannot be found in *Red on Red*.

Secondly, a reading of the actual chapter in *Red on Red* will show that not only do I include two versions of Linda Alexander's telling of the Turtle story, and conversations that lead up to and follow the story, but I also include two of Swanton's versions. And, inspired by Sarris's important work, I discuss exactly why ethnographer/fieldworker relationships are complicated by the story's many participants, demonstrating, as does Sarris, that there are many worlds that surround and intersect any given story.

Thirdly, Pulitano, typical of her ahistoric and abstract critical mode, ignores incredibly important facts about the Turtle story, one being that the ethnographer John Swanton "collected" only an English version of the story, whereas I listened to Linda Alexander tell a Creek version and attempted an English translation with the help of Pam Innes— the very first English translation of this important story. (Now, I am glad to say, there are other versions translated from the original Creek in *The Creek Stories of Earnest Gouge*.) The other interesting thing I did was have Linda tell an English version of the story so that she was translating it herself. I felt it was important to include her as a translator, again calling into question certain ethnographic relationships.

Fourthly, when Pulitano rejects my claim of persona writing as a quintessentially Creek literary form, then she needs to provide an explanation as to how one accounts for the historical reality that persona letters in dialect have provided a major forum for Creek literature with many Creek practitioners from the 1880s until today, including Charles Gibson, Acee Blue Eagle, Thomas E. Moore, Tulmochess Yahola, Fus Harjo, and Jesse McDermott. Does Pulitano deny the fact that dialect writing in the form of persona letters has constituted a major body of Creek literature? Elvira Pulitano has not done enough homework to make statements about these, and many other, matters. She needs more reading in the primary literatures and the historical contexts that surround them.

As far as colonizing the story, fixing it in the past, turning it into an artifact, and so on, how does she justify these statements? It seems I am a colonizer simply because Elvira Pulitano says I am one and because I am not Greg Sarris, Louis Owens, or Gerald Vizenor. Especially hollow is the criticism that I provide no historical reading of the Turtle story when I do. (I talk about Turtle stories in relation to colonial themes of forms of resistance when the power structure involves a "little guy" and his larger opponent, and I have an entire chapter on the way in which history and politics are too often left out of oral story analysis, Chapter Two, "Reading the Oral Tradition for Nationalist Themes: Beyond Ethnography.") This is another pot calling the kettle black accusation since Pulitano never historicizes anything.

Red on Red concerns itself with the ethics of the relationship between a text and the community it claims to represent, and my position on the matter is that Native writers cannot simply bow out of this discussion in exchange for hybridity and other theories. The dialect letters are an attempt to imagine how a Muskogee Creek audience might respond to the book Red on Red. Admittedly, this response is symbolic because it "only" occurs in my head since real Creek people did not send me these letters; I made them up. Let us remember, however, a Native American nonfiction classic, the essay "The Man Made of Words." The young Kiowa author N. Scott Momaday protests to the old woman Ko-sahn that "all of this, this imagining . . . has taken place—is taking place in my mind. You are not actually here, not in this room." Ko-sahn answers, provocatively, "Be careful of your pronouncements, grandson . . . You imagine that I am here in this room, do you not? That is worth something. You see, I have existence, whole being, in your imagination. It is but one kind of being, to be sure, but it is perhaps the best of all kinds. If I am not here in this room, grandson, then surely neither are you."[65]

Imagining a Muskogee Creek audience response in the form of dialect letters forced me to confront the question of how Creeks might react to the way they are depicted in Red on Red. There is no doubt that this is an imperfect act of the imagination. I knew I could not send out a survey and compile the results to see how Creeks responded to the book; it would have already been in print by then and beyond alteration, not to mention the impracticality of a social science methodology to "measure" community satisfaction, dissatisfaction, and other types of responses. The symbolic act, nonetheless, of an imagined Creek audience response underscores one of the most challenging ethical questions for me as a scholar: How might the people we theorize about respond to our theories? *Red on Red*, to a degree that far exceeds simply labeling scholars "privileged" as Pulitano does, tries to confront the issue of privilege in the very structures of the text itself. While the dialect letters symbolize, rather than directly embody, a Creek audience, most students of literature are able to admit that symbols matter.

I want to do a little bit different kind of reality check now in relation to privilege. Anyone who describes a position teaching in the reservation community (where I taught at the time *Red on Red* was published) as "privileged," probably has never been to Lethbridge, southern Alberta, or anywhere within Blackfoot territory. More privileged than what, teaching at the University of Geneva in Switzerland? One might imagine that a job teaching in Switzerland may isolate Pulitano somewhat from Indian realities. In the end, her separatism may be even more stringent than my own given the ocean that separates her from Indian Country, which seems to loom rather large both geographically and metaphorically in regard to her distance from us.

While it is obvious I cannot have perfect knowledge about my culture, or any culture, it should be equally obvious that it is ridiculous to assert that all my knowledge is canceled out by university press contracts and gainful employment. I am not altogether convinced I would have written a better book if I was unemployed, living in a trailer in the Creek capitol of Okmulgee. Pulitano's point, however, is even more extreme. No matter how close I might be to my culture, it is not good enough because of the impossibility of a Creek perspective. My years of involvement as a full-fledged member of one of the Creek grounds where I touch medicine, the volunteer work I do inside Oklahoma prisons with Native people, and a lot of other stuff I try to avoid talking about publicly are nothing more than delusions I have fostered on myself and the public about being involved in communities. Pulitano's theories, it should be noted, actually fracture communities, even discourage participation in Indian communities by relegating it to the realm of denying one's European inheritance. One is allowed to claim only one kind of community: a hybrid one. This is a self-fulfilling prophecy since, if one gives up on the viability of participation in Indian communities, one's cultural inheritance may in fact seem increasingly European. I take a much different stance, and I hope my work stands for something clearly distinguished from the hybridist camp, a deviant viewpoint that I wanted to underscore when I titled my book *Native American Literary Separatism*, a choice I will explain in the concluding section of this essay.

The deviant line of reasoning I adhere to is this: I argue that my experience as a Muskogee person in a lived relationship with my community counts for something in spite of whatever degree it is problematized by what Pulitano claims are distancing factors. She needs to also take into account proximity factors, an area of inquiry her methodology seems ill-suited for. Hers is the deficit approach to theory, more adept at locating what is missing rather than what is there, at least when applied to those of us in the lower echelons of her critical hierarchy. It is telling that hybridists have yet to apply their theories to their own positionality, declaring themselves ill-fit to make claims about the Indian world. Evidently, this deficiency is only an "Indian problem."

o

Having spoken at great length in a defensive posture, I want to conclude by discussing what *Red on Red* does rather than what it does not do and thus consider what it means to be a tribal literary nationalist, our aim in presenting this book. I was formally schooled in Native literature in the early nineties, during a time period that I consider a turning point in the discipline. When I say I was "formally schooled" this is something of a misnomer. Like many of us who would go on to teach and write about Native literature, I would do so with no graduate classroom training in the field whatsoever. My MA is from South Dakota State at Brookings. I readily admit I was not schooled at fancy places; however, there were Indians at the schools I graduated from. In my MA work, although I wrote a thesis on Native literature, I did not take any graduate level courses in the field because none were offered. I received first-rate advising, however, from Chuck Woodard, a strong proponent and teacher of tribal literature. There was a graduate seminar on Native literature given the semester after I left Brookings and took a job. Chuck had already developed a fine undergraduate program years earlier in which he constantly sought to link literature with regional issues of jurisdiction and redress.

The same scenario repeated itself at the University of Oklahoma. During my time there, no graduate-level courses on Indian literature were scheduled. A course was offered the semester after I was ABD, but I had taken a job at the University of Nebraska. As at SDSU, I received first-rate supervision from Cherokee-Quapaw critic Geary Hobson, who played the major role in my consideration of focusing a study on Muskogee literature. Today there are many more graduate course offerings in Native literature at both Brookings and Norman, and I am proud to say at OU we offer at least one graduate seminar in Native literature every single semester—a brief plug for those thinking of graduate studies.

While I wrote both an MA and PhD on Native literature, I managed to graduate with no courses in Native literature at the graduate level. I had one undergraduate course in Native Non-Fiction. I am not trying to disqualify my credentials. I do not want anyone to sue me for malpractice or take away my license to preach. My point is that, like many of my colleagues during this time, those of us who would go on to teach Native literature were schooled in the good old humanistic literary tradition of great authors, including minority writers, given the concerns with multiculturalism in the 1990s.

I say this time period was a kind of threshold because things are different now. There are places where a person can get a PhD specifically in Native American Studies such as the University of Trent in Canada and the University of California at Davis in the United States. At some schools, such as the University of Georgia where coauthor Jace Weaver teaches, students can get a PhD in any traditional discipline such as English, history, or anthropology and receive a certificate in Native American Studies.

In the English department at Oklahoma we will be turning out a new generation of Native literature scholars who have actually studied Native literature as part of their graduate degree program and who have not only strong readings in the primary materials of the field but theoretical foundations that are developed enough that they can challenge the hybridists, and others, who have kept Native literature stagnant. People doing Native literary criticism in the future may also be trained in federal Indian law, Indian history, Indian-white relations, Native art, Native philosophy, Native literature, Native languages, and so on, especially if they come from these PhD programs in Native American Studies. This is a different kind of training than I received in "the great authors" school. The effectiveness and impact of these new programs remain to be seen, especially in light of the way in which the very theories I am examining in this essay provide so much resistance to the idea of foregrounding Native knowledge.

What is, in fact, becoming apparent to me is that two schools have emerged: those who teach Native literature as NAS practitioners and those who teach Native literature from English department perspectives (either group could be in English or Native Studies—the philosophical mode is not necessarily the same as one's home department). Pulitano's book, like my own book *Red on Red*, does not do much to scrutinize the emergence of these two approaches and what they mean—their mission, their audience, the ways they are compatible and incompatible. Such questions, I believe, will have increasing importance. It disturbs me that Pulitano so aggressively opposes modes of analysis that are the very analytical tools that legitimate NAS as an academic discipline: studies of sovereignty, federal Indian law, and history. Celebrating Vizenor, which seems to be her intention, may not be the only effect of her study. I am much in favor of celebrating the considerable accomplishments of Gerald Vizenor—not, however, at the cost of dismantling Native American Studies.

A history department cannot exist if its members are not allowed or able to express historical perspectives, nor can an English Department continue if it adopts a stance that perspectives on language are not possible. Neither can a Native American Studies department exist unless perspectives on Native issues are both a theoretical and lived reality. By making Native perspectives implausible, Pulitano, even if unintentionally, questions the very validity of NAS as an academic discipline. Her work is dangerous and not for the subversive reasons she likes to think. It has the potential to quell Native voices and hinder the growth of NAS. Further, Pulitano's study is flawed even as an example of English department approaches, given her failure to read closely and make theoretical arguments.

The old humanistic and multicultural school that I was trained in, like everything else, has its advantages and disadvantages. Part of the craft, the technique, the training of being either a novelist or a literary critic is simply reading lots and lots of novels and literary criticism, everything a person can get his or her hands on. Being an Indian is not the only issued involved in being a literary critic, though for me it is a most important one.

While I was coming up in the discipline as a PhD student in the early 1990s, a particular dissatisfaction existed among us that related to our training. Because we were doing Indian literature in a non-Indian environment, taking classes on everything under the sun other than the subject most central to our literary lives, many of us tended to feel surrounded, to quote a title. Surrounded by the legacy of literature departments that were telling us how to teach our own Native texts (while not offering them to us in graduate courses) and feeling like we had inherited a critical tradition we had no investment in. Surrounded by all the isms: postmodernism, poststructuralism, postcolonialism. Surrounded by administrations that did not even recognize the existence of indigenous knowledge, much less value it. Surrounded by irrelevance in terms of matching our intellectual experience with what we knew from home. Theory became a threatening Other, European and foreign. While not entirely an accurate perception, it was certainly a powerful one.

In expressing our frustrations about the way in which the academic world failed to illuminate our Indian worlds, our dissatisfaction was real enough, but we failed to see our own role in creating these dilemmas. What was not being articulated was what *would* in fact shed light on our experience. Many of us started to sound a little like the song— nobody loves me; everybody hates me; I'm gonna eat a worm. In those instances when we tried to brainstorm alternatives, often they were so pan-tribal, generic, or essentialized, that they were worse than the ill-fitting theory we were seeking to replace.

This was the time period when all Indian writing was claimed as being based on oral tradition and ceremony, yet there was little actual tribally specific analysis or consideration of how oral tradition itself has a literary history and has changed over time. Avoidance of these issues diverted attention to superficial generalizations about the Indian mind, whatever that is. Indian writing became circular, non-Aristotelian, lacking a beginning, middle, and end, since oral stories, supposedly, do not have linear plots, and what else could Native writing be based on if not oral stories? Textual contributions from earlier generations of Native writers were seldom considered in relation to today's literature.

Every Indian story was actually about tricksters. There were tricksters in every teapot. The job of the critic was to locate the trickster in the story. The simple fact that there is no such thing as a trickster in indigenous cultures, that tricksters were invented by anthropologists, that no Indian language has the word trickster in it, that many people from home would not know what we were talking about if we mentioned the word trickster, were simply ignored. Of course, Native cultures, and many cultures around the world including European ones, have story characters that behave in ways that are very much like what we often call tricksters, and my point is a simple one about making assumptions apart from historical, cultural, and other forms of specificity. No doubt a lingua franca with terms like "trickster" was necessary, but we had not considered the possibilities, and limitations, of our terminology, having assumed its universal applicability.

Native writings that failed to measure up to their supposed oral tradition roots or trickster roots were simply ignored or made to fit. We outlined a lot of literary approaches without any attention to history, politics, language, or other factors that could move them beyond clichés. Even today, obviously, many of these problems still need to be worked through.

In writing *Red on Red* I knew I wanted to do something different, but I did not quite know what it was. There were two authors, however, who were particularly helpful to me. One was Robert Warrior and his two books *Tribal Secrets: Recovering American Indian Intellectual Traditions* (1995) and *Like a Hurricane: The Indian Movement from Alcatraz to Wounded Knee* (1996). Both of these works rely on the thesis that Native authorship has an intellectual history that ought to be considered in contemporary criticism (in his work on activism Warrior argues, similarly, that the Indian movement was preceded by shifts in internal perspectives caused by historical changes).

I was also strongly influenced by Greg Sarris's attempts to allow Pomo culture to generate a theory of itself in his work *Keeping Slug Woman Alive*. The significance of Sarris's book in light of the environment I just described is that it is not written in a rejectionist mode. He is influenced by reader response theory, but he asks the question, how might reader response ideas be transformed when Pomo culture is taken into consideration instead of the "recipient only" theories that assume Native culture can only be altered, and they cannot alter anything outside themselves. Sarris uses Pomo basketmaking, for example, as a way to understand how readers might approach Pomo written texts. Instead of the bicultural, hybridity, and mediation emphases that have taken over much of Native literary criticism, he seemed to be saying that Indian literature could just as easily transform other literatures as be transformed *by* them and turned into some kind of melting pot mess. Native literatures could be the active, not just the passive, partner in any literary encounter. I drew a very different lesson from Warrior and Sarris then Pulitano does, thank God, or I might have given up.

I was especially inspired by Sarris's concentration on a body of Pomo texts and stories. This struck a resonant chord within me. Whatever questions I might attempt to answer, I needed to do so in relation to my home community. The field was simply too big for me. I did not know how to take on all of Native literature. I could not wrap my mind around it, as the cliché goes. Even considering the literary output of Creeks seemed impossibly broad, but such a task was at least more contained than something calling itself Native literature.

Over a period of time I became increasingly convinced that one of the strongest possibilities for transforming this huge field existed at the grassroots and local level. Specifically, I had the sense that there were powerful sources, especially unpublished ones, in the form of biographies, autobiographies, tribal histories, oral stories, family histories, genealogies, letters, and so on. Part of this experience had to do with being a student at OU where the Western History Collection, an amazing tribal repository, was part of the resources available, and in it were all kinds of documents about my own tribe. I had never, then or now, conceived of these sources or sources I use in *Red on Red* as "pure." Another reason I started to understand that there were undervalued resources in our own backyards was a growing level of participation in the ceremonial life of the Creek Nation during Green Corn and other aspects of the stomp dance religion, where I was constantly amazed at the breadth of knowledge among local people that had the potential to inform my thinking on literary issues.

The issue was what kind of language was appropriate for this kind of study? Like so much else I was experiencing during this time, the question was overwhelming. Part of the distrust of theory that I described, so much so that it became a joke among us in hallways in the department or when we were partying or just having fun, was this tendency of theorists to speak on behalf of the Other in a language that the Other could not possibly understand. In reality, given the directions of poststructuralism, the issue was probably speaking in a language that *nobody* understood, and we laughed about wondering if we were the only ones who didn't get it.

One of my fears was the very real possibility of writing a book about Creek literary history in a way that would not resonate at all with Creek people back home. This was a fundamental contradiction for me, even though this particular question of accountability to audience did not seem of much concern in regard to the theory I was being exposed to in graduate school.

I had a big head start; otherwise, these questions would have simply overwhelmed me. Other Creek authors had tackled the language and audience problem as early as the 1880s in terms of producing a body of literature for Creek people, one such writer being Alexander Posey, although many preceded and followed him in the dialect tradition. I was interested in the stylized language Posey uses in his Fus Fixico letters.[66] Like most caricatures that rely on overkill, it is an exaggeration of the way Creek people sound who speak English as a second language. Nonetheless, there are features in the dialect that are immediately familiar and recognizable to Creek readers. In the kind of critical environment that surrounded me, my most likely choice would have been to examine the so-called "trickster" elements of the letters and Posey's guise of writing to the editor of the *Eufaula Indian Journal* when Posey was, in fact, the editor of the *Eufaula Indian Journal*, taking on a persona, pretending to be a Creek full blood speaking broken English when, in actuality, he was very literate.

Posey's trickster stance, however, was not the main thing that captured me. I was fascinated by a storyteller who, to a certain degree, invented the language in which he would tell his stories. (Posey was not the first dialect writer, so this claim has its limitations, but certainly he brought Creek dialect to new heights). I was interested in Posey's willingness to imagine a specialized Creek literary language that went beyond its oral tradition roots, given it deviated from normal speech. It was a language specially designed to present Creek written literature. Further, it was a language developed to enhance a particular political viewpoint that had to do with fighting against the extinguishment of tribal government. While deviating from the actual speech of the community, the quality of the caricature was such that the community would, nonetheless, immediately recognize itself in the speech. It was this paradox that had me hooked. It seemed relevant to the daunting chore of presenting a literary criticism that might diverge from the typical language of the community by taking up theoretical literary concerns yet still retaining some feature the community could appreciate.

Posey's letters had profound implications for a Muskogee Creek literary nationalism, and a language that might describe it, in which Creek people, on some level, could be participants in the process, at least to the degree that they recognized themselves in the stories and laughed at what they saw. Laughter is, after all, a form of participation. Caricature, ingeniously, provides points of recognition, even while distorting them.

This is why I structured *Red on Red* on the literary conceit borrowed from Posey. I wanted to put at least one thing in the book that many Creek readers would immediately recognize, and the letters perform that—even those Creeks who have not read Posey or other dialect writers have often heard someone who talks something like that.

When I conclude the letters with "Sincerely, Jim Chibo," this is a moronic pun in Creek that sounds like "your ass." Of course, I knew that many of my non-Creek readers would have no way of recognizing the Creek joke in that. So, it was a little gift, probably a somewhat juvenile one, thrown in for Creek people reading the book. Somehow "fumbee" humor, stink and talk of asses, often plays into jokes, and this is good for a laugh for folks from home. Signing, "your ass," is consistent, also, with the spirit of the Fus Fixico letters, the wise fool commenting on the politics of statehood, and it characterized what I felt at the time—that I had fallen into something really profound, but I did not know exactly how to articulate it or what all of it meant or whether any of it was philosophically consistent or shot full of holes. I really felt like I was the ass, the fool, wise or not, signing the letters, as well as authoring a book.

I use the dialect letters to indulge my literary imagination with a bunch of "what if" scenarios: What if Alice Callahan, a Creek author who wrote a really terrible novel in the early 1890s had a near violent confrontation with the characters she created? What if Alexander Posey was taken on a raft trip down his favorite river, the Canadian, and interviewed about his motivations to write for a Creek audience when he could have had a much larger following? What if the contemporary Creek author Louis Oliver, who passed away in recent years, had met Alexander Posey in his childhood; what might have transpired?

In a way it was a kind of advanced form of cheating, getting the characters to say what I needed them to in order to back up my theories in the literary chapters. This also felt consistent with Posey's own use of his cast of full bloods to make political arguments in his favor in relation to Oklahoma statehood.

Unlike Posey's letters, mine tend to unfold a little more like short stories. I was a burgeoning fiction writer, still am, and this was happening at the same time that I was beginning to write literary criticism. Further, my inclusion of the letters is based on a musical idea. I am a musician, a jazz guitarist. Southeastern Indian music, like jazz, is based on a call and response structure. Jazz and stomp dance songs share a history of influence on each other that is fascinating but beyond the scope of this chapter. (In Armstrong Square, across from the French Quarter, in New Orleans, a square often claimed as the birthplace of jazz because under Napoleonic law slaves had to be given Sundays off and they came there and made music, there is a plaque that tells how, before the slaves started congregating there, this was the site of a Houma Green Corn ceremonial ground, an amazing revelation for me.) Anyway, at Creek dances, women shake shells attached to their ankles, and men sing the songs. A song leader calls out a verse that is echoed back; sometimes it is repeated exactly, other times the melody or words are altered.

The persona letters in *Red on Red* are the response to the call of the conventional chapters of literary criticism. I wanted these letters to function not only as commentary on the chapters they follow, but also to take the ideas off into new directions so they have that musical feeling of both repetition and improvisation. Jazz improvisation always depends on the old and the new, on stuff some cat has worked out ahead of time but presents in fresh ways when he stands up to solo. Or when *she* stands up to solo. A woman trumpet player is always a possibility. The chapters followed by letters, the call and response, appeal to both my Creek sensibility and my sensibilities as a jazz player. It also places within the book a structure that I hope many Creek readers find familiar, whether on a conscious or unconscious level.

It is discouraging to me that Pulitano sees so very little in these letters. Her avoidance of them may have something to do with the way they challenge her most strident claims. One of the letters, for example, in its entirety, is about Alfred Hitchcock's film *Strangers on a Train*. Does this not count as some kind of engagement with other cultures, even Western discourse? On a language level, a better hybridist than Pulitano might spot John 3:16 lurking in the words of this rewritten biblical quotation: "... for Stijaati so loved his *sofki* that he gave his only begrudged jar that whosoever come over to his house should not perish from hunger and throw an everlasting fit."[67]

If turning the Incarnation, the central event in Christian history, into a jar of sofky is not subversive in relation to things European I wonder what is, what it would take to get Pulitano's attention, a literary moment that would put me in the league of her holy trinity, Vizenor, Owens, and Sarris. These alterations of mine of sacred Western textual and cultural moments occur everywhere in the book. Perhaps it is not my fault that Pulitano simply could not detect them, or could not understand them, or that the great universal übercritic, finding that they did not speak to her, simply ignored them.

Such subversions have a serious intent. Posey's letters demonstrate that transformation may more accurately describe the way Indian people adopt and adapt literary forms than hybridity. Posey so skillfully Indianizes quotes from Shakespeare, the Bible, Robert Burns, popular British and American aphorisms, and many other sources that many readers do not realize their points of origin; they hear them as thoroughly Creek, and, in fact, they become Creek after Posey is through with them because he enables Creeks to recognize and own them. Posey demonstrates that Indians can just as easily assert influences *on* other literatures as be influenced *by* other literatures. In terms of these arguments, I cannot do better than what Simon Ortiz did years ago in his essay "Towards a National Indian Literature," which this volume commemorates for its twenty-fifth-year anniversary.

Considering the prominence of the dialect letters in my text, it is ironic, to say the very least, that Pulitano frequently tells her readers that one of the factors that makes Vizenor's, Owens's, and Sarris's work superior to my own is that they use stories to illuminate their criticism. Given the emphasis on Bakhtinian dialogism in the hybridist school, the call and response nature of these letters that actually perform a dialogue should be of some interest to them, one might think. Pulitano includes a discussion of dialogism, claiming it for Vizenor, Sarris, and Owens. Her demands that Native authors play by her rules, however, sounds to me more like a monologue than a dialogue. Dialogists are much better at talking about it than doing it. Pulitano cannot, in my view, lay claim to a Bakhtinian commitment to dialogism, plurality, multiplicity of voices—and then insist there is only one correct way to write, best exemplified by Vizenor, Owens, Sarris, and Krupat, that supersedes everyone else. This constitutes a most egregiously un-Bakhtinian study.

I realize *Red on Red* has its failings. An obvious one is subtitling the book "Native American Literary Separatism" and never defining what I mean by this term anywhere in its pages. There are a lot of different approaches to separatism. If we take well-known African-American separatist Malcom X as an example, we might note that the Malcolm after Mecca was a very different separatist than the Malcolm before. In using the term separatism in the subtitle, I wanted to signal, strongly, that my study would not be business as usual. I wanted a title that would, immediately, differentiate the book from the hybridist and mediation approaches that had taken over. I have already described the "surrounded" feeling, accurate or not, that characterized my critical environment at the time, and I wanted a title that would indicate I would be taking up Indian concerns as a central rather than peripheral endeavor, and this comes out of an environment in which many of us felt we were studying "everything but." We had been schooled in all else; now it was time to study something Indian.

To say my position in *Red on Red* reinscribes European hegemony ignores history, the role critics play who are writing from cultures who have been spoken for instead of being allowed to speak on their own behalf, and the critical moment we are still in when Indians are far from dominating anything, even Native literary criticism. I can certainly say my separatism has never meant a "categorical denial" of the relevance of Western discourse, but, I admit, I was less than responsible when I threw a term like separatism out there without defining it within the book.

This came about in a particular way. The press did not like my own choice of title, *A Creek National Literature: Making a Return to American Indian Communities*. It was too plain to their way of thinking, and they liked the phrase "red on red" that occurs in one of the earlier dialect letters in the book. I liked the phrase too and agreed. They also said they wanted a subtitle, something that would get people's attention, raise their blood pressure a little. I said, "put something about separatism in there, that always gets everybody going." In spite of this somewhat flippant response, I still stand by my title and by the concept of separatism if it is defined as working toward getting Indian people interested in the literatures of their own tribes. I wanted to send a signal to both Native and non-Native readers that Indian studies is not merely courses on federal Indian law, that creative literature has a central role as well. This is another characteristic of my separatism as I choose to define it: a sociologically based literary criticism, as well as some hope for a more literary sociology.

I was more concerned with concentrating on a local, grassroots level (more appropriately on a national tribal level in relation to one specific tribe) than on a "Native literature" level. Of course, Creek literature and Native literature are interdependencies, not oppositions. Reading Creek literature in isolation from a consideration of other tribal writers would be a mistake. I do not think *Red on Red* does this, given, as I have already mentioned, the forty-nine non-Creek Native authors who are cited in the book. My idea of separatism involved focusing a critical study on works authored by Muskogee Creek people rather than thinking of any particular audience to exclude.

The department I teach in, like most English departments, is a place where, to borrow Jace Weaver's phrase in this book, a thousand separatisms bloom. Six of them include dividing literary studies into the following area concentrations students choose for a major: Modernity and Theory; Composition, Rhetoric, and Literacy; Native American Literature;

Women's Writing; Early Modern; Medieval and Renaissance. Yet no one is accusing these folks of categorically dismissing contact with other areas of knowledge, of setting themselves up as privileged insiders, of claiming a Medieval literature perspective that is impossible because Medieval literature can never exist as an autonomous literature, or other sins of exclusion.

Briefly, I would like to say something about canonicity. I concur with Jace Weaver that Native literature is distinctive enough that its autonomy should be upheld. It should constitute a separate concentration in English departments. I am also convinced, however, that no one can graduate with a legitimate degree in American literature (though it might be recognized by various institutions) if that person has not studied the literatures of the Americas. I think that Native literature should be taught in American literature courses and anthologized in collections such as *The Norton Anthology of American Literature*. It is to everyone's detriment if it is not. Such a claim is well supported by nationalist ideology: the tribes constitute autonomous nations within the boundaries of the United States. Like tribes, American Indian literature has a unique status, different from any other ethnic literature in the U.S. canon. It is the product of legally defined political entities that exist in government-to-government relationships with the United States. This means, while it may seem strange to argue for both independence from and inclusion in the American canon, in the case of Native literature's unique status, it is entirely consistent.

No doubt there is danger in canonical inclusion: the possibility that only a very few popular authors will be published; the literature may be underrepresented; discussions of literature could be watered down; specific tribal contexts ignored; the unique legal status of tribes traded for some vague sense of minority status—all real problems, and ongoing ones. The solution to this dilemma of asymmetrical power relations, however, is not for the tribes to withdraw from America and go elsewhere, nor for Native literature to withdraw from inclusion in the American canon. It is our America, after all, and our canon, and we should stay put since it is our home. Rather than withdrawal, the solution is seeking greater and higher quality literary autonomy.

The point is, one I made in *Red on Red* and still adhere to, Native literature cannot withdraw from the American canon because it *is* the

American canon, the foundation for it, the literatures of the Americas. The question is not so much whether Native literature should be recognized in the American canon but whether anything else should be (and, of course, I believe there is also room for American authors in the American canon since they have also become part of the history of this place). The real debate has to do with proportionality: the *Norton Anthology of American Literature* and American literature courses would have to be predominated by American Indian literatures if they were to ever actually live up to their titles. While I have always worked for an autonomous Native literature component in the English departments where I have been employed, I have not then asked American literature professors or Canadian literature professors to cease teaching Native literature or editors of anthologies to stop including it.

In regard to the larger environment of dissatisfaction I described as part of what seemed to surround those of us doing Native literature during the time I was considering these ideas in the nineties, the subtitle of *Red on Red* referring to separatism related to the feeling that it was finally time to turn to things Indian—especially if one was going to write about Indians. Sure, anyone can argue that *Red on Red* should have discussed European theory. I was aware, however, of certain historical realities. There were hundreds (thousands?) of books on European literary theory at my disposal. There was not a single work analyzing Muskogee Creek literature. I simply chose a focus. Given the balance of power it might make more sense to demand that some famous theorist should be writing about Muskogee Creeks than Pulitano demanding that a virtually unknown tribal writer take on Euro-theory. In light of the number of non-Native works on theory, it is hard for me to imagine how one book that concentrates on the Creek Nation becomes guilty of so many sins of exclusion. Indian scholars cannot focus on their own work without being attacked, but non-Indians can concentrate on the most mundane minutia in their own studies and be considered rigorous scholars.[68]

Pulitano's critique of Allen, like other critics, has focused on the way in which Allen pits Native cultures against a totalized western Other as the center of her study, that is the oppositional mode Allen writes in that insists on an Indian purity versus a corrupted European legacy. Yet when a critic like Robert Warrior comes along and chooses to concentrate on

Indian sources in his bibliography rather than attacking the non-Indian world or non-Indian books, and a few years later I analyze Creek literature in relation to Creek history, culture, and politics rather than comparing it to some kind of corrupted "white" Other best distinguished by its incommensurability with the Indian world, we are guilty of all these sins of exclusion—of ignoring the non-Indian world. It would seem that the non-Indian world cannot be totalized and dismissed (Allen's sin), nor can it simply be allowed to exist as the focus of other people's books as we turn our attention to Indian matters (Warrior's and my own sin).

Pulitano offers us a third option. What is left is a radical embrace of the non-Indian world and its pervasive integration into one's work on the deepest level possible, or more to the point, a confession that it is already profoundly embedded in everything one does. This, she claims, is the approach of Vizenor, Sarris, and Owens. *Red on Red*, as I have indicated by offering a very substantial body of page numbers, already includes references outside the Indian world even if it does not make a metadiscursive discussion about non-Indian influences its main point. Why do non-Indian influences have to be the dominant thesis of every book? Can a few of them, at least, turn to other matters? Pulitano's insistence on a single destiny for all Native critics sounds a lot like "drawing a line between those . . . being on the right and the wrong sides of American Indian Studies."

Other practical considerations abound. A good number of people who incorporate theory into their work—I would say most of us in English departments—are dabblers, dilettantes in the theoretical world. In my department of twenty-six tenure-line faculty, there are two people who could probably be considered theorists. Not that many scholars have a sufficient background in the history of philosophy to really understand the implications of theory. I do not write well about literary theory.

Vizenor's own relationship to theory is a haphazard one in that not all notions of poststructuralism are compatible with the philosophies he seems to endorse. Approaching poststructuralism from a predominantly celebratory rather than selective perspective creates a good deal of inconsistencies in his writing. Vizenor's stylistics, for better and worse, involves telling compelling stories and letting readers draw their own conclusions about the tensions and contradictions. He is not a theorist in the sense of articulating a philosophical basis for these notions in terms of working out their relationship to literary theory in a consistent fashion. His particular genius is creating a mosaic of ideas rather than stepping back and explaining the picture he has drawn for his readers in terms of scrutinizing the underlying theoretical assumptions. I could have made poststructural theories the focus of *Red on Red*, but I think I would have done a rather poor job. I do not think it would have had the thought-provoking quality of one of Vizenor's collages; instead it would have just been a mess. Why should I do this? Pulitano's book is a case-in-point about someone who tries to launch a theoretical discussion and cannot pull it off.

One particular fictional depiction I regret—when Hotgun claims that trying to educate non-Indians about Native people is like "teaching hogs to sing." Arnold Krupat picked up on this in his review of the book for the May 2001 issue of *College English*, and I admit, with some chagrin, that these are not the best lines I ever wrote. My embarrassment, frankly, is that this is bad fiction. It sounds like something one might see on a coffee mug at a Cracker Barrel restaurant if such places had any interest in representing Indians on cups (we have these restaurants in Oklahoma and throughout the south). The "teaching hogs to sing" comment occurs in a fictional story, however. Hotgun is a character, not Craig Womack. Like his namesake in the Fus Fixico letters and in keeping with his very name, he tends to shoot off at the mouth. The statement is consistent with Hotgun's character, though I wish I would have had him state this a little more creatively, especially given the artistry of the Posey original that I need to honor. My particular brand of separatism does not equate to a denial of the validity of non-Indian involvement in literary criticism of Native works. Certainly the "teaching hogs to sing" line is not the center of *Red on Red*, and I wish Krupat would not have used it to conclude his review, but I wrote the damn line, so there you have it—seems like fair game. Reservations about the line do not change my conviction that a work that focuses on Creek concerns and hopes for a Creek audience is just as legitimate and theoretically defensible as one that focuses on confessing complicity and hybridity.

I have written a companion volume to *Red on Red*, the novel *Drowning in Fire*, which Pulitano never alludes to a single time, even as much as to mention its title (while referencing both Vizenor's and Owens's fiction). One of my novel chapters concludes thusly,

> There's a story about a Rabbit, call him Jimmy, call him *Choffee*, call him Chebon or Dear Hotgun. This Rabbit liked to mouth off to guys who were a lot bigger than he was. A kick, a shove, and before he knew it, Rabbit was up to his elbows in Tar Baby. You can call this Tar Baby Josh, if you want, or you can call him Jimmy if it'll make you feel better, or not call him Jimmy if you see that as some kind of racial slur. Because I'm not thinking about that, I'm talking about the birth of the Tar Baby, a story maybe you never heard. Some might say a Tar Baby isn't born, he's made, fashioned from human hands, to scare off crows and other thieves. But he's born, all right, shaped out of words. An invented history, a history of invention. A choice to invent your own history. As early as birth, there's the danger of getting stuck to a bad story if you stick your hands inside the wrong words. You could wake up inside the belly of a whale, boiling in a black kettle of sin, instead of glued to a Tar Baby. Or you could come unstuck and just float away without changing anything. And there's the real Tar Baby, too, stuck to a Rabbit, but he's a little more tricky to locate. Tar Baby talks Rabbit into a boiling pot by telling him a story. Now, you might ask, given our story inside a story, or stories inside stories, who is the inventor, and who is invented? You might even wonder which parts I made up and which actually happened.
>
> I didn't know the answer. I only knew at that point that I wanted out of the kettle, especially if someone else was going to be throwing logs on the fire. The way out wasn't by leaning over the side and spitting on the flames. I'd have to climb out, up over the words, and into a new story. I was still here, Jimmy was still in Weleetka, and Creek land was still waiting for us to take it back.[69]

Hell, I called the thing Native American literary separatism because I

wanted a new story, and I was tired of the one I was stuck to. The meaning of the tribally specific approach of *Red on Red*, and the challenges
of such an approach in an era dominated by pan-tribalism and Native
diaspora viewpoints, is part of a criticism of difference, rather than same-
ness, I was searching for. These points seem lost on Pulitano.

What happened to the promise, when we first started hearing all about
hybridity, that this kind of theory was going to liberate us, free us from the
dominance of master narratives? It seems like the freedom train pulled out
of the station with no Indians on board. One of the reasons I am a tribal
literary nationalist is because I know we cannot rely on these folks, with
their failed commitment to pluralism, to take good care of us; we have to
tend to ourselves. In focusing on the needs of our communities, it does not
follow that our belief in nations, sovereignties, Native perspectives, and
Indian claims are synonymous with exclusion. Tribal literary nationalism
allows me to speak as an Indian. Hybridity theory dictates the terms of my
speech. The choice is not very difficult. All speech communities have normative guidelines in regard to speech acts, but I prefer ones in which I have
some voice in formulating the rules. I am from a constitutionally based
tribe. What can I say? I like democracy. It's a tradition.

The publication of this volume marks the twenty-fifth anniversary
of Simon Ortiz's ground breaking 1981 essay "Towards a National
Indian Literature: Cultural Authenticity in Nationalism,"[70] a work in
which Ortiz argues that Native literature written in English, and
influenced by European literary forms, still maintains its American
Indian integrity. Ortiz analyzes processes of transformation through
which Native people "Indianize" the world of contact they have inherited. In those five pages Ortiz does much more for the empowerment of
Native literature than hybridist theory does. I am interested in the kind
of work that Ortiz pioneered that continues to function as a catalyst for
new forms of Native literature; this is to say I want to put my energies
into areas of growth rather than areas of deficit.

I would like to suggest some flexible tenets for a compassionate
American Indian literary nationalism, and for those who might want to
be our allies, a set of principles open to further discussion:

1. Just as tribes are related to the outside world of local municipal-
ities, state governments, federal Indian law, and international relations

(American Indian presence on U.N. task forces on indigenous peoples being a key example), literary nationalism can do local work with global implications, thus demonstrating a more profound cosmopolitanism than has been argued for to date, one with strong roots at its base.

2. Our criticism can grow, and we can learn to interrogate each other's work as much as celebrate it, while keeping up such a discussion at the level of ideas rather than personal attacks. The backslapping that has characterized our discipline has not gotten us very far, any more than the occasional ad hominem attacks. Whatever else we might think about the work of critics like Krupat and Pulitano, we should appreciate the fact that they refuse to simply trade in unmitigated praise of what we do. As Lisa Brooks points out in regard to her metaphorical table, which stands for the exchange of Native ideas, such a gathering place is not safe or comfortable, and the conversation may very well be contentious. Yet people are fed.

3. A compassionate criticism, to continue the Brooks analogy, gathers people back together, seats them at the table, feeds them, and they, in turn, give something back. Feasts, to mix metaphors, are a two-way street. My house today, yours tomorrow. One measure of the nationalist's literary commitment is the degree to which he or she finds a way to turn over some of his or her own work to the younger generation of critics who are coming up in the discipline. This is as much a measure of the effectiveness of one's criticism as its actual content. Theory does not exist only on a philosophical plane; it is embodied in actions that measure the effectiveness of the philosophy. A senior critic does not have to edit every volume or contribute to it . He can pass on some of this work to younger critics. This is, after all, how nations are built, by training the next generation to take over your job. Simply put, some among us are willing to do this; others are not, making deliberate choices, instead, to "hog up" the discourse. Some critics, both Indian and not, who have been exemplary in giving chances to younger writers include Alan Velie (who is always asking me which graduate student he can pass things on to), Chuck Woodard, the late Elaine Jahner, and the late Louis Owens. In some cases, the very reason the generous critics have not become "famous" is because they turned over many of their opportunities to Indian people.

4. Critics can recognize the validity of the work of those who have chosen to work within tribes as much as those seeking to establish Native literature as part of broader multicultural movements in the United States.

5. The compassionate nationalist cannot simply walk away from those things that are killing us in Native communities. We all know the statistics: shorter lives, higher unemployment, younger suicides, and a host of other depressing realities. It should be obvious by now that casinos, essential as they might be as economic resources, are not going to save us; thinking must save us, and this is where critics come in, in concert with other thinkers. We know the foundation of the crisis is loss of land, and the possibility of turning around these statistics is only available through its return, a grim reality in light of the unlikelihood of land reform in America. A major strategy for the compassionate literary nationalist is commenting on social policy and articulating community strategies for increased health, in one's art, while keeping it artful. While finding ways to increase his or her commitment to social realism, the compassionate literary nationalist will also strive for artistic excellence and experimentation. This may seem a rather tall order or even a contradiction. But think of it this way: some people might claim that if you write metered or rhymed poetry, formal constraints limit your word choices. Those who have tried it, however, know that it also causes you to choose words you would not have considered without the metrical or rhyming structures. Sociology is not, by default, the death of art any more than meter is the death of poetry. Bad sociology is the death of art (also of sociology), and bad art is the death of art. The question "What might a land reform novel look like?"—one that has been intimated by Elizabeth Cook-Lynn over the years—is certainly intriguing and asks us to find new ways to be artful rather than making art impossible. It is an endeavor that requires vision, dreaming of things that do not yet exist. The compassionate literary nationalist builds on dreams as much as realities, her biggest challenge toward a theory that both depicts the world as it is and looks beyond it to what it might be.

6. A compassionate literary nationalism makes religious studies a key feature of its interests. I see two reasons for this. Whether or not it is true, America claims to be a Christian nation, now more loudly than

ever. The deplorable situation in Indian Country is a spiritual crisis that has to do with the radical disruption of the relationship between humanity and creation. Land theft was engineered by the Christian church from the very beginning, a fact that can be established by simply reading the papal bull after first contact calling for conquest of the so-called New World. The church has not only offended Indians; it has cut itself off from a relationship with the God it says it serves who claims, among other things, to be a God of justice, to have created peoples for a reason, and to have put them in particular environments according to Her will. This means the church not only needs to reconcile itself with Native peoples but with God.[71] Until the church rectifies this situation it is fraudulent. Early Christian Indian writers like William Apess understood that the American public was more likely to respond to a breach in its relationship with God than a breach in its relations with Indians. The church has severed a fundamental relationship with creation and its Creator through its massive disruption of the environment of the New World and its inhabitants. The second, and equally important, reason for making religion a cornerstone of a materialist theory is because spiritual matters are paramount for Indian people themselves and no discussion of art or politics can proceed without referencing them. In Indian Country a materialist criticism cannot function by abandoning spirits.

7. A compassionate literary nationalism must engage in challenging historical work. Often those areas that present the biggest obstacles to historical inquiry are the very ones that are most needed in scholarship. We need to prioritize dates, events—in short, history. Not just distant history but recent events. Instead of making universal, overarching assumptions about Indians, the compassionate critic should delve into historical particulars. We need an improvement over the kind of literary work that has been so very popular in relation to Native literature in which people avoid historical research and base their criticism exclusively on tropes and symbols. The compassionate critic needs to show some kind of commitment to archival sources and other kinds of knowledge rather than atemporal, nonhistorical analyses such as, "Well . . . I think the frybread probably symbolizes . . ." The literary nationalist must develop historical methodologies since Native literary criticism has too often been scrutinized along thematic lines rather than historical details.

Such strategies can proceed without abandoning close readings of creative work or theoretical formulations.

8. The American Indian literary nationalist serves double duty as an activist. The literary nationalist, potentially, could provide movements with what they have sometimes lacked in Indian Country: a philosophical basis from which to justify or call into question political acts. Neither activism nor criticism should be a mutually exclusive endeavor. This is not the only way to do literary criticism, but we need some people with this kind of commitment in the field. We need an interventionist approach to theory. In Terry Eagleton's recent book *After Theory* (2003), which is an attempt to predict what is next after the decades of French, and other, theories in the 1970s and 1980s, Eagleton moves away from a detached hypothetical analysis of the effects of colonialism and toward an advocacy that names specific ways the United States must change its imperial thinking and practices, specifically questioning U.S. policies in Iraq. Political outcomes are as important as underlying philosophies and neither endeavor should be abandoned; which is to say, we hope for both a smart theory and praxis.

9. Literary nationalists need to demonstrate more close reading strategies. Some have said sovereignty theories are vaguely defined. In order to address this issue, I believe the next step is to begin applying a theory of jurisdiction to Native literature. Jurisdiction, it is important to note, is not the same thing as ownership. In Oklahoma, for example, tribes do not have a land base, since it was allotted under the Dawes Act, yet they have governing powers over traditional areas and administer services to their members. Key questions relevant to a more clearly defined sovereignty theory should include "when did it occur?" "Can you locate it on a map?" "How is jurisdiction exercised in this particular space?" One of my favorite stories, "Summer Water and Shirley," by Creek author Durango Mendoza, available in Natachee Momaday's collection *American Indian Authors*, contains three intersecting jurisdictions that are central to the events that unfold: the activities of Creek Christians that center around Thewarle church outside of Dustin, Oklahoma; the traditions that have their central locus in the Creek square grounds; and the dark practices of a Creek witch by the name of Ansul Middlecreek, which take place in the woods surrounding the

church. Jurisdictional spaces of the Christians center around the church camp houses the kids play around and the deacons who are responsible for keeping order in these places they are given jurisdiction over by Creek pastors, elders, and God, Hessaketemessee. Ansul Middlecreek, on the other hand, has a certain kind of jurisdiction in the woods that Shirley violates when she addresses him inappropriately on his own turf down by the creek, distant from the church house. Both Ansul's and the church community's spaces are deeply interrelated and central to the story and the inevitable conflict. Part of the problem is when Shirley removes herself from one space (the church house where adults could watch over and counsel her) and acts too freely in a distant geography. The irony is that Shirley, like all humans, must enter other geographies away from home. So the idea is not the stereotypical "stay at home and listen to the elders" but more along the lines of how to act appropriately, given the inevitability of various departures and returns, and knowing how the rules change on new turf. In Creek culture one can also observe individuals with granted jurisdictions at the ceremonial grounds: the Dokpalas (I don't know the English word here), for example, who keep order inside the consecrated arbors that are set apart from other spaces at the ground, leaders who are given their authority from the Micco, the grounds community, and, ultimately, Ofunka, the creator. They have their counterparts at the Creek churches, the deacons, whose authority comes from pastors, elders, the church community, and God. Varying jurisdictional responsibilities are evident in the roles of special leaders, men, women, children, everyone who goes to the grounds or church. This is a case in point that recent arguments that sovereignties are of European origins and irrelevant do not hold up very well, at least if one is speaking of the jurisdictional element of sovereignty. There are very significant possibilities for applying jurisdictional notions to Native literature and doing closer sovereignty readings of creative texts more generally. One of the greatest problems in Native Studies has been attempts to make one kind of jurisdiction fit everything. Hypothetical example: "White feminism is irrelevant to my tribal ceremonial traditions; therefore, I reject white feminism." But what about other jurisdictions inside and outside the tribal world? Can a "one-size-fits-all" rejection of feminism serve all tribal people in all geographies and all cultural spaces?[72]

10. We need to scrutinize theory based on what we *do* as much as what we say and write. Anyone who has taught or studied theory knows that radically different conclusions can be drawn from the same theory depending on how one argues it. No doubt those criticized in this chapter will mount a spirited defense of their work just as we have here. We can keep arguing about who won the debate or turn our attention to what we're actually doing in the Indian world. In scrutinizing our involvement in the tribal world, our support of the tribes need not mean always agreeing with them—they do not need that kind of help. In a recent speech at the University of Georgia on April 21, 2006, coauthor Robert Warrior reminded us that scholarly nationalism can take the form of advocating for disenfranchised people in ways that might involve speaking against tribal government positions that endorse the Iraq war, that legislate against gay marriage, or that disenfranchise African-American tribal citizens. Serving tribes is not the same thing as submitting to them. I hope for an experience-based criticism that looks at actions alongside words.

The title of my chapter is an obvious reference to the Stanley Kubrick film *Dr. Strangelove*. One of Kubrick's most enduring images is Slim Pickens straddling the bomb like a bull rider just before the chute is thrown open, then his trip down, falling from the hatch of a B-52 and waving his cowboy hat as he plummets through the clouds. Embracing my hybridity is about as sexy as wrapping my legs around an H-bomb. While you might get a big tingle during the initial descent, it's the impact that will kill you.

C. S. W.

O

Notes

1. Elvira Pulitano, *Toward a Native American Critical Theory* (Lincoln: University of Nebraska Press, 2003), 13.

2. Ibid., 185–86.

3. Ibid., 14.

4. Ibid., 59.

5. Ibid., 27.

6. Ibid. 76.

7. Ibid., 77–78.

8. Ibid., 79.

9. Ibid., 77–78.

10. It seems like some such courses are developing at OSU-Okmulgee, certainly a strategic location within the Nation.

11. Robert Dale Parker, *The Invention of Native American Literature* (Ithaca, NY: Cornell University Press, 2003), 196.

12. Pulitano, 13.

13. Ibid., 60.

14. Ibid., 79.

15. Ibid., 94.

16. Ibid., 96.

17. Craig S. Womack, *Red on Red: Native American Literary Separatism* (Minneapolis: University of Minnesota Press, 1999).

18. Pulitano, 105.

19. Ibid.

20. Ibid., 54.

21. Ibid., 141.

22. Ibid., 180.

23. Ibid., 74.

24. Ibid., 75.

25. Ibid.

26. Ibid., 95.

27. Ibid., 95–96.

28. Ibid., 96.

29. Ibid., 63.

30. Ibid., 15–16.

31. Ibid., 2–3.

32. Ibid., 99.

33. Ibid., 79–80.

34. Ibid., 70–72.

35. Ibid., 82.

36. Ibid., 81.

37. Ibid., 158.

38. Ibid.

39. Ibid., 90–91.

40. I am indebted to Daniel Heath Justice's reading and feedback for this particular sentence, inspired by his response to the essay.

41. Pulitano, 111.

42. Ibid., 40.

43. Ibid., 74.

44. Ibid., 85.

45. Ibid., 86.

46. Ibid., 62.

47. Ibid., 153.

48. Ibid., 70.

49. Ibid., 66.

50. Ibid., 88.

51. Ibid., 34–35.

52. Ibid., 78–79.

53. Ibid., 44.

54. Claudio Saunt, *Black, White, and Indian: Race and the Unmaking of an American Family* (Oxford: Oxford University Press), 58.

55. Pulitano, 55.

56. Womack, *Red on Red*, 2.

57. Pulitano, 73–74.

58. Ibid., 92.

59. Ibid., 99.

60. Womack, *Red on Red*, 65.

61. Pulitano, 89.

62. See Womack, *Red on Red*, 119–20, as well as other parts of the chapter.

63. Ibid., 142.

64. Pulitano, 85–86.

65. N. Scott Momaday, "The Man Made of Words," in *The Remembered Earth*, ed. Geary Hobson (Albuquerque: University of New Mexico Press, 1979), 164.

66. Daniel F. Littlefield Jr. and Carol A. Petty Hunter, eds., *Alexander Posey's Fus Fixico Letters* (Lincoln: University of Nebraska Press, 1993).

67. Womack, *Red on Red*, 173.

68. The last sentence of the paragraph owes much to Daniel Justice's written comments on my essay.

69. Craig S. Womack, *Drowning in Fire* (Tucson: University of Arizona Press, 2001), 246–47.

70. Simon J. Ortiz, "Towards a National Indian Literature: Cultural Authenticity in Nationalism," *MELUS* 8.2 (1981): 7–12.

71. This observation was born out of a conversation with pastor and drug and alcohol counselor Ron Blackburn when we were flying back from the Claremont Theological Forum the summer of 2005. The idea that the American public has offended God, not just Indians, is his.

72. In these regards I find myself influenced by a groundbreaking essay authored by Cheryl Suzack and entitled "Land Claims, Identity Claims: Mobilizing Indigenous Feminism in Literary Criticism and in Winona LaDuke's *Last Standing Woman*." This essay is in a forthcoming edited volume entitled *Reasoning Together: Native Critics in Dialogue* (University of Oklahoma Press).

Chapter Three

Native Critics in the World

Edward Said and Nationalism

When Edward Said died in September 2003, I experienced his passing at a personal level. Along with his work making constitutive contributions to the way I think about criticism and its connection to politics, Said was one of my teachers in graduate school. In considering this chapter on the relationship of Native American nationalism to my work as a scholar and intellectual, I have found myself recalling my interactions with Said as a student and have decided to frame my comments here with a sort of intellectual memoir of this great intellectual figure who was a tremendous, generous teacher.

Beyond his masterful work dissecting the ways western modes of representing colonized peoples have served the purposes of imperialism, Said has provided for me a primary example of the importance of dissent—especially dissent from the ideas of those who share a critic's political commitments. His insistence on dissent, importantly, derived from his complex position on problems that can and do arise when religious ideas are central to the critical field a critic examines, something that is certainly the case in considering the contemporary climate of the Middle East, the United States, and the indigenous world. My first book, which I was working on as a dissertation during the years I knew Edward Said, deals with these issues, but here I want to focus on them in a way that I did not over a decade ago when I was writing it.

| 179

Tribal Secrets: Recovering American Indian Intellectual Traditions
(1995), benefited immeasurably from my understanding of Edward Said
as a nationalist. That may be jarring for some readers, since the Edward
Said I knew from my studies as a critic and that I came to know as my
teacher and the Edward Said I have read others commenting on or discussing usually seem at odds with each other. That speaks to the complexity of Said. But to me it also speaks to the insidious way some
scholars, American ones especially, have been highly selective in their
reading, focusing on the Said who loved opera, talked in broad terms
about imperialism and his own conservative critical impulses, and quoted
at least as often from Vico, Foucault, or Raymond Williams as he did
from from Arab nationalist writers. This selectivity is unfortunate insofar as nationalism is a topic that appears as often as any in Said's work.

Said agreed with nearly every critic of nationalism that perhaps no
form of political ideation has been so pernicious in its effects as the modern concept of the nation. Yet he also points out that nationalism is "neither monolithic nor deterministic."[1] Said was a devoted, even strident
critic of Yasir Arafat, Idi Amin, and others who lead nationalist movements and postcolonial governments. But his opposition to them was
based in their corruption and cravenness rather than the fact that they
were nationalists.

Following Frantz Fanon, Said understood nationalism as something
problematic, but also something necessary to the mobilization of groups
of people toward political goals. Nearly all the great decolonization
struggles of the twentieth century, in fact, were nationalist ones, and Said
clearly understood his own commitment to the struggle for a homeland
for his own Palestinian people in the light of those other struggles. Yes,
he loved opera and played classical piano, but he was also a member of
the Palestine National Council (he eventually resigned), an outgrowth
of the Palestine Liberation Organization. He disavowed the violent tac-
tics of many people in the movement for Palestinian justice and abhorred
political extremism, but he believed in an unwavering way in the peoplehood of Palestinians and the rightness of their struggle for a land they
could call both home and, importantly, nation.

As Said read the history of imperialism, decolonization has been
intertwined with nationalist movements. The important thing to note in

this context is that Said saw criticism as one of the remedies for the excesses of nationalism, part of what he saw in his Palestinian commitments as the development of an "enlightened nationalism." As Aamir R. Mufti argues convincingly, Said's deployment of what he calls "secular criticism" is a direct effect of the nationalist milieu in which he engaged in the politics most personally immediate to him—the Arab world.[2] Said's sense of secular criticism and its opposite, religious criticism, came out of the world of his politics and the politics of his world.[3]

ℴ

This coupling of enlightened nationalism and secular criticism is what is centrally important about Said's work to what is happening in contemporary Native Studies and is the focus of where I am headed in this chapter. To obviate this connection, I want to use three examples that illustrate issues that arise in thinking through what nationalism has come to mean in the Native world and how Said's work leads me to argue that critics ought to respond to those meanings. The first example comes from the very persistence of nationalist discourse and the growth of discourse on the subject over the past three decades. Second is gender analysis and its role in the development of nationalist discourse. The final of the three examples comes from the increasing call for Native people to implement means of control over the research that occurs in their communities. I will discuss each of these examples briefly and then return to them after discussing the impact of Said's work on the way I think about criticism.

Rather than lay out the twists and turns of recent Native discourse on nationalism, I will take the liberty here of using one writer, Taiaiake Alfred, as an exemplar of where this discourse finds itself at this point in the arc of its history. Alfred has been perhaps the most important recent scholar to theorize nationalism in the Native context. His first book, *Heeding the Voices of Our Ancestors: Kahnawake Mohawk Politics and the Rise of Native Nationalism* (written under the name Gerald Alfred) takes up the idea that "Native societies . . . are re-examining the roots of their own Native political institutions and the canon of Native thought in a conscious effort to re-discover a set of values and political principles."[4]

While in this first book Alfred takes on the role of charting the prospects of nationalism in Native communities, in his second book,

Peace, Power, Righteousness: An Indigenous Manifesto, Alfred strenuously advocates particular forms of retraditionalization of Native politics, directly engaging in "a traditionally rooted philosophical reflection intended to give voice to a long-silenced wisdom."[5] *Heeding the Voices* brings Native politics into interaction with contemporary theories in political science. *Peace, Power, Righteousness* brings political theory into a framework that Alfred adapts from the Mohawk ceremony of condolence, the most basic source of historical and contemporary Mohawk politics.

[Alfred's manifesto is a powerful critique of contemporary Native politics in Canada and the United States, not only calling into question hegemonic Native political concepts like sovereignty and the efficacy of treaties, but also modeling through its ceremonially derived rhetoric the shape of the alternative it proposes. Young people who aspire to take part in Native politics, according to Alfred, need to redefine leadership in line with Native traditions, and scholars who aspire to be intellectuals of use to Native communities need to value those same traditions. As he writes, "A real Indian intellectual is proud of our traditions and is willing to take a risk in defending our principles.... The traditions are powerful, real, and relevant. As intellectuals we have a responsibility to generate and sustain a social and political discourse that is respectful of the wisdom embedded within our traditions; we must find answers from within those traditions, and present them in ways that preserve the integrity of our languages and communicative styles. Most importantly, as writers and thinkers, we should be answerable to our nations and communities."[6] Alfred's work represents the aggressive edge of a Native nationalism seeking adherents.]

Indigenous feminisms, the second issue I want to raise here at the outset of this chapter, are present in the communities Alfred writes about and presumably are also a part of the sorts of accountability Alfred calls for. Importantly, though, in spite of there being significant numbers of Native intellectuals, including novelist Louise Erdrich, who profess feminism or an equivalent, Native Studies has most typically been a site in which discourse that self-consciously addresses the patriarchal oppression of women has been rejected in favor of analysis that focuses on indigenous women and men at the same time.[7]

Laura Tohe's influential article "There is No Word for Feminism in My Language" sets out the parameters of this approach.[8] Eloquently tracing out her experiences of growing up and coming of age within the context of Diné (Navajo) traditions, Tohe argues that the Diné do not share in the gender problems that prompted the rise of feminism in Anglo-American culture. Instead, she writes of how she grew up understanding her fundamental worth as a caregiver in her Diné family and as being part of a female power dynamic that is integral to her people's creation stories and philosophy.

That traditional culture, the practices that derive from it, and the national culture that continues to be part of it shore up a world in which "a young person grows up knowing that the women are quite capable of being in charge. . . . The men in our family understood this, and we all worked together to get the work done . . . no resentment, no insecurity about male roles."[9] Arguing that she has seen similar dynamics among other Native women, Tohe claims that she and other Native women have "no need for feminism" because of the strength of the matrilineal cultures that "surround[] us constantly."[10] Those who cross the boundary to live in the Western world "must confront and deal with the same issues that affect all women," but the traditional Diné world remains a haven in which no word for feminism exists because no such word is needed. Tohe's essay is couched in cultural, autobiographical language, as is much of the discussion of the need for respect, informal or formalized, when doing academic research in indigenous communities.

I would like to suggest, however, that these are arguments that are every bit as related to nationalism as Alfred's work. That is, in both writers we find a clarion call for the affirmation of Native ways of knowing and doing and a call to reinforce a heavy boundary between Native nations and the larger polities that have dominated them in history. This highlighting of discrete Native political structures reflects a genuine need on the part of those who study the contemporary indigenous world to consider the social implications of what it means that these political entities continue to have a separate status.

Another area in which Native nationalism has been part of contemporary Native intellectual work has been indigenous control over the research that occurs in indigenous communities. Linda Tuhiwai Smith, er groundbreaking work *Decolonizing Methodologies: Research and Indigenous Peoples*, argues that centuries of disrespectful, disempowering scholarship by nonindigenous researchers has created an enormous credibility problem for those seeking to do academic work in indigenous communities.[11]

Leaders in those communities have responded with demands for greater respect for the needs of their communities from scholars. Smith, speaking from a New Zealand/Aoteoroa context, describes this as a matter of researchers developing relationships of respect similar to ones from indigenous cultures involving "the protocols which govern our relationships with each other and the environment. . . . Respect is a reciprocal, shared, constantly interchanging principle which is expressed through all aspects of social conduct."[12]

Others have suggested that such protocols be much more formal, and many tribal governments in the United States have established research offices and other programs to regulate the academic work done in their communities. At least one group of indigenous researchers has gone so far as to suggest that suspending academic freedom as it has come to be practiced in the United States is called for, and that tribal government appointees be allowed to shape not just the way research is conducted, but also the conclusions that researchers publish. Spero Manson, Eva Garroutte, R. Turner Goins, and Patricia Nez Robinson argue that such entities make certain published research is "conducive to the best interests of the tribes" based on the extent to which it "yield[s] direct and immediate benefits to [Native] people."[13]

These examples augur the direction in which academic discourse on Native nationalism seems to be headed as increasing numbers of scholars find these positions and others like them attractive. I want to dissent from what each of these authors argues. More than that, though, I want to argue that dissent is perhaps the primary sign of good health in nationalist discourse, a position, once again, that I find articulated most compellingly by Said. After working through my experiences with Edward Said and the ways those experiences prompted for me particular ideas about the need for criticism in Native Studies, then, I want to return to these three examples to discuss some ways that a more clearly defined critical practice helps to speak to these important issues.

o

I had two classes with Professor Said at Columbia University in the late 1980s, when I was across the street working on my PhD in systematic theology at Union Theological Seminary. Having by then read some of Said's work, the possibility of taking courses with him had been one of the reasons I had opted to go to New York for graduate school rather than staying at Yale, where I had done a master's degree in religion at its Divinity School. By that time, I was becoming less and less interested in classical and contemporary theology and more and more interested in pursuing questions about literary theory as it pertained to Native American writing and politics, an area I had started studying in earnest while in New Haven.

My hope of taking a class with Said became a reality my second semester at Union, when I was among those he chose to let into a graduate seminar comparing American and French literature. About 120 people showed up the first day of class seeking the coveted eighteen spots in the seminar. We had to make our case on index cards for why we should get in, then stop by Said's office door the next day to see if he had chosen us. I was one of thirty students he let in.

The class was held in a seminar room inside of an institute that was in a secure building in which everyone who entered had to show a school ID. This, it turns out, was a matter of security that Said took quite seriously. The first Palestinian intifada was in full swing, and he was a regular commentator on television news shows, generating controversy as he presented his positions on the brutality of the Israeli occupation, which, of course, continues to this day.

That semester he would show up for every class purposely at least five minutes late, stand at the doorway, and scan the room for faces of students he did not know. He asked those he didn't recognize why they were there. I remember one day a student answering when asked that she was a prospective graduate student who was hoping it would be okay if she sat in for the day. Said didn't hesitate in asking her to leave. That day and the others, once he checked the room, he would come all the way in, take off his olive green wool cape (during cold weather), and start teaching.

ᴐ

By the time I got to New York for graduate school, I was thoroughly engaged in the project of understanding the scope and breadth of the history of American Indian writing and the implications of that history for contemporary scholars. While still in New Haven, I had encountered Carlos Montezuma, Charles Eastman, Gertrude Simmons Bonnin, and others from the turn of the twentieth century and had read autobiographies, novels, and other writings by nineteenth- and twentieth-century Native authors. New York's excellent bookstores and libraries increased the texts available for my consideration, and I read a steady stream of titles by well-known and not-so-well-known Native authors.

The last years of the 1980s were an interesting time in Native letters, and I watched some of the assumptions about, for instance, what Native novels should be about crumble as the literature (as we should hope its does) outpaced the machinations of readers and critics. N. Scott Momaday's *The Ancient Child* and James Welch's *The Indian Lawyer* came out around the same time, and I still recall the way these texts examining the lives of middle-class, professional Indian people struck me as innovative and important. Louise Erdrich, at the same time, had gained a foothold in the American literary establishment and Leslie Silko's *Almanac of the Dead* was just on the horizon. Gerald Vizenor's collection, *Narrative Chance*, demonstrated that Native literature could be considered from a postmodernist point of view. I walked through bookstores on the Upper West Side several times a week on the lookout for new books, and nearly every weekend I would be at Saint Mark's Bookstore in the East Village combing first through its small Native American section before looking for the latest books in its massive section on theory.

Beyond books, though, those years in New York also showed me the extent to which Native literature was happening in ways that are hard to find. Native poets and theater companies came through town regularly. Some even lived right there and were active in the American Indian Community House, including the actors from Spiderwoman Theater, the Winnebago poet Diane Decorah, and others who have been mostly lost to obscurity. Native politicians, community organizers, academics, models, and performers joined steelworkers, street people, and church bureaucrats and came together temporarily or permanently in the midst of the teeming masses of Manhattan. There were fund-raisers for Leonard Peltier, previews of Hollywood's new Indian movies, gallery openings of Indian artists, and a constant procession of people passing through town for meetings at foundations.

It was all a valuable education, and I gained perspective as a result on the largeness and variety of the Native world. Through contacts I made while a graduate student, I spent one whole summer traveling by bus, plane, and car to far-flung corners of Native America, including Robeson County, North Carolina, and various reservations in South Dakota, Arizona, and Oklahoma. Later I traveled as far as Ecuador and Malaysia in official and unofficial capacities. Whether just outside my door or two thousand miles away, I came to see the Native world as a place where an immense amount of activity was taking place with hardly anyone being aware of and next to no one being able to speak to how it all fit together.

I was pulled in three directions. My readings in Native literature opened a world of language and self-representation that helped me see some of the ways that Native writers had found to represent their realities in writing. My ongoing interest in and love of theory reminded me of how far I and other Native scholars needed to go in confronting the intellectual challenges the Native world was facing. My increasing awareness of the complexities and variety of Native communities was a constant reminder that a real world was and is at stake in the process.

o

The subject of that first seminar I had with Edward Said was a comparison of intellectual responses to empire in American, French, and British/ Anglophone literature, with special attention to writings having to do with North Africa and the Arabian Peninsula. We read, among others, André Gide's *The Immortalist*, Tayib Salih's *Seasons of Migration to the North*, Herman Melville's *Moby-Dick*, Jean Genet's *The Balcony*, T. E. Lawrence's *Seven Pillars of Wisdom*, Ernest Hemingway's *The Sun also Rises*, and Abdelrahman Munif's *Cities of Salt*. Careful readers of Said's masterpiece *Culture and Imperialism* will note that nearly all of these books are among the hundreds he writes about in that study, and indeed Professor Said tried out on us most of the major themes of this book he was drafting.

Sitting at the seminar table during those class sessions I took notes furiously, attempting to keep track of the critical strands that emerged from Said's readings. Telling us he was really nothing of an Americanist, he would dazzlingly expound on the "how-to" tradition that runs through *Moby Dick* (for which he had just done an introduction to a new edition) and Hemingway, mentioning various other figures who helped make his point. He seemed to rattle off the titles of at least a dozen new books a week, books that were germane to our discussion and that he talked about with a specificity that made it seem as if he had just completed them before coming over for class. Through my first years of classroom teaching, I referred to those notes regularly, devising my own pedagogy in light of Said's.

One of the main things I took from Said's approach to graduate teaching was his refusal to allow students to throw around jargon in his classroom. As in his writing, in his teaching he demanded that even complex formulations make unmuddled sense and not be reliant on the gnosticism of critical shorthand that doesn't convey meaning so much as send messages, messages that would be puzzling to most educated users of English. Whenever someone in Said's classroom would launch into a post-Althusserian, neo-Bakhtinian, pre-proto-poststructuralist statement, Said would stop and ask the student to explain each piece of the jargon-laden phrase he or she had just uttered. Sometimes students would merely amplify their jargon with more jargon, but Said would keep pressing until students used as many words as it took to communicate their ideas clearly.

Though challenging students to avoid obfuscating language cut against the grain of stereotypes of a literary critical classroom, Said was not above indulging some others. One day, for instance, as we all settled into listening to a fellow student make a presentation on the reading for that week, Said produced a pipe and lit it. As thick smoke curled into the air, several of us who were smokers exchanged inquiring glances, then reached into pockets and bags for Gauloises (standard issue, I used to joke, at orientation for Columbia literature graduate students) and (in my case) Marlboros and lit up. It was the only time I ever smoked in class and must have been among the last instances of smoking in an American classroom.

The next academic year I took another class with Said, this one team-taught by him and Jean Franco, a terrific scholar of Latin American literature. This class on Third World intellectuals was also billed as a seminar, and well over two hundred students showed up looking for spots in it. Said and Franco chose seventy of us. The two of them provided marvelous interaction that was much more instructive than anything we as graduate students could have done, so I don't recall anyone complaining that we were really a few too many for a seminar. Our teachers traded off each session, with one speaking for twenty minutes, the other responding for ten minutes, then back and forth until it was time to go. Halfway through the semester, Said in one of his openings said that he already knew what Franco was going to say in response. "Yes, Edward," she said, "I'm so transparent, aren't I?"

In those two courses, I spoke a total of two times, including once when Franco called on me by name to respond to a reading on Derrida's response in *On Grammatology* to Levi-Strauss's famous "Violence of the Letter" episode from *Triste Tropiques*. I have to say that two years at Yale and then being among the cream of Columbia's critical crop in Said's classes hadn't done much to untie my tongue in situations like that. I managed to mumble something that satisfied Professor Franco, but have always wished that I could have said the smart things that came to mind immediately after and in the weeks to come.

The year before I had in a rare moment been much more articulate when I blurted out a response to Said's discussion of the biblical figure of Ishmael and Melville's use of that name in *Moby Dick*. The biblical Ishmael, of course, is the son of Abraham and the Egyptian woman Hagar, the slave of Abraham's wife, Sarah. In the religion of ancient Israel that became Judaism, Abraham and Sarah have a son together who is younger than Ishmael, but whom Abraham's god, Yahweh, favors. In the Islamic tradition, Ishmael is the one who finds divine favor and is the progenitor of the Arab people. As Said pointed out, Ishmael the rejected son of Abraham (at least in the Jewish and Christian versions) becomes a rich narrator for this story of Ahab's obsession, an obsession that C. L. R. James and others have read as being rooted in the errand of imperialism.

Listening to this, after a couple of months of steady silence and frantic scribbling, my mouth opened and I injected into Said's train of thought the idea that Yahweh's rejection of Ishmael can also be thought of as his being elected for something else. This is certainly the upshot of the Muslim version of the story—Allah chooses both sons of Abraham, with Ishmael taking the primary role. Various strands of Christian and Jewish thought have also opted for Isaac and Ishmael both being predestined. The other choice, theologically speaking at least, is for God (Yahweh or Allah) to appear on the vengeful side, choosing some people for salvation and others, through no real fault of their own, for damnation.

This is fairly heavy theological stuff, which I was steeping myself in as part of my graduate training in theology, with the theme of divine election being of special interest to me as I sought to understand the confluence of religious and nationalistic ideas in the unfolding of Native history. Said responded favorably, though I had to add that no religious tradition that relies on the idea of divine election has moved very far beyond the chauvinism of deific preference for a particular set of people. Saying some other people are differently elected has a certain anti-xenophobic attraction over thinking of the other as always already rejected and damned, but the exceptionalism of divine favoritism, whether expressed through religious bigotry or nationalism, remains.[14]

o

Outside of class I found myself much less reticent in my interactions with Professor Said. I saw him occasionally during his office hours and every now and then I would run into him on the Upper West Side. He always seemed happy to talk to me, though I am sure he had many better things to do. I was always just happy that he recalled who I was.

Said in his office was a flurry of activity. The office was separated from the hallway by an anteroom, with both rooms protected by a protective metal door. His assistant would lead me in for my meeting while Said was still on the phone, often switching between English, French, and Arabic. He would hang up and we would begin to talk, usually about my growing assessment of where Native critical discourse found itself in the early 1990s.

I remember trying to do a shorthand description of where all my reading in Native writing had taken me. In short, I was not satisfied with any of the models that had presented themselves thus far. The postmodernism that some were gravitating toward tended to lead to social disengagement and disembodied relativism. On the other hand, writers who were engaged with the social implications of intellectual work tended toward reliance on cultural models that were difficult to defend—unified indigenous worldviews, a posited but unprovable Native consciousness that transcended history and tribal differences. What posed as political radicalism too often came down to flimsy philosophy that I considered to be a plague on Native intellectual work. The alternatives were just as unsatisfactory, though, and represented to me the entrenchment of scholarship that reveled in its lack of awareness of its imbrication in the structures of contemporary Native life.

I was looking for something different than the positing of grand schemes and systems that describe the general features of indigenous life around the world or the positivist pretension that scholarship could be something that was just sitting there like an empty vessel waiting to be filled, in this case with factoids of Indianness. Said was sympathetic, and I found value in those meetings if for no other reason than having to learn to articulate the parameters of Native discourse for someone so august. Plus, I left those meetings not only having had Said's ear for a moment, but sometimes he would also give me photocopies of his writings that he considered to be germane to the issues I had brought to his office.

Not every professor, of course, could get away with that—diagnosing someone's intellectual afflictions and then prescribing and dispensing his or her own work as therapy—but this was not just any professor. I nearly wore out those copies reading and rereading them.

O

Said's articles were included in the one box of research papers and two boxes of books that I mailed to myself when I moved to Pawhuska on the Osage Reservation to draft my dissertation in the spring of 1990. I can still remember agonizing in my Manhattan apartment over what to include in those boxes and what to leave behind.[15] I can also remember comparing what I was doing to Said's description in the beginning of

The World, the Text, and the Critic of the impact of exile on Erich Auerbach's *Mimesis.*

In his monumental study of western literature, Auerbach describes the difficulty of composing so ambitious a book after having fled from Nazi Europe to Istanbul, a great city, but one with no library to support such an effort. In moving to Pawhuska, I was the opposite of an exile, someone returning home to do what Taiaiake Alfred would later advocate for Native American Studies, that it come from "someplace Indian."[16]

Someplace Indian—more accurately, someplace Osage, in this case—meant limited access to the scholarly resources to which dissertation writers in my program were accustomed—hence my three boxes of books and articles. Thinking in Pawhuska of Auerbach in Istanbul and the importance of that to Said's self-conception of exile in his life of criticism, I thought of the ironies of how I had come home to the national capital of the Osages only to be reminded of the underdeveloped nature of our life as a nation without, among other things, a library. I had come as an Osage national to Osage homelands to reflect on the Osage future and what that might imply for other Native intellectuals. The way most of my colleagues in the academic world thought of what I was doing was that I was somehow engaged in fieldwork. An exile in his own land, that shopworn phrase, came to mean something to me in those months.

Reading and rereading *The World, the Text, and the Critic* as I worked in Pawhuska helped me learn one of the enduring lessons I took from my work with Edward Said. That was the idea that it is possible to be a critic, a nationalist, a cosmopolitan, and a humanist all at the same time. Yet I also came to be committed to the idea that nationalism and criticism not being mutually exclusive did not mean I should think of myself as a nationalist critic doing nationalist criticism. For Said, nationalism is worth engaging in only insofar as concomitant institutions of criticism arise to challenge its excesses and temper its corrupting power. Some of the most important of those institutions arise within the nationalist struggle itself. Thus, following Said, I think of myself as a nationalist and as a critic, but I don't put the two together.

This is a distinction that I am not certain I share with my coauthors, nor do I suspect that it will be well received by some people whom I consider allies in Native Studies. But in deploying this formulation I am not seeking to give comfort and aid to those who would make critical discourse a place devoid of politics. Thus, much of what I would like to do in the remainder of this chapter is work through implications that arise from the way I follow Said in envisioning this relationship of Native nationalism and Native criticism, a relationship that I will maintain throughout should not be elided: first, I want to discuss some of the themes of *Tribal Secrets* as they came out of my engagement with Said and his work; second, I want to describe more plainly and directly than I have done in my previous work my own sense of intellectual work as sharing in Said's notion of secular criticism; and third, I want to return to the three issues I outlined at the outset of this chapter, giving lie in the process to the idea, more and more prevalent in the Native scholarly world, that intellectual work is something that should focus on the immediacy of goals like the development of technical skills and the gathering of information rather than focusing on creating frameworks in which to understand the broad ways in which knowledge has operated ideologically and politically in bringing the Native world to the state in which in currently exists. After discussing these points, I want to conclude with a return to Said's work on what he called, late in life, "lost causes."

o

Professor Said saw my book *Tribal Secrets* when it was a still a dissertation, though I never had a chance to discuss it with him. When it appeared that I would be competitive for jobs in literary studies, he agreed to write for me in spite of the fact that he was not on my committee. We arranged all of this by telephone through his assistant, and I vaguely remember trudging through bad weather on the Upper West Side of Manhattan to deliver a copy of my recently defended thesis to his office. Once I got a job and set about depositing the dissertation and planning a move, I never got a chance to sit down with Professor Said to see what he thought. I was grateful, though, that he had taken the trouble to write for me, which I can only imagine made a world of difference to those who were trying to make the case to hire me.

Tribal Secrets, dealing as it does almost exclusively with authors outside the European or Amer-European canons and issues particular to authors who share, as Native Americans, a minority identity, is nothing

:e most of what Said did in his scholarly work. The book's method-ological thrust of privileging the works of Native authors in the development and deployment of critical ways of understanding Native texts further flies in the face of Said's basic impulses to draw on any and every historical and contemporary theorist in deriving an understanding of texts and their place in the world.

Though I sometimes wonder how my career and work might have unfolded differently had I decided to position my work more toward the model of Said's, directly engaging deconstructionists, postcolonialists, Third World critics, and even holdovers from the New Criticism, the highly particularized agenda I chose to pursue in *Tribal Secrets* seems entirely justifiable nearly fifteen years since I conceived of it and over ten years after publishing it as a book. Indeed, much of what bothered me then both about academic discourse on Natives and intellectual discourse by Natives remains true today.

I don't want to rehearse too much of a decade-old book here, but much of my motivation to fashion it the way that I did came from my sense that people doing work in Native American Studies, including most Native scholars, didn't have much regard for the work of Native scholars in formulating their approach to their work. When I was in graduate school, I used to comb through the bibliographies of books of criticism and theory, totaling the number of Native critics (as opposed to creative works of fiction and poetry) that appeared. Few such items, if any, appeared, even in work that billed itself as being self-conscious of the need to include Native voices in academic discourse.

The great irony, at least to me, was the extent to which Native scholars failed to cite each other, even as they themselves complained about being ignored. Why should non-Native scholars take Native scholars seriously when Native scholars don't take each other seriously, I remember asking myself repeatedly. My corrective was to focus tightly on the work of two Native intellectuals, John Joseph Mathews and Vine Deloria, Jr., and use their own work to comment on themselves and each other's work to comment on each other. I also focused, though not exclusively, on Native scholars whose work helped me elucidate what Mathews and Deloria were doing and how it might be helpful to furthering a Native intellectual agenda.

All these moves were part of what I thought of as a self-conscious hermeneutics of inclusion and were reminiscent of the school of discourse analysis I had studied while an undergraduate first learning to read texts critically. The idea of privileging the voices of Native intellectuals also came from my engagement with liberation theology, which was a major concern of the graduate programs in theology I worked in, though in liberation theology privileging was an expression of what was called a divine "preferential option for the poor" that helped guide the reading of biblical texts.[17]

For me, privileging Native voices was not a matter of infusing Native perspectives with an infallible access to truth, but a recognition of the need to be methodologically self-conscious in attending to perspectives that had been ignored, debased, discounted, and marginalized. Interestingly, what has always been for me methodological—almost to the point of being procedural—has seemed to some readers more ideologically driven by identity politics than anything else.[18]

Including those perspectives in a proactive way, then, brings new insights into Native Studies, and, if Satya Mohanty is right that there is such a thing as "epistemic privilege" through which people can be supposed to know things about their own experiences exactly because they are their own experiences, some such insights may only be available through the work of Native scholars. More, though, I have advocated the inclusion of Native voices in criticism because the Native world needs models for inclusive, incisive critical discourse that is Native-led. Nothing seems to lead more easily to hurt feelings, injured poses, and bruised egos than the suggestion that one of the things that is wrong with contemporary Native Studies is that not enough Native people are involved. At the same time, nearly everyone agrees that solutions to the problems of the Native world require Native leadership. To me, a logical extension of this easily agreed upon point is that Native people need to be leaders in all aspects of Native life, including the world of scholarship.

When I first got involved in the scholarship on Native literature in the mid-1980s, I picked up repeatedly on an attitude through which some people saw Natives as good at creative tasks like fiction, poetry, and even essays, but not very astute at criticism. I remember a conversation about Paula Gunn Allen with a non-Native scholar of Native literature (someone I liked then and still like now) in which Allen was admittedly a very good poet and an interesting novelist, but not much of a critic or thinker. Like many, I have found the essentialist frame of Allen's work to be problematic, but I found it amazing then and still do now that her obvious mastery of so much knowledge of so many things could be so easily dismissed.[19]

Unfortunately, such attitudes are still present and are, in fact, part of a very old tradition of racism toward Indians and other colonized people— we are the sort of people who are good with their hands, clever in their crafts, nimble on their feet, and delightful in their imaginations, but not so strong on the heavy lifting of philosophy and other higher order tasks of the mind. Feeling the brunt of those attitudes as a graduate student, I was intent on demonstrating the pernicious error of those who held them. Becoming a theorist who could discuss Bakhtin, Vico, Foucault, and Saussure would have done the trick, of course, but I was intent on bringing others like me along for the ride and creating, at least in the space of my critical work, the sort of discourse that I believe needs to be going on in Native communities.

That was the main reason I was interested in drawing so much on the work of Native writers in developing criticism—it was a calculated effort at undermining the thoroughgoing binarism of recent Native thought. The "death dance of dependence," as I call it in *Tribal Secrets*, expresses itself in white versus Indian, good versus bad, Eurocentric versus indigenist, and various other forms of narratives and mirror-image counternarratives.[20] Deloria and Mathews were both too smart for that, and I thought that by holding up their work and scrutinizing them together, I would be able to find a way of gaining the benefits of the particular insights others had missed in Native figures like them while also giving two examples from different generations of how some of the smartest people in the history of Native writing demanded of themselves a more complex view of the world than the one inherited from generations of the corruptions of colonialism.

This was, again very self-consciously, an attempt to work within Said's position on nationalism, that it was necessary to raise nationalist consciousness in order to mobilize toward decolonization, but it was concomitantly necessary to see that moment as a beginning point rather than an end unto itself. I thought of myself as engaging in an intellectual version of that process. I didn't harbor any illusions, especially once I was working on the manuscript as a book, that I was involved in some sort of mass intellectual movement or that bunches of other Native scholars were going to sign on to my agenda. But still, it was important to me that I had come up with an approach through which I was able to remain in conversation with a broad array of Native scholars while at the same time not merely engaging in my own private ethnic cheerleading clinic. I didn't want to become what is known in the African-American context as a "race man," but I did want to infuse my work with a strong sense of standing in an historical line of Native writers and scholars.

I should say before going further that I have always found it interesting that naming that history "American Indian intellectual history" has seemed odd or off-putting to various people (including Deloria, who seemed confounded by my work).[21] It has confused me most of all when this topic has arisen in the field of Native literature. Here we have a field of inquiry that nearly everyone who engages in defines as being works of literature by American Indian authors. But to suggest that there might also be something worth calling American Indian intellectual history that is made up of the intellectual work done by American Indians, or Native criticism that is made up of work by Native critics, prompts suspicion, accusations of essentialism, and questions about who is qualified to write about American Indian issues.

o

At this point, so as to avoid being misunderstood, let me say as clearly as possible that not only do I agree with my coauthors that anyone can write about American Indian issues, but I also share their hope that more people of every background will do so. I may not have always been able to say that with as much enthusiasm, but my position on that issue has not changed in any significant way over the course of my scholarly career.

Deeply misguided books like the one by Elvira Pulitano discussed in the previous two chapters temper that enthusiasm somewhat, but other books by non-Native scholars, such as Maureen Konkle's *Writing Indian Nations* (to give but one example) demonstrate that someone doesn't have to be Native to write well and effectively about these issues. One thing that me about these two books and my new one on Native criticism ll three focus on Native critical writing as a major resource for understanding the intellectual world of Native people. While I can see Konkle's critical insights (not all of which, I should say, I agree with) having an impact for a long time, I think it is more likely that scholars several generations from now will put together panels at conferences on criticism by Natives rather than panels in which they consider the work of everyone in any particular generation who is writing about Indians.

[Having said that, I still want people all over the world to read Native American and other indigenous writing, teach it in their classes, make it part of their scholarly perspective, and write about it. The problem on this point, of course, has historically always been how much of the work—nearly all of it by non-Natives of European descent wrapped up in the colonial enterprise—that has been done over the past several centuries has been untrue, ideologically motivated, and racist. Anyone who enters the field of Native Studies inherits this history.]

Linda Smith argues that formalized European systems of knowledge about indigenous people are based on "early fanciful, ill-informed" travelers' accounts, missionary reports, and other suspect documents that "are now taken for granted as facts and have become embedded in the language and attitudes of non-indigenous people toward indigenous people. They continue to frame the discourses on indigenous issues of a particular society and account in part for the very specific use of language, including terms of abuse, the sorts of issues which are selected for debate and even the types of resistance being mounted by indigenous people."[22]

Smith argues that this history has established a dehumanizing impulse to Western knowledge regarding indigenous people that shapes and molds what sorts of research and theory scholars produce about the indigenous world. This is, of course, in many ways an old point and one that a great number of those who work in Native and indigenous studies would agree to. What I don't want to miss about Smith's argument, though, is the forceful way that she reminds us that this history of work has a living legacy for everyone who comes into the field.

This link to the ongoing project of colonialism and imperialism is the primary reason, as Smith writes, "the word . . . 'research' is probably one of the dirtiest words in the indigenous world's vocabulary. When mentioned in many indigenous contexts, it stirs up silence, it conjures up bad memories, it raises a smile that is knowing and distrustful."[23] Everyone, then, who takes up the task of researching and writing about the indigenous world comes into an arena of inquiry already left in ruins by generations of bad faith.

Too often, focusing on the colonial history and context of knowledge creation in the indigenous world has elicited a defensive response centered on the fact that contemporary, individual scholars are not responsible for this history of scholarship and are not to blame for its excesses. This speaks to the invidious form of white liberalism that affects Native Studies—the promotion of the idea of the innocent non-Native scholar who just wants to help but can't figure out why so many Native people she encounters are so angry, so suspicious, and so resistant to the wonders and insights of contemporary theory.

I am much more interested in understanding how the history of bad scholarship and bad writing continues to impact my work than in attaching blame to any specific scholar or writer. As I have said, I want more people to write about indigenous issues. What I want even more than that is for the scholarly and intellectual discourses on indigenous issues to be sufficiently healthy so that those things that are published or otherwise disseminated in the field are thoroughly reviewed, disputed, and discussed.

These were the two things, then, that I found most dissatisfying about Native Studies when I was writing the dissertation that would become *Tribal Secrets*—the paucity of Native scholarly voices making their way into the academic context and the lack of a healthy tradition of dispute through which the weight and merit of ideas could be shared, assessed, and wrestled over. I often envisioned being a Native scholar as a matter of standing in a tiny circle of other Native scholars, standing shoulder-to-shoulder and facing outward against a world of non-Natives.

This was an extension of the world of Native political activism as it had evolved in the 1980s after the tumult of the late 1960s and early 1970s. Radical scholars, like radical activists, were a remnant standing against the ravages of racism in colleges and universities, policing the borders of our discourse against the slings and arrows of scholars who were not with us but against us.

Tribal Secrets was my attempt to envision Native intellectual work differently, to work through what happens when Native scholars turn inward instead of outward. This had important affinities with work by George Lindbeck, a theologian with whom I had studied at Yale Divinity School, and Alasdair MacIntyre, a philosopher who has advocated communities of virtue defined by their commitment to shoring up their own members in the face of modernity.[24] Like MacIntyre, I saw the situation of Native intellectuals as being a moment in which I and others needed to expend effort to understand what we as Native intellectuals had to offer each other in our work. Ojibway scholar Scott Lyons is troubled that my approach creates what he calls an "endgame" of Native scholars paying exclusive attention to each other. Had I advocated my approach as an end to itself, Lyons would be on target in his criticism. My sense, however, was always that Native scholars consider each other's work as a starting point, especially given the regularity with which one or the other of us demanded of non-Native scholars more attention to Native work.

Ten years later, the most striking thing I find about the agenda I laid out in my first book is that I still feel the need for its proposed remedies so acutely. A lot of terrific work has appeared since, some of it directly in the wake of *Tribal Secrets*, most not. The world of Native Studies has grown, with more Native scholars than ever being part of the academic world as professors, graduate students, and undergraduates. If I were writing the book now, I doubt it would be recognizable in most of its parts. At the same time, the need for more Native scholars engaging in intellectual exchanges with each other as part of the development of a healthier intellectual world in Native communities seems just as vital today as it did then.

o

My engagement with the work of Edward Said helped me develop an agenda in *Tribal Secrets* that allowed for the embrace of the impulse toward nationalism that had been growing among some Native scholars for the previous generation. His basic logic, that struggles against colonization required the galvanizing energy of affirming national histories, cultures, and identities, allowed me to understand what I was doing as something more than lionizing Native culture. But if Said's argument, following closely on the heels of Frantz Fanon's analysis of national culture in *The Wretched of the Earth*, posited the nationalist moment as a starting point, what was the next step?

Where I found myself looking again and again in his work was his definition of criticism as he lays it out in *The World, the Text, and the Critic*, the same book that presented such a compelling portrait of Auerbach in exile in Turkey. At the outset of that book, Said argues that criticism needs to be secular, by which he means it needs to understand itself as both taking as its subject and being in its own practice something created, shaped, and guided by human action. For Said, texts and the critics who read them "are worldly, to some degree they are events, and even when they appear to deny it, they are nevertheless a part of the social world, human life, and of course the historical moments in which they are located and interpreted."[25]

Criticism, for Said, is secular insofar as it refuses "either to validate the status quo or to join up with a priestly caste of acolytes and dogmatic metaphysicians."[26] The term itself, secular, seems throughout Said's work to be intended to be taken in the most general way, in the sense of worldly as opposed to otherworldly, and is opposed in *The World, the Text, and the Critic* with religious criticism. In articulating my sense in *Tribal Secrets* of what criticism should be in Native Studies, I hesitated to use Said's terms secular and religious, a hesitation that came from the way that scholars in Native Studies, especially Native scholars, have defined themselves in relation to cultural traditions and spirituality.

For a lot of good reasons, Native ceremonies, oral traditions, and other forms of indigenous spirituality have been regarded in various ways as key to the future development of American Indian communities. The Good Red Road to Sobriety, a catchall term for lots of different approaches to culturally based substance abuse treatment—many of them quite successful—is one example of how a turn to indigenous traditions is contributing to the improved health of Native communities. Inflecting Native educational institutions and programs, from Head Start to survival schools to tribal colleges, with Native culture and language instruction is another.

These programmatic efforts to bring the insights of Native ways of life and living into programs and institutions have taken place during a period of growth in specific tribal traditions, including the training of medicine people and other leaders, membership in ceremonial and dance societies, and participation in forms of indigenous spiritual life that just two generations ago seemed to many to be passing away. Nearly all North American Native languages continue to have declining rates of use, but even there unprecedented efforts have been undertaken to shore up the linguistic heritage of tribal groups so that the grandchildren of current tribal members will be able to learn and hear the languages that many consider to be their birthright.

The blossoming and flowering of Native culture that has taken place over the past four decades has been nothing short of astounding. Just a half-century previous to the point in the 1960s where one can say that things started to turn around for Natives vis a vis culture, the widely held assumption in white America was that Native ways were passing from modern life, never to return. In 1945 John Joseph Mathews, making a point that I take issue with in *Tribal Secrets*, writes that remaining instances of traditional Native life are but a few strongholds left over from a battle, long since lost, just waiting to be rooted out by the steady onrush of modernity.

N. Scott Momaday has pointed out that the history of colonialism has been a process of sacrilege for Native people, sacrilege being for him the "theft of the sacred."[27] One way to understand what has happened in Native cultural life over the past several decades is as a response to that theft. As Momaday says, "Inexorably the Indian people have been, and are being, deprived of the spiritual nourishment that has sustained them for thousands of years. This is a subtle holocaust, and it is ongoing. . . . We, Native Americans in particular, but all of us, need to restore the sacred to our children."[28] The restoration of tradition, then, is a crucial form of resistance to a history of loss and oppression.

Something similar is happening in indigenous communities all over the world, communities that share a history of experiencing the cultural plundering of colonialism. [As Linda Smith has argued, "The cultural and linguistic revitalization movements have tapped into a set of cultural resources that have recentered the roles of indigenous women, of elders and

of groups who have been marginalized through various colonial practices.
These groups in the community were often the groups who had retained
'traditional' practices, had been taught by elders, were fluent in the language and had specialized knowledges pertaining to the land, the spiritual
belief systems and the customary lore of the community."[29] Though certainly not always the case, much of what Smith describes as traditional
practices and specialized knowledges are based in spirituality and require
a high level of belief in what is usually understood as the supernatural and
the extra-worldly.

Unlike nationalism, Said does not embrace religion. As he says of
religious beliefs, "Like culture, religion . . . furnishes us with systems of
authority and with canons of order whose regular effect is either to com-
pel subservience or gain adherents." Yet, this does not mean that Said is
antireligion. He recognizes, for instance, that religious beliefs and the
shoring up of cultural traditions are responses to "the need for certainty,
group solidarity, and sense of communal belonging." Such responses, he
points out, can be and often are "beneficial."[30]

Mufti argues that much more is going on in Said's work, then, than
a simple rejection of religion. He points out that while Said's particular
ideas on secular and religious criticism have not often captured the attention of scholars, they are central to the way he envisioned his work.
Following Bruce Robbins, who suggests that Said intended secular criticism as a response to beliefs in nations and nationalism, Mufti argues that
Said's deployment of the secular is a way of problematizing the persistence
of minorities within modern nations, a concern that of course resonates
specifically for him as a Palestinian.[31] Returning to Auerbach's exile in
Istanbul and the hold it had on Said's imagination, Mufti argues that a
Saidian secular critic moves beyond mere recognition of the presence of
minority points of view to a taking up of a position through which a critic
defines him or herself as always occupying such a position.

Mufti describes the Saidian position of secular criticism as "adopt[ing]
the posture of minority, renounc[ing] one's sense of comfort in one's own
(national) home," and engaging "in a permanent and immanent critique
of the structures of identity and thought in which the relative positions
of majority and minority are produced."[32] It would be easy to dismiss Said's
use of the term secular in this regard as an attempt to remove spiritual

realities from scholarly discussions, but that would, I think, miss the more important point he makes about criticism, that it ought to be inclusive of experiences and points of view that are on the margins, that get left out even of communities of resistance. Given my concern when I wrote *Tribal Secrets* and now for criticism that includes voices that have usually been ignored in Native intellectual work, Said's position has obvious attractions.

Still, I hesitated to use the term secular not because I feared associating myself with the secularism of American academic culture. I wanted to be free to address myself to people who hold strong religious and spiritual beliefs without demanding that they check those beliefs at the door of the discourse I imagined. I was also reluctant to associate historical and contemporary Native thought with the sorts of abuses and ravages I associated with fanatical believers from American evangelicalism, radical Zionism, extreme forms of Islam, virulent strains of Hinduism, and others.

North American indigenous systems of belief by and large have been rather tolerant and benign, especially in comparison to these other examples. My own tribal nation, the Osage, has developed an inclusive ceremonial dance society that draws strict traditionalists, peyotists, Roman Catholics, Quakers, Baptists, and others. That society, I should say, has historically been open only to men. Women also dress in traditional clothes and dance, but the society remains a men's tradition for which there is, as of yet, no strict equivalent among Osage women. This and tribal traditions like it can prompt interesting and important questions regarding gender, class, and other issues (as do Christianity, Judaism, Islam, and other religious traditions, though of course on a much larger institutional level), but I don't want to lose the point that many tribal ceremonies include a healthy sense of tolerance of various kinds of differences. While among some people there is an insistence on maintaining strict boundaries between adherents of various contemporary belief systems, nearly all North American followers of ceremonial tradition practice toleration of the beliefs of others as a primary virtue.

In a related way, Native political radicalism has only rarely engaged in the sorts of brutality and repression that have so often been part of militant social activism. The recent indictments of the alleged murderers of American Indian Movement activist Anna Mae Pictou Aquash (who was murdered in 1975) and the subsequent trial and conviction of one of the accused stands out as a chilling reminder of the fact that Native politics is not immune from the worst aspects of movement politics, as is the seemingly equally brutal case of the disappearance and assumed murder of African-American activist Ray Robinson during the 1973 siege at Wounded Knee that has only recently come to light.

As inexcusable as these and other instances of internal repression and violence are, they do not come close to the record of brutal intimidation that took place throughout the Third World and here in the United States among the Black Panthers and other radical groups. Corruption, however, comes in many forms, including less immediately violent forms of the gender oppression that killed Aquash, moral and political hypocrisy, fiscal malfeasance, and the homophobia that has become all too common in Native communities. My point here is that the rise of traditional culture and spiritual practice as a way of ameliorating problems in indigenous communities takes place in a broader context that creates plenty of opportunities for tradition, culture, and religion to be used as cover by those who lack scruples.

One of the conclusions I drew during my graduate training in systematic theology is that the Native American religious traditions that I have come to know best do not need theologies attached to them in the same way that Christianity, Judaism, and Islam do as book-based religions. (I am, of course, excluding indigenous expressions of these religions, such as Native Christianity, from this assessment.) Theologies emerge as part of these book religions as systems of internal inquiry, posing and asking higher order questions that arise in the living out of these traditions in a way similar to the way precedents and legal theorizing operate in written systems of law.

When a book becomes a sacred text in a religious tradition, the tradition generates more texts, many of which have as their main purpose the justification and explanation of how something so finite and corruptible as a written text can contain something so ineffable and holy as divine will. A ceremonial tradition, for all its imperfections, is usually an end in and of itself, leading to a direct experience of itself rather than mediating, and thus representing, something else. I stand by the conclusion that such traditions do not need theologies, perhaps even more strongly than when I first drew it, when I was immersed in such questions in seminaries and divinity schools. While such traditions might inform deep questions about life and its meanings, I would argue that codifying those traditions would be antithetical to what makes them work.

The corollary is not true, though, vis a vis criticism. I see a permanent need for criticism of various sorts in the Native world, and Said's notion of that criticism being secular is something I am now prepared to argue for strenuously. As Said argues, only critical investigations that take place outside "the domain of sacred history" make the truth of criticism available to the people in need of that truth. While not denying what can be beneficial in religious traditions, Said writes "that what a secular attitude enables— a sense of history and of human production, along with a healthy skepticism about the various official idols venerated by culture and by system—is diminished, if not eliminated, by appeals to what cannot be thought through and explained, except by consensus and appeals to authority."[33]

To suggest as I am doing here that Native intellectual work can and should be done in a number of different ways with discrete senses of what different modes (the cultural, the philosophical, the historical, the critical) can lead to will be anathema to some who argue that indigenous ways of knowing ought to reflect a more holistic, unified approach. This is the sort of perspective that disciples of shopworn versions of postmodernism continue in graduate seminars to point at as being essentialist, but my objection comes not from a sense that such appeals are distasteful. Instead, I would say that such a position fails to account for the contemporary reality that Native people face.

The Native world needs criticism that is self-consciously and aggressively radically inclusive. That is the model I took from Said in what he calls secular criticism, though I might suggest that Said could have just called it criticism and left it at that. To echo a point Jace Weaver has already made, it could be said that religious criticism is to criticism what military music is to music. The point here is not so much how we name it, but that we confront the need for intellectual work that reflects primary allegiance to its own independence of thought and a willingness to take stands that oppose not just those who hold political power, but also those who wield considerable spiritual power as well.

Absent the sort of critical perspective I am describing and championing here, I don't know how to address some of the questions that arise in modern Native experience. In the second paragraph of *Tribal Secrets*, committed myself to "addressing such issues as economic and social class, gender, and sexual orientation within Native life" that I found nearly all previous work to ignore. Then, as well as now, I considered Native criticism worth engaging in only insofar as such issues had a place.

The fact is I can pursue my vision of nationalism and my vocation as a critic within the realities of what it means to be Osage in 2006. Homophobia, classism, racism, sexism, patriarchalism, and even xenophobia exist among us as a people, but in the institutions we have created for ourselves as a people and in the formal and informal associations I engage in as an Osage individual, I do not feel any need to hide my commitments to inclusive justice for all. I would like to believe, however, that if this situation were to change or if I found myself in a different one, I would not hesitate to seek out or create alternative communities from which to realize my Osage vision of justice.

Simon Ortiz, whose work has been a beacon for what my coauthors and I are attempting here, provides an excellent example of just this sort of thing in his writing. He speaks forcefully as a member of the Acoma community throughout his work in spite of the fact that his way of understanding economic exploitation and oppression no doubt differs from that of many people there. Tribes, like clans, have gotten a bad rap in the West since even before Europeans arrived in the Americas, which no doubt has something to do in its ancient forms with the rise of monotheism and in more recent centuries with the rise of individualist and liberal ideologies regarding how we as people belong to each other in the communities to which we are born or in which we other- wise come to live. My understanding of what it has meant to be Osage now and in history does not involve walking in lockstep with others or their ideas. As with so much else from the tribal world, the reality is more complex than most people have allowed it to be. The criticism for which I am advocating here is deeply marked by the conditions of modernity, but that does not mean that criticism came to Native people only with the arrival of the modern in the form of colonialism. Various forms of deliberation, critical judgment, dissent, and intellectual independence have existed among Native people, I believe, for eons.

Of course, as the forces of religious conservatism become more and

more powerful in the United States, only independent critical position-
ing can stand effectively against the corrosive effects of Christian funda-
mentalism on civic life and civil rights. To use the term secular is not a
matter of invoking the godlessness of secularism, and I believe that a secular critic can maintain a life of faith and belief. The difference here is
between having religious beliefs and invoking those religious beliefs and
demanding of others agreement with them in intellectual discourse.
Doing so shuts down discussion, removes the possibility of communication across differences in beliefs, and can and often does create an atmos-
phere of dogmatism (just as the corollary move of declaring religious
beliefs wrong or false also shuts down communication).

Having endorsed this idea of criticism, I now want to return to the
issues briefly outlined in the beginning of this chapter to discuss in
specificity some of the reasons why this sort of criticism is so crucial to
the ongoing intellectual struggle for an indigenous future.

o

Taiaiake Alfred suggests that a new generation of Native leaders needs to
work toward decolonization "in concert with the restoration of an indigenous political culture within our communities."[34] Restoration, for Alfred,
is not a matter of nostalgia or any other sort of uncritical attempt to cap-
ture the past in the present. It is, instead, a sincere attempt to find ways to
use insights, practices, and structures from indigenous traditions as the
basis for contemporary forms of democratic polities in the Native world.

Given the prevalence of similar claims in the material practice of
Native politics over the past several decades, Alfred's willingness to work
through the intellectual issues that arise in the midst of such advocacy
is welcome and important. Indeed, it augurs the state of Native politics
that *Peace, Power, Righteousness* has in over five years made little impact
even in the academy, much less among a more general audience in the
Native world. When I teach this text, which I have done now almost half
a dozen times, I engage my students on the issue of why there are not
more texts like Alfred's that strenuously argue for specific points of view
in Native politics.

Alfred's work is valuable because he does more than argue for the
efficacy of Native philosophies in the development of contemporary

politics. More than that, he lays out some of the important steps that would go into actualizing such developments. He focuses on the ways leadership in general and specific kinds of leaders in particular help and hinder movement toward what he calls for. He calls for a stronger sense of what it means to be a Native intellectual as a means of providing crucial aspects of the conceptual underpinning of his ideas. And, perhaps most important of all, he suggests that today's young people, especially those in colleges and universities, consider themselves the harbingers of the program he lays out.

What is so refreshing about *Peace, Power, Righteousness* is the way Alfred treats the Native political world as something worth having intense, passionate opinions about. In a field littered with books that focus on describing Native politics without raising the importance of prescribing what needs to be done in Native politics, Alfred makes demands and poses challenges. The Native world he describes is not just out there someplace but is, rather, a place or set of places that needs and deserves the results of better and stronger thinking by those who purport to care about it.

This is not to say that Alfred's arguments are airtight—far from it. At times he slips into a broad generalizing of indigenous political systems that undercuts his powerful elucidation of the Mohawk political traditions he is most familiar with through his upbringing and subsequent study. The rhetoric he employs sometimes makes his ideas come across as, at worst, sacrosanct, or at least irritating.

The weaknesses of some of the arguments, however, is not my primary concern. Rather, I am struck in reading Alfred's text at the complete lack of discussion of how someone might evaluate the efficacy of his call for a restoration of indigenous structures of governance. That is, it seems to me that such a clarion call to restore indigenous systems of governance would simultaneously prompt a need for a critical framework for working through crucial, contentious issues of difference, including differences between and among various indigenous traditions. Instead, though he admits to the diversity of indigenous traditions and cultures, he claims that "we share a common bond that makes it possible to speak of a 'Native American' political tradition: commitment to a profoundly respectful way of governing, based on a worldview that balances respect for autonomy with recognition of a universal interdependency, and promotes peaceful coexistence among all the elements of creation."[35]

I can imagine plenty of contemporary readers accusing Alfred of essentializing on this point, and I would agree that the logic he deploys leaves him open to questions about, for instance, what happens if a particular cultural group lacks one or more of the traits Alfred enumerates. Are they still part of the tradition? Yet, a larger problem is that Alfred's proposals fail to address more important contingencies. For instance, how can someone whose upbringing and experiences have led them to other belief systems participate in the governance of their own indigenous communities? Adherence to nonindigenous belief systems is not always a matter, as Alfred argues, of finding "sincerity and comfort in the oppressor."[36] There are American Indian Buddhists, agnostics, Baptists, Roman Catholics, and Muslims. Even if some of these have direct ties to the cultures that have dominated Natives, the comfort some Natives derive from these belief systems are real.

What Alfred argues, in the end, is that indigenous belief systems are the necessary basis for reforming the institutions that govern Native communities. I have deep, personal sympathy for that idea, and I believe that Native traditions of governance can be crucial to developing Native communities. I fail to see, however, how I can ask Native people of sincere belief to abandon those beliefs. I would much prefer to come up with an approach that defines people not on what they are, but on what they do in relation to what our communities need.

Alfred does not, I should say, present indigenous political traditions as being hermetically sealed against outside influences and new ways of addressing social issues. But he does create a strong argument for the idea that taking up what he calls indigenous ways is sufficient in and of itself for the task of political reform in Native communities. The upshot of this approach is that there are those who follow indigenous traditions and those who don't. While Alfred argues that indigenous traditionalists can and should be respectful of those who have a different view, he also clearly advocates restoration of tradition as a singular solution to Native problems.

As I have already said, though, won't there always be people who do not sign on to the traditionalist project? Mightn't some of those people bring important perspectives and, perhaps more importantly, commitments to the table of the collective work of liberation? At the end of his book, Alfred calls on his readers to follow four principles as part of following a restorationist path: "First, undermine the intellectual premises of colonialism. Second, act on the moral imperative for change. Third, do not cooperate with colonialism. Fourth and last, resist further injustice."[37] Isn't it possible to do all of these things without adhering to traditional beliefs? Aren't there plenty of sincere and politically committed Native Christians, for instance, who have done many of these things while retaining a strong sense of their faith? Would there be room in the political world Alfred proposes for the Mohawk equivalent of thoroughgoing secularist Jawaharlal Nehru, that patriot-nationalist from that other Indian world? A Mohawk Buddhist, Jew, or Muslim?

More to the point, Alfred outlines a system among the Iroquois of female clan mothers selecting male leaders and deselecting them if and when those male leaders stop working on behalf of the good of their clans, communities, and confederacy. What happens if someone has respect for that tradition as a historical means of incorporating female power into the life of a community, but argues that contemporary women need to play a more direct role in decision-making? What about someone who respects the people who hold a belief in this traditional system, but believes that contemporary Iroquois people need a system that doesn't split men's and women's roles in politics?

One might raise a similar question in light of Laura Tohe's contention that Diné people do not have a word for feminism in their language because, at least in their traditional world, they do not need such a word. Both Alfred and Tohe demonstrate the powerful arguments that can be mounted in favor of indigenous traditions. Yet both also demonstrate the rhetorical ease with which the material realities of Native life can get lost amidst calls for culturally based responses to the modern situation of indigenous people.

For Tohe, this is a matter of rhetorically reading the experiences of all Diné women through her own. She discusses her own upbringing in a traditional family, including the ceremonies and other cultural practices associated with women and their role in the Diné world going back to the creation of the world in the mind and actions of Thought Woman.

Then, in discussing the general irrelevance of American feminism for Native women in the 1970s, she makes the point that Diné women entered the modern world of work and wages "in low-paying, dead-end jobs that offered few benefits." Diné women may need feminism at that point, she argues, because they have "left their traditional world."[38]

Her statement is, of course, exceptionally broad, especially given that it fails to note where, exactly, this moment of passage from the world of Diné tradition into the western world in which all women might need analytical tools for understanding the reasons why they are disempowered in the ways that they are. "In the Diné world," she goes on to say, presumably referencing the world of tradition, "a young person grows up knowing that the women are quite capable of being in charge."[39] The Diné are one of the most culturally intact Native groups, which is remarkable given their numbers. However, the idea that this equates with all or even most Diné people being raised with the same robust sense of tradition as Tohe is hard to defend.

My point here is not to articulate my disagreements with Alfred or Tohe. Cheryl Suzack, for one, has already ably defended the need for forms of feminist analysis in the Native world more incisively and credibly than can I, and Alfred's ideas have not been as well received as they might be, I would argue, because of the rhetorical excesses in which he engages (several people I know, including some like me who teach the text, call it "Peace, Power, Self-Righteousness"). Suzack argues for "the importance of gender identity to a reading of community relations and tribal histories" and the need for "American Indian feminist critics . . . to theorize a relationship between community identity, tribal history, and women's collective agency in connection with gender identity so as to create an oppositional space from which to restore gender identity as an analytical category to discussions of tribal politics and community values."[40] Though she does not use the term, Suzack argues that Tohe's argument creates a false consciousness that says such oppositional space is not necessary when, in fact, it is, if one is to "work against asymmetrical power relations" in the Native world.[41]

What interests me more for my purposes here is the way both of these scholars write in such a way that readers agree with them or don't. Tradition, for Alfred, is the singular key to an indigenous future, and those who disagree are benightedly wandering in servitude to western paradigms. For Tohe, tradition creates impermeable boundaries around indigenous communities and renders analytical tools like feminism unnecessary. The need for disagreement and dissent, for both, are seemingly subsumed by adherence, participation, and belonging.

I intend this to be a strong critique, but in making it I want to stress that I see enormous potential for good in the ways that Alfred and Tohe prompt us to think about tradition in contemporary Native discourse. Alfred's championing of traditional forms of political systems is backed up by numerous examples from Native communities of people who are meeting the demands of their modern existence through just such traditional forms. Tohe's explication of how Diné beliefs about gender equality have informed her life speak to the continuing power of traditions from a number of tribal systems that sustain gender relations in much more healthy and just ways than what happens in most places on this continent. We need more work in Native Studies that helps us understand how these traditions can be effective in addressing the problems of contemporary Native life. Such work, after all, would show us the extent to which Native traditions offer genuine alternatives to hegemonic forms of modern life.

The way we go about doing that work says a tremendous amount about what we believe such work can and should do. At some point, though, either through the good sense and wisdom of the person who presents the work in public or, more likely, through forms of critical discourse that come in the wake of such work, dissent, disagreement, and the questioning of orthodoxies and received wisdom must be valued.

Unfortunately, the trend in Native Studies and among Native intellectuals seems to be away from rather than toward an embrace of the sort of criticism I have described here. This is the problem with the sorts of institutional review Manson, Garroutte, Goins, and Henderson have called for in their formulations of what it means to engage in consultation and collaboration with indigenous communities in conducting and disseminating research. While Linda Smith is surely correct in her assertion that indigenous people need to address the still-prevalent attitude among academics that indigenous communities are somehow just sitting out there for the academy to exploit for its purposes, I fail to see how that has come to mean for some people that freedom of expression and academic freedom are worth sacrificing.

Manson and his coauthors champion the development of "agencies that function not only as institutional review boards (IRBs), but also control access to the entire population within their jurisdiction. They demand that proposed research show relevance to local priorities, reserve the right of review and approval of all publications prior to dissemination."[42] Through three case studies, they provide a sort of how-to guide for working with such agencies.

Much of what these authors describe as coming out of tribal research offices is positive and forward thinking. Requiring discussions with local stakeholders, suggesting formal settings like talking circles in which community concerns can be voiced, and the transfer of assets, especially technological ones, are all ways of creating new sorts of research to counter the sad history Smith chronicles.

Though my work has been mostly in the humanities, my second book required IRB approval since it involved doing oral histories. I have since guided a number of students through the process of institutional review and can say that I am a strong believer in the principle of institutional review of research protocols and the development of tribal IRB and research policy offices. Not only does institutional review provide protection of research subjects, it also can lead to the creation of new and innovative ways of researchers working among indigenous people.

Yet, when researchers cede control or are expected to cede control of the conclusions they draw in their work, I can't imagine what good end is being served. Clearly, indigenous people have suffered at the hands of unscrupulous, biased research for generations, but I would suggest that those same people stand to suffer nearly as much or more from scholarly work that, by fiat, reflects the prescribed points of view of appointed research police. In the section about Eva Garroutte's research among the Cherokees, the authors advocate such practices as sending "personal courtesy notes" to tribal officials with influence over such boards and enlisting relatives to come along to meetings, I assume to demonstrate the filial ties of the researcher to the community. "Simple gestures of courtesy and goodwill," they write, "are important" in producing what they call "short-term deliverables."[43]

The Osage do not yet have an IRB, but if it did and I sat on the board, I can only imagine how incensed I would be at the idea of someone submitting a proposal while also currying favor with elected tribal officials to grease the skids of the approval process. If someone showed up with their aged aunt to a board meeting, I would like to believe I would question the petitioner on what they considered the scholarly merit of the presence of such a person to be for their proposal. I might ask myself if the aunt's presence is an attempt at coercion. In other words, I can't imagine a way of making institutional review less serious than through such machinations.

Manson and his coauthors couch their proposal in terms of protecting tribes from researchers. What I have always found the most compelling about institutional review is the idea that its main purpose is to protect vulnerable populations. Tribal governments might be underfunded, embattled, or weak, but they can be and often are corrupt, retaliatory, and inept. Anyone who takes these comments to mean that I think Native people are not capable of taking responsibility for themselves in areas like academic research are missing my point completely. Rather, I am trying to say that the issue calls for a much more complex, nuanced approach than what Manson and his coauthors propose.

"Short-term deliverables," after all, sound like something that come out of a manufacturing plant, and I know of plenty of tribal politicians who would love nothing more than to have academic experts deliver to them the same sorts of conclusions that tobacco companies pay scientists for. If that's what a tribal council wants, I say let them find someone willing to say what they want for a fee. I don't see the point in any self-respecting scholar volunteering for that sort of service, especially when actual people with real vulnerabilities (abusive spouses, homophobic schoolmates, sexist employers, for instance) are regularly ignored by nearly every tribal government on the continent (much in the same way, I should add, that such people everywhere are cast aside in contemporary political discourse).

In spite of my disdain for such developments, my sense is that the world of Native intellectual work is heading more toward Alfred, Tohe, and Manson et al. than it is toward me and my coauthors. Rather than making this seem like a meager attempt to stem the tide of these dynamics that seem to be growing rather than diminishing, let me instead offer once more the idea that the most effective counter to these dynamics is a critical discourse that is willing and able to stand against the tide, calling into question the moral and ethical basis of the assumed authority of every and any claim to power. That, then, is what Mufti calls the minority perspective that Said embraces, a position and positionality he calls secular criticism.

o

Though I did not know it at the time, some months previous to my 1992 request that he write in support of my efforts to gain an academic position, Edward Said was diagnosed with leukemia, the disease that would claim his life nearly a dozen years later. In spite of this illness that was often debilitating, his published work appeared in an astoundingly steady stream that continued until the very end. *Culture and Imperialism*, which had been in the works for years before the diagnosis, joined *Orientalism* as another magisterial work of importance, while books like *Representations of the Intellectual, The Politics of Dispossession*, and the memoir *Out of Place* demonstrated the great breadth and variety of Said's engagement with the world in which he lived.[44]

Toward the end of his life, essays like "Thoughts on Late Style" and "Between Worlds" referenced his own mortality (as does *Out of Place*).[45] For my purposes here, another of these late essays, "On Lost Causes," provides a fitting end point for both my memoir of my former teacher and my thoughts on how his example informs my own sense of the critical needs of intellectual work in the indigenous world.[46]

Published in *Raritan* in 1997, the essay reads as a reflection on the cascade of defeats stalwarts of the Palestinian cause have faced in the aftermath of the 1993 Oslo accords through which, in Said's opinion, Yasir Arafat and the leadership of the Palestine Liberation Organization abandoned the most profound aspects of their nationalist struggle for a Palestinian state in favor of an Arafat-led dictatorship serving as a vassal to Israel. Confronting the bitterness of this defeat was often the subject of Said's work in his last dozen years, much of it appearing in the Arab world. Said, who had joined the PLC and worked closely with the PLO leadership, including Arafat, for many years, spent tremendous amounts of what must have been already flagging energy being a voice of opposition to a situation that was, for him, complete capitulation of the dreams and hopes of a dispossessed people.

For Said, Oslo was a betrayal of the movement that had taken flight in the wake of the 1967 Arab-Israeli War and given Palestinians hope they had not had since before the U.N.-sanctioned creation of Israel in 1948. "We saw ourselves as a Third World people," he says, "subjected to colonialism and oppression, now undertaking our own self-liberation from domination as well as the liberation of our territory from our enemy."47 As Said traces out the life of this nationalist movement and his part in it, he also comments on the problem of how people in the West, especially Americans, perceived Palestinians and their struggle. As he says,

> The distorted view of us as a people single-mindedly bent on Israel's destruction that existed in the West bore no relationship at all to any reality I lived or knew of. Most of us, the overwhelming majority, in fact, were most interested in the recognition and acknowledgement of our existence as a nation, and not in retribution; everyone I knew was flabbergasted and outraged that the Israelis, who had destroyed our society in 1948, took our land, occupied what remained of it since 1967, and who bombed, killed, and otherwise oppressed an enormous number of us, could appeal to the world as constantly afraid for their security.48

Though engaged in an uphill struggle, Said portrays his fellow travelers for the Palestinian cause as willing to work to overcome every obstacle in their way. With the cooperation of their nationalist leaders, Oslo marked for Said the end of that struggle in its former mode. He writes, "Now we had conceded that we were prepared to exist not as a sovereign people on our land but as scattered, dispossessed people, some of whom were given municipal authority by the Israelis, with very little to check further Israeli encroachments against us or to prevent violations of the ungenerous pettifogging agreements they tied us into."49

At this point, Said makes one of his few allusions to American Indian history, referring to Norman Finkelstein's suggestion that Palestinians after

Oslo were proceeding down the same road the Cherokees had traveled in the nineteenth century.[50] Said calls this "a harrowing portrait of the defeat of the Cherokee Indians."[51] The comparison is a striking one, and, though I find Finkelstein's portrayal of Cherokee history to be seriously underinformed (Teddy Roosevelt is his major historical source), the idea that the Palestinians may now find themselves in a similar predicament as Native North Americans find themselves in is provocative.

As Said works through what he fears is the lost cause of Palestinian liberation in his essay, he makes several other references to indigenous people supposedly being lost causes. In pointing out how what seems now like a lost cause might be different in the future, "Many times," he writes, "we feel that the time is not right for a belief in the cause of native people's rights in Hawaii, or of gypsies or Australian aborigines, but that in the future, and given the right circumstances, the time may return, and the cause may revive."[52]

Those of us who work in Native American and indigenous studies might immediately want to point out that various Native people in Hawai'i and many Aboriginal people in Australia wouldn't consider their cause in need of revival given that, for them, it has never been lost. That would better nuance Said's argument, but I hope it wouldn't blind us to his larger point, which is to suggest that a cause seeming lost or not is a matter of many things, including the juncture in history at which the determination is being made, the sort of narrative the determination is part of, and the perspective from which judgment on the cause is being pronounced. Standing disappointedly in the lengthening shadow of the complicity of Palestinian leadership in capitulating the goals of national liberation (while presumably also confronting his own mortality) creates crucial context for why Said takes up the topic of lost causes in the way he does.

Said speaks as someone who had participated in an active movement for national liberation that made its followers see themselves with something in common with "the Vietnamese, Cubans, South Africans, Angolans, and others in Third World."[53] After Oslo, he indicates with his comparison to the Cherokees and in other references a discomfort and fear that the Palestinian struggle had joined those, like that of American Indians, who had become "dispossessed and forgotten."[54]

In my one-on-one conversations with Professor Said, I don't recall that we ever had an extended discussion of American Indian history or politics, though my own sense of where Native intellectual discourse was headed was a subtext for me whenever we talked. If we had discussed in detail the situation of Native people in North America and he had described us as a lost cause as he does in this essay, I would have been tempted to respond in a number of ways—providing a short course of lectures on the contemporary realities of American Indian people, or inviting him back home for some meat gravy and fry bread and a weekend of Osage dancing. Even now that he is gone and all responses are limited to the imagination, I would love to see him rehabilitated so wonderfully as Craig Womack does for Alice Callahan in *Red on Red* so that he could envision the depth of hope that has emerged in our unfortunate history as people who continue to live on this continent.[55]

But then I am reminded of the difficult truth that Said confronts in this essay, a truth that Palestinians, Native Americans, and other indigenous people around the world share. That is, we are a people who live in shadows of defeat under the sign of modernity. However much we hold to hope for the future, we must also see the extent to which the past centuries have been an unmitigated disaster for us as peoples in this world. He asks a question in his essay that some may bristle at, but that contains an important truth: "Do many people now believe that the gypsies or the Native Americans can get back what they lost?"

"On Lost Causes" points from its start to a reconceptualization of its subject, which is the main reason I think it bears our consideration. In the midst of answering back to Said that many Osages and other American Indians have never lost some fundamental things, like the relationship to their homelands that many have always regarded as a gift of their Creator, I see that he also offers an important way of thinking about all of this. That is, for Said, no cause is ever finally lost until its hope is extinguished in the last person who holds it in her or his consciousness.

That hope, like the nationalist struggle for liberation, needs critical consciousness to realize its greatest potential. For Said, this is "a means of affirming the individual intellectual vocation, which is neither disabled by a paralyzed sense of political defeat nor impelled by groundless optimism and illusory hope."[56] As much as I would like to believe in an easy way out of the various conundrums we find ourselves in as Native people,

I find in these late words of Said's a compelling description of where we now stand as Native intellectuals. Like him, I see in the willingness to speak truth to power, and to stand against whatever diminishes us in our quest for justice (including our own misbegotten ideas) a way of "blunting the anguish and despondency of the lost cause, which its enemies have tried to induce."[56]

Native intellectuals on this continent have been vying in the arena Said describes already, many of them for a long time. While I wished for him while alive and wish for his people, the Palestinians, now a better result than they have as of yet been able to achieve in regaining power in their homelands, I also welcome them to our world, the fourth world. May a new world of justice focus the energies of our intellectual lives. May a new world of justice in our Native Nations be ever in our grasp.

R. W.

o

Notes

1. Edward W. Said, *Culture and Imperialism* (New York: Knopf, 1983), xxiv.

2. Aamir R. Mufti, "Auerbach in Istanbul: Edward Said, Secular Criticism, and the Question of Minority Culture," in *Edward Said and the Work of the Critic: Speaking Truth to Power*, ed. Paul A. Bové (Durham: Duke University Press, 2000), 229–56.

3. See Edward W. Said, *The World, the Text, and the Critic* (Cambridge, Mass.: Harvard University Press, 1983), 1–30, 290–92.

4. Gerald R. [Taiaiake] Alfred, *Heeding the Voices of Our Ancestors: Kahnawake Mohawk Politics and the Rise of Native Nationalism* (Toronto, ON: Oxford University Press, 1995), 7.

5. Taiaiake Alfred, *Peace, Power, Righteousness: An Indigenous Manifesto* (Toronto, ON: Oxford University Press, 1999), xviii.

6. Alfred, *Peace, Power, Righteousness*, 143–44.

7. See Louise Erdrich, *The Blue Jay's Dance: A Birth Year* (New York: HarperPerennial, 1995), 142–48; Paula Gunn Allen, *The Sacred Hoop:*

Recovering the Feminine in American Indian Traditions (Boston: Beacon, 1986); Kathryn Shanley, "Thoughts on Indian Feminism," in *A Gathering of Spirit: A Collection by North American Indian Women*, ed. Beth Brant (Rockland, Maine: Sinister Wisdom, 1984), 213–15; and Lee Maracle: *I Am Woman: A Native Perspective on Sociology and Feminism* (North Vancouver, BC: Write-On, 1988).

8. Laura Tohe, "There Is No Word for Feminism in My Language," *Wicazo Sa Review* 15 (Fall 2000), 103–10.

9. Ibid., 109.

10. Ibid., 110.

11. Linda Tuhiwai Smith, *Decolonizing Methodologies: Research and Indigenous Peoples* (London: Zed, 1999).

12. Ibid., 120.

13. Spero M. Manson, Eva Garroutte, R. Turner Goins, and Patricia Nez Henderson, "Access, Relevance, and Control in the Research Process: Lessons from Indian Country," *Journal of Aging and Health* Supplement to Vol. 16, no. 5 (November 2004): 65, 67.

14. One result of this work on divine election was an essay I published at the time, "Canaanites, Cowboys, and Indians," *Christianity and Crisis* 49 (11 September 1989), 261–65. The essay brings together my interests in theology, literary criticism, and indigenous politics.

15. I have written about this before. See Robert Warrior, "Packing and Unpacking 'The Man Made of Words' by N. Scott Momaday," *Genre* 33, no. 3–4 (Fall–Winter 2000): 257–68.

16. Alfred, *Peace, Power, Righteousness*, 143.

17. See Gustavo Gutierrez, *A Theology of Liberation: History, Politics, and Salvation* (Maryknoll, NY: Orbis, 1988).

18. See Scott Richard Lyons, "Rhetorical Sovereignty: What Do American Indians Want from Writing?" *CCC* 51, no. 3 (February 2000): 447–68.

19. See, among others, Allen, *The Sacred Hoop*; Paula Gunn Allen, *The Woman Who Owned the Shadows* (San Francisco: Spinsters/Aunt Lute, 1983); and Paula Gunn Allen, *Shadow Country* (Los Angeles: UCLA American Indian Studies Center, 1982).

20. Robert Warrior, *Tribal Secrets: Recovering American Indian Intellectual Traditions* (Minneapolis: University of Minnesota Press, 1995), 123.

21. See Jack D. Forbes, "Intellectual Self-Determination and Sovereignty: Implications for Native Studies and Native Intellectuals," *Wicazo Sa Review* 13, no. 1 (Spring 1998): 11–23; and Vine Deloria, Jr., "Intellectual Self-Determination and Sovereignty: Looking at the Windmills in Our Minds," *Wicazo Sa Review* 13, no. 1 (Spring 1998): 25–31.

22. Smith, 79.

23. Ibid., 1.

24. George A. Lindbeck, *The Nature of Doctrine: Religion and Theology in a Post-Liberal Age* (Philadelphia: Westminster, 1984); and Alasdair C. MacIntyre, *After Virtue: A Study in Moral Theory* (Notre Dame, IN: University of Notre Dame Press, 1981).

25. Said, *The World, the Text, and the Critic*, 4.

26. Ibid., 5.

27. N. Scott Momaday, *The Man Made of Words: Essays, Stories, Passages* (New York: St. Martin's Press, 1997), 76.

28. Ibid.

29. Smith, 111.

30. Said, *The World, the Text, and the Critic*, 290.

31. Mufti, 230.

32. Ibid., 252.

33. Said, *The World, the Text, and the Critic*, 290.

34. Alfred, *Peace, Power, Righteousness*, 145.

35. Alfred, *Peace, Power, Righteousness*, xvi.

36. Alfred, *Peace, Power, Righteousness*, xi.

37. Alfred, *Peace, Power, Righteousness*, 145.

38. Tohe, 109.

39. Ibid.

40. Cheryl Suzack, "Land Claims, Identity Claims: Mapping Indigenous Feminism in Literary Criticism and in Winona LaDuke's *Last Standing*

Woman," in *Reasoning Together: Native Critics in Dialogue,* ed. Native Critics Collective (Norman: University of Oklahoma Press, forthcoming), 4.

41. Ibid., 15.

42. Manson et al., 605.

43. Ibid., 695.

44. See Edward W. Said, *Orientalism* (New York: Pantheon, 1978); *Representations of the Intellectual: The 1993 Reith Lectures* (New York: Vintage, 1996); *The Politics of Dispossession: The Struggle for Palestinian Self-Determination, 1969–1994* (New York: Pantheon, 1994); *Out of Place: A Memoir* (New York: Knopf: 1999).

45. Edward Said, "Thoughts on Late Style," *London Review of Books,* 5 August 2004; "Between Worlds," *London Review of Books,* 7 May 1998 (republished in Edward Said, *Reflections on Exile and Other Essays* [Cambridge, MA: Harvard University Press, 2002], 554–68).

46. Edward Said, "On Lost Causes," in *Reflections on Exile,* 527–53 (originally published in *Raritan: A Quarterly Review* 17:2 [Summer 1997]).

47. Ibid., 546.

48. Ibid., 548.

49. Ibid., 551.

50. See Norman G. Finkelstein, *The Rise and Fall of Palestine: A Personal Account of the Intifada Years* (Minneapolis: University of Minnesota Press, 1996).

51. Said, "On Lost Causes," 551.

52. Ibid., 527.

53. Ibid., 543.

54. Ibid.

55. Craig S. Womack, *Red on Red: Native American Literary Separatism* (Minneapolis: University of Minnesota Press, 1999). 123–29.

56. Said, "On Lost Causes," 553.

57. Ibid.

stones must form a circle first not a wall
open so that it may expand
to take in new grass and hills
tall pines and a river
expand as sun on weeds, an elm, robins;
the prime importance is to circle stones
where footsteps are erased by winds
assured old men and wolves sleep
where children play games
catch snow flakes if they wish
words cannot be spoken first
              —Maurice Kenny,
                "First Rule"

Afterword

At the Gathering Place

Lisa Brooks

*T*here was a time, in the early 1990s, when anyone who wanted to write to me, whether family, friend, or bill collector, had to address their correspondence to the Sovereign Abenaki Nation of Missisquoi, which had a zip code that matched that of Swanton, Vermont, but was (and has always been), in many ways, an entirely different space.[1] I have been thinking lately about the meaning of such an act. We know the power of words. N. Scott Momaday reminds us in his landmark essay that "we are all" people "made of words."[2] Craig Womack, in *Red on Red*, notes that "as often as not Indian writers are trying to *invoke* as much as *evoke*." For our words, he writes, have the potential to "actually cause a change in the universe."[3] In the Abenaki language, it is quite clear that the written word has the power to create and solidify changes in the landscape.[4] I have been thinking about what it meant for so many people to write those words on a daily basis. Words that enacted recognition of our nation, all over the state of Vermont, all over New England, all over the world.

It seems a strange request for me to write this Afterword in a volume on Native literary nationalism. According to the papers manufactured by the state and nation-state that purport to have jurisdiction over

Abenaki people (Vermont and the United States) the existence of such a nation is tenuous. We do not have a reservation; we do not have a casino; we are not, as of this date, a "federally recognized tribe." When Abenaki people rose up in the 1980s to assert their continuing right to fish in the Missisquoi River, a place where families such as mine have stories that suggest that fishing is as essential to physical and cultural survival as drinking water, a court battle ensued that would last for the better part of a decade. The case began with an organized "fish-in" and rested on the doctrine of aboriginal title. Although often abrogated by treaty, removal, or federal recognition, aboriginal title represents the sovereignty that is inherent in an indigenous people's relationship to land.[5] According to U.S. law, aboriginal title exists a priori; it can be extinguished by treaty or federal proclamation, but its existence does not rely on recognition by the United States or its colonial predecessors. The doctrine recognizes the jurisdictional right of an indigenous nation in the land they have inhabited and utilized over an extremely long course of time. What made the Missisquoi case so significant was the idea that aboriginal title continues to exist (if a Native nation continues to enact it), *regardless* of whether a nation-state (in this case, the United States) had formally recognized it as such.

During the fish-in trials, the judge at the district court level gave the case a thorough hearing and deliberated carefully, concluding that the Abenaki Nation of Missisquoi and its interdependent relationship to land continued to exist long into the twentieth century *despite* colonial encroachment. The court concluded that "the State [had] failed to prove . . . that the Missisquoi abandoned or ceded their Missisquoi homeland or that their aboriginal rights were extinguished by either an express act or an act clearly and unambiguously implying any sovereign's intent to extinguish those rights. Accordingly, the Missisquoi's aboriginal right to fish in their Missisquoi homeland continues to exist today."[6] This was a huge victory for the nation. It represented recognition without relinquishment. It meant families could continue to fish without interference. It solidified, in writing, a relationship that had long existed in the daily practice and stories of Abenaki families. Powerful words, indeed.

The events that occurred in the aftermath of this decision could make for an electrifying novel or political thriller. I will give you an abbreviated version. During some of those years, I was working in the tribal office. As a repatriate and an idealistic undergraduate, I felt myself a part of a transformation in the political landscape. The tribal office, housed in an old railroad depot nearby the Missisquoi River, was a chaotic but energized place. Much of our energy went to working this case. In the meantime, tribal members faced harassment from local police, fear and opposition from local landowners and sports fishing outfits, as well as the struggle with the daily battle of poverty, lack of basic health care, the increasing encroachment of development, growing reports of diseased and mercury-laden fish, internal conflict, and despair. It seemed that everything rested on this one case. Consider what it means to understand yourselves internally as a Native nation while those governmental mechanisms that directly affect your lives literally do not see that you exist. There are advantages, if you can manage to survive. But if your resources are being directly threatened by increased development and pollution, and you have no legal recourse as a political body, the future can seem bleak indeed. In the wake of the fish-in decision, it seemed that this disempowered community might actually be able to regain control.

As the fish-in case developed, a couple of words began to circulate that threatened to cause a change in the universe: "land claim." This phrase made its way into the newspapers, into gossip networks, into law journal articles and university lectures. Title insurance companies began to add clauses that protected them against land claims by the Abenaki Nation of Missisquoi. It was those two phrases together that caused all the trouble. A lot of power resides in words. Through a series of rhetorical maneuvers, the Vermont attorney general was able to seek an appeal of the lower court decision. At the level of the Vermont Supreme Court, we saw the meticulous work of the district court judge undone. In the absence of a legal doctrine that would support colonial occupation as eradication of aboriginal title, the Court invented a concept that still haunts me to this day. I remember the day the decision came in to the tribal office. I remember seeing those little words typed on paper: the judges on the Vermont Supreme Court decided that Abenaki aboriginal title had been "extinguished . . . by the increasing weight of history."[7]

Although the court did not dispute that the "tribe" continued to exist, the judges asserted that their rights to their homeland did not. How one could separate out the "tribe" from its land, particularly when subsistence was still essential to existence, was incomprehensible to me. Imagine that . . . nations could be extinguished by . . . history. It's no wonder that for those few Abenaki people who have access to academia, the bulk of us have chosen to pursue an understanding of words, and to almost obsessively comprehend the work, and the "weight," of history.

∂

To turn for a moment to the other side of my family, it has been helpful to me, in trying to understand the weight of history and the complex character of nationalism, to draw on the stories from my mother's family as well.[8] My mother was born a "displaced person" in a Nazi labor camp, the sixth child in a Polish family that had been given the choice, in 1939, to either go with the Germans to their work camps in the east or to wait for the Russians, who would arrive shortly to ship them to their work camps in Siberia. This forced submission to the will of neighboring imperial nations had a long history. For a period of some 125 years (until the end of World War I), the nation of Poland was not allowed to exist. The political map of the landscape was divided up amongst Russia, Austria, and Prussia. I have heard that it was illegal, in some areas, to even speak the word "Poland." However, in the stories and minds of Polish families, in the music and in the attachment to land, Poland carried on. If asked, my mother will always identify herself as Polish, but she has never been to her homeland. When my mother's family came to the United States in 1950, it was not to pursue some idealized version of the American dream; they simply had no other place to go. The Soviet Union controlled their country, and they could not return. The United States was the only country that would take a family of nine "displaced persons," and then only because their relocation was sponsored by a Catholic mission. When my grandmother died and was revived by paramedics at her house in Connecticut in 1995, she yelled at her surprised saviors. She told us that, when they woke her up, she had been on the hill she had grown up on as a girl in rural Koszarawa, surrounded by flowers. She had returned home, and they had taken her away, again.

Like my Polish ancestors, my Abenaki relations have also defined nationhood differently from the imperial and colonial powers that have sought to eradicate the existence of the Native nation and its inextricable relationship to land. In the Abenaki language, as Joe Bruchac points out in his book, *Roots of Survival*, the word for "tribe" is *Negewet kamigwezo*, or "those of one family." The word for "nation," however, is *Mizi Negewet kamigwezoi*, meaning "families gathered together."[9] Thus the activity of nation-building, in the Abenaki sense, is not a means of boundary-making but rather a process of gathering from within. To echo Jace Weaver's term, it is a process of "upbuilding."[10] Historically, Abenakis are famous for cycles of gathering and dispersal within particular territories, traveling to up-country havens either to get where the hunting is good, or to avoid being hunted themselves, and then returning to central village places, to fish, to plant, and to gather.[11] When calamity hits, families may disperse, but they never "disappear." Always, they end up gathering together when the storms clear.

During the 1990s, we were involved in an intense gathering time. As families within Missisquoi solidified around the fishing case, other families arrived from all over New England, carrying stories, songs, papers, and photographs. We gathered together, exchanging words, trading stories, slowly rebuilding trust. In contemplating the power of words, I've been thinking about what it meant for my father to call me every week at the tribal office and hear about the "upbuilding" project in which I was engaged, what it meant for him to come to tribal gatherings at the old fish hatchery on the shore of Lake Champlain, back to the place, at the village center, where his own grandfather had been born, how he took me upstream to the places along the Missisquoi River where he fished as a boy, the places where they gathered berries, the delight with which he recalled the stories of huge extended family gatherings. I've been thinking about what it meant when I asked my grandfather to recall the stories of maple sugaring, rum running, and rabbit tracks that linked us with other Abenaki families along the river of his birth, what it meant for my sister to visit Missisquoi, as a teenage girl, to recognize this place in a way I never would have imagined, to come to know her name. What it has meant for me, in this lifetime, to connect my family with others whose stories we share, to gather with others who understand the literature of my family, who recognize our name.

However, I have also been thinking about the dispersal that occurred after the "weight of history" decision came down. Anyone who wanted to understand internalized oppression could have come to Missisquoi, to the tribal office in 1992–3, to witness that phenomenon in action. I don't know that lawmakers fully understand the impacts of their own decisions, but that year the "weight of history" felt like lead on our shoulders. When we raised the seemingly insurmountable sum that an appeal to the U.S. Supreme Court required, and that Court simply decided it wasn't prepared to hear the case, we were left with no legal recourse. Many other options were discussed, explored, and pursued, but ultimately, the conflict and infighting that arose with that defeat, with those words of nullification (to echo William Apess), created a dispersal.[12] It is only now, over a decade later, that it feels to me as if families are beginning to come together again. Yet, I've noticed that the decision that was handed down a decade ago did not change the perception of the families from Missisquoi. In fact, if anything, that long, drawn-out legal battle only solidified the relationship between families and the land to which we belong. And what the stories that outlast the papers say is that as long as families continue to gather in place, the nation will exist. However, as Greg Sarris observes in *Keeping Slug Woman Alive*, this gathering process is never idealistic or easy:

> Families bickering. Families arguing amongst themselves, drawing lines, maintaining old boundaries. Who is in. Who is not. Gossip. Jealousy. Drinking. Love. The ties that bind. The very human need to belong, to be worthy and valued. Families. Who is Indian. Who is not. Families bound by history and blood. This is the stuff, the fabric of my Indian community.[13]

As my father's family gathered recently around the sudden and violent death of a beloved and central woman in our extensive network of relations, I was reminded once more of how very fragile our loves and lives are, how tenuous our connections to each other in this world. The words I heard like a refrain in my own mind over the course of those days were from Simon Ortiz: "We must take great care with each other."[14] After all, family gatherings can be painful, tumultuous events. When we most need diplomacy and condolence, they can foster divisiveness and anger. I am painfully aware that our eyes and ears are not yet cleared from the violence that our families have endured. But I was grateful for and proud of my family in those days as we told the stories that would make meaning from my cousin's death. We confronted the anger and violence, the madness that was the hidden fabric beneath her carefully woven life. We reminded each other of all the things she said and did that made us laugh. We told stories that envisioned better, more hilarious versions of ourselves. A huge gap in the web of our family required the mending that only stories can do; those strands reinforce the relations between us, remind us of our shared history, let loose the laughter the gives us the reassurance that we can, as a family, endure. This, perhaps, is the essence of a Native nationalist literature, a literature that gathers families together. We turn to the stories for sustenance and meaning; they enable our survival, not just as individuals, but in the words of Samson Occom, "as one family," as a "whole."[15] As Simon Ortiz writes in his seminal essay, "Towards a National Indian Literature," "Because of the insistence to keep telling and creating stories, Indian life continues, and it is this resistance against loss that has made that life possible." As Ortiz seems to suggest, the process of "story-making" and the process of nation gathering may be one and the same.[16]

o

As my family came together for my cousin's passing, I found that the deepest and most painful of stories, as well as the most hilarious strands we wove, seemed to emerge as we gathered around my cousin's table in the evening, with scraps of food and paper, old photographs, flowers scattered haphazardly (perhaps blasphemously) across the space she had kept so neatly clean and organized. Of course, this was no surprise to the women in my family, amongst whom it is a well-known secret that the kitchen is where all the stories are made. When my sister-in-law revealed to me some time ago that she felt a little out of the loop when we went to the big extended family gatherings, I told her, "Just go help out in the kitchen." Sure enough, she returned from a gathering for which I was absent to tell me, "You're right. Everything happens in the kitchen." Once she made her way to the village center, and got in on the conversation, she felt included in the gathering. And my aunties later said to me, "You know, it was so nice that Amy came into the kitchen this year..." Tellingly, it was my cousin's unusual absence from the kitchen at the last family gathering that was the biggest signal to us that there might be something wrong. As Joy Harjo writes, reflecting a reality I now know too well: "The world begins at a kitchen table. No matter what,/we must eat to live."[17] The women in my family would surely recognize themselves in her poetic lines:

> *Our dreams drink coffee with us as they put their arms*
> *around our children. They laugh with us at our poor*
> *falling-down selves and as we put ourselves back*
> *together once again at the table...*

> *Perhaps the world will end at the kitchen table,*
> *While we are laughing and crying,*
> *Eating of the last sweet bite.*[18]

I remember well the experience of sitting at Chief Homer St. Francis's kitchen table at the village center during those turbulent years at Missisquoi. There was always lots of food (whether it was Patsy St. Francis's homemade rabbit stew or "breakfast for dinner") and lots of conversation to go around. You never knew who you might meet there, could be a fisherman who you didn't recognize at all but who turned out to be one of the guys who instigated the fish-in for which you were fighting every day. Could be a leader from another nation who came to consult or commiserate. Could be a relation, could be an enemy, could be a hungry stranger off the street. Everyone, it seemed, was welcome at Homer's table; everyone would be fed, but that didn't mean you were safe from confrontation. Many a fight broke out at the table, many a man was challenged. I remember hearing that the heads of families gathered there in the seventies and eighties to discuss their rights as Indian people. I remember the first night I sat at that table, and I stayed so late talking, I was invited to stay over, take up an extra bed, but I declined the offer. For some reason, I wanted to walk back to the tribal office, walk by the river, even though it was around 3:00 or 4:00 AM. There was something about the quiet of the night on the river. I stopped by the bridge, peered over the edge, listened. All around me, it was dark, silent, except for the ebb and flow of the water below. It was like I could hear the weight of history running past, traveling downstream.

ʘ

Many years later, when I was still trying to figure out that history, still attempting to understand the forces that seemed to tear the gathering apart, I found myself at a lot of kitchen tables, all over Indian Country. At the same time, there were gatherings of Native writers erupting in universities and conference centers, and I found myself drawn into those conversations.[19] It was interesting to me, when I later entered graduate school, that while literary critics in English departments were battling each other in the so-called "theory wars," Native writers and literary scholars were gathering together, engaging in "upbuilding," discussing the interrelatedness of their work and its implication for and in their home communities. I saw creative minds from Alaska to Mexico discussing what it meant to be a Native writer, the responsibilities and potential conflicts with home communities, the joy at reading each others' work in print, and the exhilaration of hearing those words come to life. The exchanges at those gatherings were nothing short of a feast.

When I first read Craig Womack's *Red on Red*, I recognized his voice from those gatherings, and I admired deeply the bravery of his project. To me, he was daring to bring the conversation at the kitchen table to print. At the time I was engaged in graduate study at Cornell. I remember feeling that being in a university was something akin to being in the belly of the beast, but it also offered a haven, a place away from the village where I could take the time to think. I remember being energized by a meeting in the Green Dragon Café with Robert Warrior just prior to reading Womack's work, discussing my ideas for writing a "creative" dissertation that would revolve around the voluminous writings from the Native northeast that had been repressed by the nineteenth-century American literature of vanishing. I remember him telling me that he thought many people beyond my own region would be interested in coming to know the Native northeast, that people would want to know what it was like to be Samson Occom sitting in the study of his house on Mohegan Hill, what it meant to be a writer, teacher, and leader in the midst of the Mohegan nation. I remember being grateful for his encouraging words, but I also remember doubting whether anyone would let me do this, particularly under the auspices of a department of English literature. And then I remember how reading *Red on Red* suddenly made my own project seem more possible, more achievable, more acceptable in what I perceived to be a somewhat hostile academic environment. Womack's writing enabled my own articulation, helped me to "find my talk," to echo Jace Weaver's citation of Rita Joe's poem. In short, his work gave me hope.

To turn to the subject of Womack's essay herein, I should note that my reaction to reading Elvira Pulitano's book was entirely the opposite: not only was her work discouraging, but it seemed to me that she and I had read entirely different books. I remember immediately driving over to (Abenaki poet) Cheryl Savageau's house, sitting down at her kitchen table, and before she could even make me a cup of tea, launching into what her husband Bill recognizes as a quintessential Abenaki woman's rant on what I regarded as Pulitano's ravaging simplification of Native critical perspectives (note the plural). I believe Womack does a fine job of fully articulating the problems of that text, so I won't belabor the point. In short, Pulitano's work diminishes my belief in the prospect of real dialogue, makes me *less* hopeful that our voices will be heard, and fearful that the complexity and depth of what many of us are writing about will be simplified, translated and tossed back to us in a form that says much less than what we had intended. To me, this kind of critical activity seems too close a kin to the ethnographic translation of Indian "myths," reminding me of the way those old stories got translated, simplified, slaughtered, stripped of context and meaning, to be reshaped into a recognizable artifact. It may be appealing to facilely characterize and dismiss work such as Womack's (or Warrior's, for that matter) as "nativist" or "essentialist," but to do so would be to misrepresent, or at the very least, misread the work. I would hope that sophisticated literary scholars would take care to do what I suggest to all of my students who are reading historical and literary criticism: strive to comprehend what the author is trying to communicate or argue first, before deciding what you wish to agree with or critique. I would hope that they would seek to fully understand the author's framework before applying their own critical lens to any work. One of the great privileges and downfalls of contemporary intellectual life is that we all have too much to read, and therefore, we sometimes hastily categorize a work in terms that are already familiar. I want to caution against this impulse, for my fellow critics as well as myself, because if we follow it too quickly, we might miss out on the most original and provocative of burgeoning ideas in our fields.

I suspect that critics like Pulitano, who admit to few interactions with Indian students, scholars, or their friends and families, have little conception of the pressure that is on Native scholars to conform to the models for which she advocates. I was lucky. Unlike Womack and other folks in the generation that preceded me, I was trained in a PhD program where I could take a graduate course in Native American literature every semester, with students and professors, both Native and non-Native, who had spent a lot of time at the kitchen table. I had courses in Native history and linguistics and participated in Cornell's first graduate seminar in American Indian studies, which formed the core of a newly developed graduate minor. I was interested, too, in exploring postcolonial, feminist, and other cultural theories that might help me to unpack and understand the internal dynamics that had thrown my nation into turmoil, the colonial politics that allowed for a state to erase us with a phrase as enigmatic as "the weight of history," and the stories that would allow for restoration. I did a great deal of gathering in those years. Many of my professors insisted that the theories they taught would provide the best route for my thinking, and I was told over and over again that my work needed to be comparative and had to engage with critical theory, so that my scholarship would be "marketable." But, to paraphrase Scott Momaday (quoting William Gass), I wasn't writing for myself (and my potential career), because that would have been "self-serving"; I wasn't writing for my audience (here, I suppose, literary critics and the departments that might or might not offer me a job), because that would be "pandering." I was writing "for the thing that was trying to be born."[29] Like Robert Warrior (in his discussion of Said), I learned from and drew on what I learned in those classes in literary and cultural theory. But those theories were not enough. Ultimately, I had to return to the gathering place in order to find the theories and methodologies that allowed me to answer the questions with which I was most concerned. I found those answers in Native space, in the networks of Native

writers in the northeast, in the complexity of language and oral literature, and in conversation with the network of relations, writers, and
intellectuals that is alive and flourishing today. Without them, without
those kitchen table conversations both inside and outside of class, this
thing called "The Common Pot" would not have been born. Perhaps
those models for which Pulitano advocates seem quite radical and liberatory in relation to the mainstream, or to the history of European and
American philosophical thought. That, I'm sure, is true. However, if we
limit ourselves to the culture of academia, or to that of literary criticism,
those methodologies for which she advocates seem to me fairly conventional, even hegemonic, to use the lingua franca of our discipline. To
strike out on our own self-determined paths, developing methodologies
that seek to interpret and read literature of our own choosing based on
models drawn from our own, often collective, knowledge and experience, that seems pretty liberating to me. I think I can say that all six of
Pulitano's chosen subjects have done just that, and I would honor them
all for that achievement. Thankfully, I find myself able to do this without creating a hierarchy of difference, or a "great chain of being," as
Craig Womack suggests herein, a methodology, I should note, which has
fairly ancient roots itself.

Returning fondly to my graduate school memories, I want to contrast Pulitano's organizing framework with that of Jace Weaver's in his
introduction to *That the People Might Live*. I remember sitting in that
first graduate seminar in American Indian studies discussing the book
with my colleagues. I told them that one of the reasons I liked Weaver's
work was because he seemed to bring the conversation amongst critics
and writers in Native American literary studies to the page. I could see
the way he was drawing lines between them, setting voices up in dialogue with each other, creating a space for interaction and even, perhaps,
synthesis. Over the years, I've found Weaver's introduction particularly
useful for teaching students who are new to the field, giving them the
opportunity to pick up on the conversations in the landscape of Native
literature and providing a foundation from which to begin addressing
the critical and historical problems with which, as Robert Warrior points
out herein, all of us who enter the field are faced. In contrast, Pulitano's
framework fails to create a space where multiple voices can be heard.

Instead, she assumes the role of ventriloquist and puppeteer. Rather than placing the work of Native literary critics in dialogue, in relation to each other, in a network of critique and exchange, she divides these critics into individual slots, and then puts them in a hierarchical order, performing, to my mind, a recolonization, an allotment and redistribution, a process of ordering and containment. The worst part is that I have my doubts as to whether Pulitano is aware of the implications of her own methodological framework. If she had brought her work to the kitchen table, however, she certainly would have become aware of those implications, and quite early on. She might have found herself sitting there alone until she made some really good stew that drew everyone back to the table. I hope that, given her level of intelligence, she would have come to understand far more before she decided to commit this work to print. You see, I am advocating that she should have come to the kitchen table not for our sake, but her own.

⟡

To turn from theoretical grounds to more pragmatic ones, I want to speak to the usefulness of literary nationalist approaches in teaching. I now find myself back in New England, living close to my family, and teaching Native American literature and history to a mix of Native and non-Native students who constantly keep me on my intellectual toes.[21] I cannot express how valuable it is to have tribally specific readings of Native texts in the classroom. I can give my students an incredibly rich, complex, and detailed understanding of the political, cultural, historical, and literary landscape of the northeast, but when it comes to other regions, I am particularly grateful for the guidance of scholars such as Craig Womack and Daniel Justice, who are immersed in those areas. Although I am not Creek or Cherokee, I teach Creek and Cherokee literatures, and the work of these scholars has enabled me to teach them in a way that is much more complex, profound, and knowledgeable than before these books existed. Maybe other gatherers are more skilled, but I could not possibly develop a full knowledge of all of the regions about which I teach, even if I had a lifetime's worth of traveling and the trust and opportunity to learn from the best plant folks around. I find the accusations of isolationism and exclusiveness to be particularly ironic given that one of the most encouraging aspects of this field is the generosity of its practitioners in their willingness to gather and distribute for us all.

This past fall, I taught a course called "Native American Literature: Narrations of Nationhood," a seminar that was built around the idea that the imagination of nations is a continuing communal process, in which narration, including writing and literature, plays a strong role. It was organized regionally and relied on tribally specific readings and criticism. As a newly conceptualized course, it was an experiment in which the whole class was engaged. During the course of the class, I noticed that the Native students in particular were especially pleased to see theirs and others' tribally specific traditions explained eloquently and with complexity in texts like *Red on Red* (which, you all know, is not always the case with academic texts about Indians). So many of my questions from Native students reflected their own interests in finding out how things are done in different nations, and what the histories and cultural traditions have been in different regions, as well as their desire to increase their knowledge and engage in analysis of their own regional and tribal histories and traditions. They were equally interested in thinking about how other Native intellectuals have grappled with the problems and questions with which they are faced and did not hesitate to challenge those with whom they disagreed. While I certainly deal with issues of representation, most Native students already know way too much about how they have been represented, stereotyped, and utilized by American literature and history. In fact, this is something that I always have to teach with a strong sense of irony and humor, because on so many levels, the figure of "the Indian" is just tired. In my experience, non-Native students, too, are often intellectually paralyzed by the endless circular gymnastics of representation, but find themselves empowered as writers and scholars when they can rely on the political, historical, and cultural traditions of specific nations to guide their readings and their writings. They can put writers from particular regions and nations in conversation, in conflict, use them to illuminate each other. With the aid of tribally specific teaching and criticism, students can, with great skill and complexity, unpack the many layers of a poem like Harjo's "The Flood" or "A Map to the Next World" with an understanding of the many overlapping worlds that exist simultaneously in the space of the poem, speaking to Creek, Navajo, Iroquois, and urban Indian contexts that intersect with and illuminate each other, without needing to rely on a simplifying framework that suggests that the characters, speakers, or authors of the poem are "caught between" anything. All of the students in this course seemed to prefer grappling with the complexity of the texts on their own terms, rather than moving to explain them only through the frameworks they have gained from studying cultural theory.[22] What is most interesting to me is the way the students in the class turned that lens around, as they took frameworks drawn from treaty literature, oral traditions, and contemporary criticism and began to apply them to other literatures, histories, and contemporary issues, treating Native American writers as sophisticated intellectuals who have something to say to the world at large, as well as to their tribally specific communities.]

I remain befuddled as to why literary nationalism represents such a controversial approach for literary studies. To compare to another field, it has long been accepted practice for scholars to focus on particular regions or nations when doing Native American history.[23] Furthermore, we have long had fields designated British, French, and German literature, so why would writing a book on Creek or Cherokee literature, particularly given the extensive literary output of these nations, be so controversial? And who better than someone who is from that nation to write about its national literature? Why would suggesting that these literatures might be able to stand on their own as literary traditions be a move that suggests alienating or excluding someone? I am Abenaki, and I do not feel excluded by such work (and I'm a fairly sensitive person). Nowhere does Craig Womack say that only Creeks can write about Creek literature, or that only Natives can write about Native literature. If some critics *feel* excluded, or sense that exclusion is *implied*, perhaps it would be a useful exercise to engage in the kind of personalized critical exploration exemplified by Greg Sarris in *Keeping Slug Woman Alive*, where he explores the feelings and senses he experiences in reaction to statements made by Pomo grandmothers like Mabel McKay and Violet Chappell. (I am not being facetious here; I truly think this would be worthwhile.) Just as I admire Womack's boldness in bringing the kitchen table to academia, I admire Sarris's brave honesty in revealing and discussing his own position at the kitchen table, his willingness to expose his inability to peel potatoes, his lack of knowledge, and his attempts at gathering. However, I would never want Womack to write Sarris's book, or vice versa. I would never suggest that either is the "more subversive" way to do Native scholarship. I am thankful for the presence of both of these models in the world. But, to return to my own befuddlement, I want to ask, why is it so offensive to suggest that a Creek might have more insight into Creek literature than a non-Creek, or that contemporary Creek concerns might be relevant to Creek literature and literary scholarship, particularly given the invisibility and displacement of such literatures and concerns from the mainstream? Is it not a worthy goal to attempt, as Warrior suggests, to "be methodologically self-conscious in attending to perspectives that ha[ve] been ignored, debased, discounted, and marginalized"?[24] Is it the tone of Womack's book that gets under people's skins? Again, to me, that tone is recognizable, because it comes directly from the kitchen table. In my family, if you are getting teased, you know you are part of the group. Or is it the insistence that the group, the family, the notion of nationhood still exists? Is it the refusal to be the subject of the scholar and the State? Is it the very persistence of indigenous nationalism in the age of globalization that remains a disturbing reminder of what many wish to regard as the colonial past?

o

I want to turn now to the notion of hybridity, and to a concept that I believe may be much more useful for conceptualizing the ongoing activity of transformation within Native space, including those changes that have taken place in relation to colonization. One of the central problems with the way hybridity theory has been applied to Native texts is that it does not seem to account for the relationship between community and land. Rather, culture and identity seem to rest within the individual "subject," who seems oddly out of place, displaced, caught between two assumed worlds or perspectives that are so intertwined that they no longer exist independently of each other. Okay, fine, but where does relationship to land figure into all of this? Is this a way to basically say that we are all native to this land because European and Native American cultures are so intertwined as to melt together into a single multicultural mass? Has assimilation and the extinguishment of aboriginal title been accomplished? Should we just drop our tribal delusions and go home? That is . . . if home could then ever be found.

When I was a visiting instructor at Colorado College, I was very grateful that my apartment was located nearby a pond that had a resident heron, as well as a family of beavers. I admit that I only liked it because it reminded me of home, made me feel less out of place in that wide expanse of a western city. I took my students there on the last day of class so they would understand what I was talking about when I emphasized the notion of adaptation.[25] Those beavers who moved into that tiny man-made pond made that place their own. Like the beavers back home who reclaim a marshy field once occupied by their ancestors by recognizing beaver space, those western victims of relocation and termination, logging and development, were able to recognize a beaver pond, whether they came from up in the mountains or a nearby urban haven. Pretty good deal, too, considering how little dam-building would be involved. Visitors to the park usually wouldn't see the family there, because they didn't expect to see beavers in their landscape, and that family, they kept to themselves. They would usually only come out when no one else was around. Even their lodge was carefully disguised to become a part of the small brushy island that afforded some cover. My students didn't see them at first, either, and then they couldn't figure out how those beavers, assumed vanished, had gotten there in the first place. "They must have been relocated from elsewhere," one said. Another responded, "But why would they want beavers here? They will probably block the drains and eat up the vegetation." "And why would they stay?" another wondered. That's when we turned to the reading for the day, Leslie Silko's *Gardens in the Dunes*, to the pages at the end of the novel that describe young Indigo's garden, a lovely working mix of indigenous plants and transplants she's gathered in her travels, where "bright ribbons of purple, red, yellow, and black gladiolus flowers" are "woven crisscross over the terrace gardens, through the amaranth, pole beans, and sunflowers."[26] This place in the desert dunes of the Arizona/ California border is a location that Silko purposefully does not name, evoking all of those Native places and histories that were not marked by reservation boundaries or American catalogues, that remained *recognizable* only to those families who had always gathered there.

The novel begins with a portrait of the child Indigo amongst her Sand Lizard family in the dunes, learning to tend plants under her grandmother's tutelage. Although the family must disperse when the forces of colonization enter their Native space, its members separated and displaced, Indigo and her sister find their way back to the gathering place and begin to build a new family from within. Drawing on the knowledge she has gained during her travels across two continents, Indigo finds new uses for "the old gardens," cultivating the seemingly ornamental gladiolus as companions to the indigenous plants, and as the irises transform in relationship to the landscape and to Indigo's tending, the extended family finds the new plants useful for trade as well as food. Their friends, the twin sisters, use the flowers' unusual beauty to repair relations with the churchgoers in the city, a move that protects them in their place, and Indigo offers the twins a stew made with "tasty" gladiolus spuds when they come to visit.[27] In the changing landscape, "those flowers turned out to be quite valuable after all." Silko's vision of adaptation and regeneration within the landscape is encapsulated in one of the novel's final passages:

> When the girls returned to the old gardens the winter before, Grandma Fleet's dugout house was in good condition but terrible things had been done at the spring . . . Strangers had come to the old gardens; at the spring, for no reason they slaughtered the big old rattlesnake who lived there; then they chopped down the small apricot trees above Grandma Fleet's grave.
>
> That day they returned, the twins helped Sister Salt and Indigo gather up hundreds of delicate rib bones to give old Grandfather Snake a proper burial next to Grandma Fleet. They all wept as they picked up his bones, but Indigo wept harder when she looked at the dried remains of the little apricot trees hacked to death with the snake.
>
> Today Indigo and Linnaeus ran ahead of the others with the parrot flying ahead of her. At the top of the sandy slope she stopped and knelt in the sand by the stumps of the apricot trees, and growing out of the base of one stump were leafy

green shoots. Who knew such a thing was possible last winter when they cried their eyes sore over the trees?[28]

Silko's imagery—of springs, of snakes, of leafy green shoots—speaks of the regenerative capability of this particular landscape, which is nothing more, or less, than the combined activity of all of its inhabitants, including humans, who can tend it like a garden or conquer it like an enemy, who have interdependent relationships with the plants and other living beings that grow up from within the place, regardless of whether they acknowledge those relationships or not. All of these beings adapt and change within the landscape, thereby transforming the "garden" itself. This is an ongoing activity in which we have always been engaged, and in which we will engage as long as we are part of this earth. As I've learned myself, from watching those closest to me regenerate and die, the hope for transformation and adaptation, for survival within the land, lies within the regenerative ability of the land itself. And it is stories that make meaning of those changes, allow experience to be translated into expression. It is literature that gives life to the words, solidifies them in the landscape, allows them to be gathered and carried on.

Over the last few decades, we have seen a remarkable change in the landscape here in northern New England, a recovery that has paralleled the regathering of families in this place. I look out now on a forest that hosts nearly every animal and plant that is indigenous to this land, with many additions that are well adapted to its changing form. There are enduring threats to its continuance, to be sure, but who could have envisioned, a hundred years ago, that the forests would return to claim the towns and fields? That the beavers would return to re-create the marshes and ponds? That coyotes would come from the west, mate with wolves on their journey, and begin to be transformed by this landscape themselves, so that even my young nieces, when reading an old story, call out the name of the eastern coyote when they see a picture of wolf? Who could have predicted, at that moment of nadir, that Abenaki families would gather together in old village places to reproclaim their place as a nation? There will be stories told about this remarkable time, I am sure, for many generations to come. And to be truthful, there have always been stories about this time; it's just that those stories have been kept quietly, tended carefully, so that one day, they would be able to feed the whole. The process of recognition belongs to them.[29]

O

I'll admit that talk of nationalism makes me wary. For me, like many, it calls to mind the setting of boundaries, both physical and cultural, and defending those boundaries with force. It calls to mind the sounds and images of patriotism and jingoism that have been so destructive and detrimental to both sides of my family. It recalls the potential for violence. As a typical big sister, as the daughter of a war survivor, and now, as an auntie, such proclamations cause me unease. However, I have a different kind of nationalism in mind, which I hope lies in concert with the calls of those within: a nationalism that is not based on the theoretical and physical models of the nation-state; a nationalism that is not based on notions of nativism or binary oppositions between insider and outsider, self and other; a nationalism that does not root itself in an idealization of any pre-Contact past, but rather relies on the multifaceted, lived experience of families who gather in particular places; a nationalism that may be unlike any of those with which most literary critics and cultural theorists are familiar. As envisioned herein, American Indian Literary Nationalism is a dynamic model that posits the existence of a field of Native American literature and supports (but does not advocate exclusively for) scholarship that draws on theoretical and epistemological models that arise from indigenous languages and literatures, as well as the many, varied, complex, and changing modes in which Native nations have operated on the ground, in particular places, over a wide expanse of time.[30]

Like the gathering and dispersal of families, the gathering and dispersal of knowledge must be "processual," as both Robert Warrior and Jace Weaver suggest, and adaptive. As Warrior adds herein, we cannot merely focus on the "gathering of information" but "on creating frameworks in which to understand the broad ways in which knowledge has operated ideologically and politically in bringing the Native world to the state in which it currently exists."[31] Gathering is a process in which we are engaged, an activity that sustains us and our families. Yet, like the gathering of plants, intellectual and artistic gathering relies on carefully considered knowledge of the landscape and our impacts on it. Gathering without knowledge could get you and yours sick, could purge you. Gathering without foresight can destroy the roots of the very plants on which we rely for nurturance and healing. Gathering also requires distribution. One does not gather merely for oneself. Even my niece, who is only six, knows this. She is excited to share her knowledge of plants with her older cousins, but is cautionary with them, telling them how and why the plant should be taken, and what should be given back. American Indian Literary Nationalism is a model that does not view knowledge as something to be gathered within a vessel and preserved, or as a process of steady accumulation, of ever-growing accuracy or progress. Rather this gathering relies on a process of exchange, which will constantly shape and change the state of the field. It requires careful tending and nurturing. It requires a continual give and take. Sometimes it will require us to gather together; sometimes we will only want to go out in small groups, to avoid damaging the plants or scaring away our fellow inhabitants; sometimes we will have to disperse, go our own ways, with the knowledge that we will always return. I want to see what kind of "national" space we might build, if the tools, methods, and materials are not "determined for us," in Jace Weaver's words, but rather we are allowed the intellectual freedom to determine this process for ourselves.

To those who might think that I am excluding them from this process, I urge you not to jump to such conclusions. I ask you to listen for a few minutes more. To those who would dismiss this volume because it appears to advocate for an exclusionary model, or one that is isolationist or provincial, I ask you to consider carefully "the weight of history." As Robert Warrior demonstrates herein, "Everyone . . . who takes up the task of researching and writing about the indigenous world comes into an arena of inquiry already left in ruins by generations of bad faith." Undoing this legacy is a burden we all share. What happens when we consider "literary nationalism" or "intellectual sovereignty," as I believe the writers have herein, not only in relation to the ideals of literary cosmopolitanism or humanistic inclusiveness, but in relation to assimilation and its coercive, often violent, history? Can we take a moment to consider the actual experiences of Native nations in relation to this American ideal? What happens when we consider the rhetoric of deconstruction in light of the policy of Termination or the extant legal doctrine of extinguishment? Until Native literatures and histories, and in particular, Native voices, are part of the curriculum, until they rise to the surface of common knowledge, I believe we may have many misunderstandings of the intent and purpose of Native American literary criticism, as with the example of Pulitano's work critiqued herein. Despite all the rhetorical claims of "hybridity," it does sometimes seem as if we are speaking from different worlds, and it is Native critics who are so often called on to play the role of translator, who are asked to travel from the village center to the academic council and explain themselves. In writing the books that we have, and in writing this volume that you are reading now, I believe that we are inviting everyone to make their way to the kitchen table, to come to the gathering place. I am not saying that you (or we) will always be welcome there, given the weight of history, or that it will be an easy journey, but I can promise that there will be some food and good conversation waiting for those who come willing to listen, and to reciprocate, in turn.

o

Notes

1. Missisquoi is an Abenaki village on the northeast shore of *Bitabagw*, or Lake Champlain, that has been continually occupied by Abenaki families for over twelve thousand years. During the seventeenth and eighteenth centuries, it also served as a refuge for many Algonquian families who were escaping colonial wars and was the main site from which the famous war leader, Grey Lock, launched his reclamation raids of Massachusetts settlements. On paper, the "Abenaki Nation at Missisquoi" leased a large swath of land on the Missisquoi River to James Robertson in 1765, which was supposed to expire after one hundred years. In the wake of the violence of the French and Indian wars, the American Revolution, and the colonial settlement of the Green Mountain boys and their cohort, Abenakis went underground but remained steadfastly in their old territories. The subsistence and family-centered communal lifestyle of Abenaki families continued to exist, despite the development of the state of Vermont and the Union to which it belonged, long into the twentieth century, when the combined

effects of the Vermont Eugenics program of the 1920s and '30s (which resulted in the sterilization and institutionalization of countless Abenaki people), the establishment of the Missisquoi Wildlife Refuge in the 1940s, the subsequent increase in surveillance by Fish and Wildlife officials, and rising development in the region forced the leadership to seek alternatives outside of the community. At the same time, tremendous political changes in Indian Country, from the fish-ins on the Northwest coast, to Wounded Knee II, to increasing political activity amongst neighboring nations to the east and south, provided an opening for Abenaki voices to address the outside world. For additional information, see, for instance, Colin G. Calloway, *The Western Abenakis of Vermont, 1600–1800: War, Migration, and the Survival of an Indian People* (Norman: University of Oklahoma Press, 1990); William A. Haviland and Marjory W. Power, *The Original Vermonters: Native Inhabitants, Past and Present*, Rev., expanded ed. (Hanover, HG: University Press of New England, 1994); Frederick Matthew Wiseman, *The Voice of the Dawn: An Autohistory of the Abenaki Nation* (Hanover, NH: University Press of New England, 2001).

2. N. Scott Momaday, "The Man Made of Words," in *The Remembered Earth*, ed. Geary Hobson (Albuquerque: University of New Mexico Press, 1981), 162.

3. Craig S. Womack, *Red on Red: Native American Literary Separatism* (Minneapolis: University of Minnesota Press, 1999), 17.

4. I have written about the words *awikhigan* and *awikhigawôgan* in my dissertation, "The Common Pot: Indigenous Writing and the Reconstruction of Native Space in the Northeast" (PhD diss., Cornell University, 2004). While *awikhigan* represents writing that has become manifest, words or images that have taken shape, solidified (a book, a map, a letter), *awikhigawôgan* is the activity of writing, drawing, or mapping, something in which we are engaged.

5. Aboriginal title "arises from a tribe's occupation of a definable, ancestral homeland before the onset of European colonization . . . the validity of aboriginal title is not dependent on treaty, statute, or other formal government recognition . . . the phrase 'aboriginal title' or 'Indian title' describes the ownership interest retained by Native Americans in lands which European nations appropriated." *State of Vermont vs. Raleigh Elliot, et al.* (1992)

6. *State of Vermont vs. Harold St. Francis, et al.* (1989)

7. Vermont vs. Eliot.

8. This story represents only one example of how, as Womack points out herein, the concept of a monolithic Europe is just as problematic as that of a monolithic Native America.

9. Joseph Bruchac, *Roots of Survival* (Golden, CO: Fulcrum, 1996), 30.

10. Jace Weaver, chapter 1 of this volume, 6.

11. See, for example, Bruchac, *Roots of Survival*; Colin G. Calloway, *The Western Abenakis of Vermont, 1600–1800*; Gordon M. Day, *The Identity of the Saint Francis Indians* (Ottawa, ON: National Museums of Canada, 1981); William A. Haviland and Marjory W. Power, *The Original Vermonters*; and Frederick Matthew Wiseman, *The Voice of the Dawn*.

12. See William Apess, *Indian Nullification of the Unconstitutional Laws of Massachusetts Relative to the Mashpee Tribe; or The Pretended Riot Explained*, in *On Our Own Ground: The Complete Writings of William Apess, a Pequot*, Barry O'Connell, ed. (Amherst: University of Massachusetts Press, 1992).

13. Greg Sarris, *Keeping Slug Woman Alive: A Holistic Approach to American Indian Texts* (Berkeley: University of California Press, 1993), 117.

14. Simon J. Ortiz, *The People Shall Continue* (San Francisco: Children's Book Press, 1988). I first encountered this line in Jace Weaver's *That the People Might Live: Native American Literatures and Native American Community*.

15. Samson Occom Papers, Folder 16: "Records of the Mohegan Tribe," Connecticut Historical Society, Hartford, Connecticut. See also Lisa Brooks, "The Common Pot," Chapter 2.

16. Simon J. Ortiz, "Towards a National Indian Literature: Cultural Authenticity in Nationalism," *MELUS* 8.2 (1981): 11.

17. Joy Harjo, *The Woman Who Fell From the Sky* (New York: W. W. Norton, 1996), 68.

18. Ibid., 69.

19. I should relate that one gathering truly led to another. It was two writers from my own nation, Joe Bruchac and Cheryl Savageau, who were responsible for drawing me into these larger circles of

Native writers. I think it is entirely likely that without them, I would probably still be holed up in a cabin in New Hampshire, covered under pages of writing that nearly no one was reading but myself.

20. Hartwig Isernhagen, *Momaday, Vizenor, Armstrong: Conversations on American Indian Writing* (Norman: University of Oklahoma Press, 1999), 35.

21. I agree with Craig Womack that teaching about the nonexistence of the Indian in a class full of Native students would be a good way to find yourself sitting alone at the kitchen table. Again, let me remind you of the very real impact of legal decisions that seek to eradicate the existence of Indian nations, not to speak of the physical dispossessions and acts of violence that wage this battle on human bodies.

22. That Native American literatures "deserve to be judged by their own criteria, in their own terms" is one of the key arguments, of course, of Womack's *Red on Red* (242–43).

23. The well-known and well respected historian Colin Calloway began his career with a history of my nation, the manuscript of which I remember passing around during those old days at Missisquoi in a yellow three-ring binder. I remember reading it with great interest when I was working on my own undergraduate thesis in a trailer in St. Albans, Vermont; his scholarship was welcome in the community, and its impact on my own sense of nationhood was significant. I distinctly remember coming to work one day to find him sitting on the couch in the tribal office, chatting with the chief, the tribal judge, and the tribal historian. To me, the quality of his work reflects not only his own immense intelligence and aptitude for research, but his willingness to sit at the kitchen table, his engagement with Native individuals and communities over the long course of his career. My argument is not that scholars of Native American history and literature *must* engage with Native people, but rather, that, as scholars, our work is enriched when we do. This is true, as Jace Weaver points out, for both Native and non-Native scholars alike.

24. Robert Warrior, in chapter 3 of this volume, 195.

25. I purposefully want to juxtapose the linguistic roots of these two terms for your contemplation. Note these definitions from Webster's:

> *adaptation*, n. 1. the act of adapting or the state of being adapted. 2. something produced by adapting: an adaptation of a

play for television. 3.a. any beneficial alteration in an organism
resulting from natural selection by which the organism survives
and multiplies in an environment. b. a form or structure
modified to fit a changed environment. c. the ability of a species
to survive in a particular ecological niche, esp. because of
alterations of form or behavior brought about through natural
selection. 4. the decrease in response of sensory receptor organs,
as those of vision or touch, to changed, constantly applied
environmental conditions. 5. the regulating by the pupil of the
quantity of light entering the eye. 6. a slow, usu. unconscious
modification of individual or collective behavior in adjusting
to cultural surroundings. [1600–10]
  adapt, v.t. 1.to make suitable to requirements or conditions;
adjust or modify fittingly. 2. to adjust oneself to different
conditions, environment, etc. [1605–15; Latin *adaptare*, to
fit, adjust]
  hybrid, n. 1. the offspring of two animals or plants of
different breeds, varieties, or species, esp. as produced through
human manipulation for specific genetic characteristics. 2. a
person produced by the interaction or crossbreeding of two
unlike cultures, traditions, etc. 3. anything derived from unlike
sources, or composed of disparate or incongruous elements;
composite. 4. a word composed of elements originally drawn
from different languages, as *television*, whose components come
from Greek and Latin. *adj.* 5. bred from two distinct races,
breeds, varieties, or species. 6. composite; formed or composed
of heterogeneous elements. [1595–1605; Latin *hybrida*, a
crossbred animal]
Note that the word "hybrid" assumes the existence of two pure,
authentic, and disparate originals prior to the new being that is
formed, whereas the notion of adaptation relies on a dynamic,
interactive relationship between a being and its changing environment.
These reflections on adaptation and hybridity are part of a larger
project that explores the concept of adaptation as a theoretical
model for conceptualizing relational identity and cultural survival.
Random House Webster's College Dictionary (New York: Random
House, 1997), 15, 638.

26. Leslie Marmon Silko, *Gardens in the Dunes* (New York: Simon & Schuster, 1999), 474.

27. Ibid., 476.

28. Ibid.

29. The concept of adaptation that I have been foregrounding here has been prominent within Native American literary studies for some time. All of the authors herein highlight the adaptability of Native communities in their scholarship. In his essay herein, Jace Weaver notes that "Native cultures have always been highly adaptive, and they continue to evolve constantly." He rightly observes,

> Native interest in incorporating elements from other cultures long predated European encounter. Vast trading networks carried goods throughout North America, and trade argots were developed to facilitate commerce—all before any had seen a white man. Natives showed themselves adept at adopting and adapting anything that seemed to be useful or to have power (Chapter 1, 29).

This process of adaptation and adoption did not begin, but rather continued, when Europeans entered Native space. In "Towards a National Indian Literature," Ortiz writes of the way in which the incorporation of Catholic saints' days into ceremonial life at Acqumah "speak[s] of the creative ability of Indian people to gather in many forms of the socio-political colonizing force which beset them and then make these forms meaningful in their own terms." He notes that,

> because in every case where European culture was cast upon Indian people of this nation there was similar creative response and development, it can be observed that this was the primary element of a nationalistic impulse to make use of foreign ritual, ideas, and material in their own—Indian—terms. Today's writing by Indian authors is a continuation of that elemental impulse (8).

In speaking of the revitalization of Native culture during the latter half of the twentieth century, Robert Warrior writes in *Tribal Secrets*,

> The return to tradition . . . cannot in Deloria's analysis be an unchanging and unchangeable set of activities, but must be a part of the life of a community as it struggles to exercise its sovereignty. . . . To understand what the "real meaning" of traditional revitalization is, then, American Indians must realize that the power of those traditions is not in their formal superiority

but in their *adaptability* to new challenges (Robert Allen Warrior, *Tribal Secrets: Recovering American Indian Intellectual Traditions* [Minneapolis: University of Minnesota Press, 1994], 93–94, my emphasis).

Finally, Craig Womack argues in *Red on Red*,

> I wish to posit an alternative definition of traditionalism as anything that is useful to Indian people in retaining their values and worldviews, no matter how much it deviates from what people did one or two hundred years ago. The nostalgic anthropological view, by contrast, creates a self-fulfilling prophecy. Only cultures that are able to *adapt* to change remain living cultures; otherwise they become no longer relevant and are abandoned. Yet anthropology often prioritizes the "pristine." Anthrospeak claims that things must be recorded because they are soon to die out, yet the anthropological definition of culture denies cultures the very thing that will allow them to survive: the possibility of changing and evolving with the times [and the place within which they operate]. Literature . . . allows for this kind of creative change (42, my emphasis and addition in brackets).

30. Let me join with my fellow contributors in reiterating that this is not to say that Native American literature is not in dialogue, influenced by, and influential on American or Canadian literature, but rather to insist that its complexity and specificity, its diversity within, and its divergence from without warrants its recognition as a full body of literature that is much more than a margin or extension of American literature, and demands interpretation and critique, in Craig Womack's words, "in its own terms" (*Red on Red*, 242).

31. See Warrior, Chapter 3, 198–99.

Towards a National Indian Literature

Cultural Authenticity in Nationalism

Simon J. Ortiz*

*U*ncle Steve—Dzeerlai, which was his Acqumeh name—was not a literate man and he certainly was not literary. He is gone now, into the earth and back north as the Acqumeh people say, but I remember him clearly. He was a subsistence farmer, and he labored for the railroad during his working years; I remember him in his grimy working clothes. But I remember him most vividly as he sang and danced and told stories—not literary stories, mind you, but it was all literature nonetheless.

On fiesta days, Steve wore a clean, good shirt and a bright purple or blue or red neckerchief knotted at his tightly buttoned shirt collar. Prancing and dipping, he would wave his beat-up hat, and he would holler, Juana, Juana! Or Pedro, Pedro! It would depend on which fiesta day it was, and other men and younger ones would follow his lead. Juana! Pedro! It was a joyous and vigorous sight to behold, Uncle Dzeerlai expressing his vitality from within the hold of our Acqumeh Indian world.

---

*Originally published in *MELUS* 8.2 (summer 1981).

There may be some question about why Uncle Steve was shouting Juana and Pedro, obviously Spanish names, non-Indian names. I will explain. In the summer months of June, July, and August, there are in the Pueblo Indian communities of New Mexico celebrations of Catholic saints' days. Persons whose names are particular saints' names honor those names by giving to the community and its people. In turn, the people honor those names by receiving. The persons named after the saints such as John or Peter—Juan, Pedro—throw from housetops gifts like bread, cookies, crackerjacks, washcloths, other things, and the people catching and receiving dance and holler the names. It will rain then and the earth will be sustained; it will be a community fulfilled in its most complete sense of giving and receiving, in one word: sharing. And in sharing, there is strength and continuance.

But there is more than that here. Obviously, there is an overtone that this is a Catholic Christian ritual celebration because of the significance of the saints' name and days on the Catholic calendar. But just as obviously, when the celebration is held within the Acqumeh community, it is an Acqumeh ceremony. It is Acqumeh and Indian (or Native American or American Indian if one prefers those terms) in the truest and most authentic sense. This is so because this celebration speaks of the creative ability of Indian people gather in many forms of the socio-political colonizing force which beset them and to make these forms meaningful in their own terms. In fact, it is a celebration of the human spirit and the Indian struggle for liberation.

Many Christian religious rituals brought to the Southwest (which in the 16th century was the northern frontier of the Spanish New World) are no longer Spanish. They are now Indian because of the creative development that the native people applied to them. Present-day Native American or Indian literature is evidence of this in the very same way. And because in every case where European culture was cast upon Indian people of this nation there was similar creative response and development, it can be observed that this was the primary element of a nationalistic impulse to make use of foreign ritual, ideas, and material in their own—Indian—terms. Today's writing by Indian authors is a continuation of that elemental impulse.

Let me tell you more about Dzeerlai. I have a memory of him as he and other men sang at one Acqumeh event. He is serious and his face is concentrated upon the song, meaning, and the event that is taking place during this particular afternoon in early September. Santiago and Chapiyuh have come to Acqu. They enter from the south, coming exactly upon the route that Juan de Onate's soldiers took when they razed Acqu in the winter of 1598.

Santiago was the patron saint of the Spanish soldiers, and the name seemed to have been their war cry as well. On this afternoon, as he steps upon the solid stone of Acqu, Santiago is dressed in ostentatious finery. His clothes have a sheen and glitter that anyone can marvel at and envy. He wears a cowboy ten-gallon hat and there are heavy revolvers strapped to his hips. The spurs on his fancy boots jingle and spin as he and his horse prance about. As Santiago waves a white-gloved hand at the crowds of Acqumeh people lining his route and grins ludicrously with a smile painted rigidly on a pink face, the people still marvel but they check their envy. They laugh at Santiago and the hobby horse steed stuck between his legs.

Alongside, and slightly behind to his right, is another figure, Chapiyuh. His name is abrupt in the mouth. He doesn't walk; he stomps as he wears heavy leather thick-soled boots like a storm-trooper. Chapiyuh has a hood over his face with slits cut in it for eyes. He wears the dark flowing robes of a Franciscan priest secured with a rough rope at his waist. In one hand Chapiyuh carries a bullwhip which he cracks or a length of chain, and in the other hand he carried the book, the Bible. As he stomps along heavily, he makes threatening gestures to the people and they shrink away. Children whimper and cling desperately to their mothers' dresses.

There are prayer narratives for what is happening, and there are songs. Uncle Steven and his partners sang for what was happening all along the route that Santiago and Chapiyuh took into Acqu. It is necessary that there be prayer and song because it is important, and no one will forget then; no one will regard it as less than momentous. It is the only way in which event and experience, such as the entry of the Spaniard to the Western Hemisphere, can become significant and realized in the people's own terms. And this, of course, is what happens in literature, to bring about meaning and meaningfulness. This perception and meaningfulness has to happen; otherwise, the hard experience of the Euroamerican colonization of the lands and people of the Western Hemisphere would be driven into the dark recesses of the indigenous mind and psyche. And this kind of repression is always a poison and detriment to creative growth and expression.

As one can see, most of this perception and expression has been possible through the oral tradition which includes prayer, song, drama-ritual, narrative or story-telling, much of it within ceremony—some of it outside of ceremony—which is religious and social. Indeed, through the past five centuries the oral tradition has been the most reliable method by which Indian culture and community integrity have been maintained. And, certainly, it is within this tradition that authenticity is most apparent and evident.

Uncle Steve and his singer-partners were naturally authentic as they sought to make a lesson of history significant, and they did so within the context of the Acqumeh community. There is no question of the authenticity of the ritual drama in that case. But there is more than the context that makes the drama—and any subsequent literary expression of it—authentic. Steve was only one in a long line of storytellers and singers who have given expression to the experience of Indian people in the Americas. Throughout the difficult experience of colonization to the present, Indian women and men have struggled to create meaning of their lives in very definite and systematic ways. The ways or methods have been important, but they are important only because of the reason for the struggle. And it is that reason—the struggle against colonialism—which has given substance to what is authentic.

Since colonization began in the 15th century with the arrival of the Spaniard priest, militarist, and fortune and slave seeker upon the shores of this hemisphere, Indian songmakers and story-tellers have created a body of oral literature which speaks crucially about the experience of colonization. Like the drama and the characters described above, the indigenous peoples of the Americas have taken the languages of the colonialists and used them for their own purposes. Some would argue that his means that Indian people have succumbed or become educated into a different linguistic system and have forgotten or have been forced to forsake their native selves. This is simply not true. Along with their native languages, Indian women and men have carried on their lives and their expression through the use of the newer languages, particularly Spanish, French, and English, and they have used these languages on their own terms. This is the crucial item that has to be understood, that it is entirely possible for a people to retain and maintain their lives through the use of any language. There is not a question of authenticity here; rather, it is the way that Indian people have creatively responded to forced colonization. And this response has been one of resistance; there is not clearer word for it than resistance.

It has been this resistance—political, armed, spiritual—which has been carried out by the oral tradition. The continued use of the oral tradition today is evidence that the resistance is on-going. Its use, in fact, is what has given rise to the surge of literature created by contemporary Indian authors. And it is this literature, based upon continuing resistance, which has a given a particularly nationalistic character to the Native American voice.

Consider Antoine, the boy-character through whose eyes the idea of the novel, *Wind from and Enemy Sky*, by D'Arcy McNickle is realized. Antoine is witness to the tumultuous and terrible events that face and cause change among his Little Elk people. McNickle not only has us see through Antoine's immediate youthful eyes but also through the knowledge related by Bull, his grandfather, and other kinfolk. We come to see not only a panorama of the early 20th century as experienced by the Little Elk people but also of the national Indian experience. Antoine, through his actions, thought, and understanding shows what kind of decisions become necessary, and even though the novel ends with no victory for the Little Elk people, we realize that the boy and his people have fought as valorously and courageously as they have been able, and that McNickle, as an Indian writer, has provided us a literary experience of it.

Abel in N. Scott Momaday's novel, *House Made of Dawn*, is unlike Antoine, but he carries on a similar struggle not only for identity and survival but, more, to keep integral what is most precious to him: the spiritual knowledge which will guide him throughout his life as it has guided those before him. It is knowledge of this life source that Momaday denotes as the strength which inspires the resistance of the people from whom Abel comes, and it will be what will help them to overcome. Surely, it is what proves to be the element which enables Abel to endure prison, city life, indignities cast upon him, and finally it is what helps him to return to himself and run in the dawn so that life will go on. Momaday concludes his novel by the affirmation that dawn will always come and renewal of life will be possible through resistance against forces which would destroy life. It is by the affirmation of knowledge of source and place and spiritual return that resistance is realized.

Ceremony, the novel by Leslie M. Silko, is a special and most complete example of this affirmation and what it means in terms of Indian resistance, its use as literary theme, and its significance in the development of a national Indian literature. Tayo, the protagonist in the usual sense, in the novel is not "pure blood" Indian; rather he is of mixed blood, a mestizo. He, like many Indian people of whom he is a reflection, is faced with circumstances which seemingly are beyond his ability to control. After a return home to his Indian community from military service in World War II, Tayo is still not home. He, like others, is far away from himself, and it is only through a tracking of the pathways of life, or rebuilding through ceremony of life, that he is able to at last to return to himself and to on-going life. Along the way, Silko, the novelist, has Tayo and other characters experience and describe the forces of colonialism as "witchery" which has waylaid Indian people and their values and prevents return to their sources. But Tayo does return, not by magic or mysticism or some abstract revelation; instead the return is achieved through a ceremony of story, the tracing of story, rebuilding of story, and the creation of story.

It is in this ritual that return and reaffirmation is most realized, for how else can it be. Story is to engender life, and *Ceremony* speaks upon the very process by which story, whether in oral or written form, substantiates life, continues it, and creates it. It is this very process that Indian people have depended upon in their most critical times. Indeed, without it, the oral tradition would not exist as significantly as it does today, and there would likely be no basis for present-day Indian writing, much less Indian people. But because of the insistence to keep telling and creating stories, Indian life continues, and it is this resistance against loss that has made that life possible. Tayo in *Ceremony* will live on, wealthy with story and tradition, because he realizes the use and value of the ritual of story-making which is his own and his people's lives in the making. "It is never easy," Silko writes; it is always a struggle and because it is a struggle for life it is salvation and affirmation.

The struggle to maintain life and the resistance against loss put up by Antoine, Abel, and Tayo, in their separate entities, illustrate a theme, national in character and scope, common to all American native people and to all people indigenous to lands which have suffered imperialism and colonialism. In the decade of the '70s, it has been the predominant subject and theme that has concerned Indian writers. And it has been the oral tradition which has carried this concern in the hearts of Indian people until today it is being expressed not only in the novel but in poetry and drama as well.

[Nevertheless, it is not the oral tradition as transmitted from ages past alone which is the inspiration and course for contemporary Indian literature. It is also because of the acknowledgement by Indian writers of a responsibility to advocate for their people's self-government, sovereignty, and control of land and natural resources; and to look also at racism, political and economic oppression, sexism, supremacism, and the needless and wasteful exploitation of land and people, especially in the U.S., that Indian literature is developing a character of nationalism which indeed it should have. It is this character which will prove to be the heart and fibre and story of an America which has heretofore too often feared its deepest and most honest emotions of love and compassion. It is this story, wealthy in being and without an illusion of dominant power and capitalistic abundance, that is the most authentic.]

Bob Hall in *Southern Exposure* wrote, describing the textile workers' struggle in the South, that the themes of family, community, religion, humor, and rage are the most common among the workers in their stories and music. He could have added "most authentic" to common, and he could have been commenting upon Indian people for it those very themes that Indian literature of today considers. The voice given these themes is the most culturally authentic as these are fundamental to human dignity, creativity, and integrity. This voice is that authentic one that my non-literary Uncle Steve, wearing a beat-up cowboy hat and bright blue neckerchief, expressed at Acqu, as he struggled to teach history, knowledge of our community, and understanding of how life continues. Indeed, like that ceremony at Acqu, depicting Santiago, the conquistador-saint, and Chapiyuh, the inquisitor-missionary, the voice is not a mere dramatic expression of a sociohistorical experience, but it is a persistent call by a people determined to be free; it is an authentic voice for liberation. And finally, it is the voice of countless other non-literary Indian women and men of this nation who live a daily life of struggle to achieve and maintain meaning which gives the most authentic character to a national Indian literature.

Index

Abenaki, 225–46
aboriginal title, and land claims cases, 226, 227, 247n5
Achebe, Chinua, 32
Acoma: connection of Ortiz to, xvii; language and government policy of assimilation, ix–x; language and indigenous identity of, xi–xii, xiv; Ortiz on correlation between Native literature and ceremonialism in, xviii–xix, 33–34, 253–54, 259–60; and Ortiz on cultural authenticity, 253–56, 259–60; Ortiz on spiritual traditions of, vii; relocation programs and government policy of assimilation, x
activism: and commitment to Native community, 15, 170; evolution of in 1980s, 199; and Native political radicalism, 204–5; and relevance of realism, 94; and tenets of compassionate American Indian literary nationalism, 172, 174
Adair, James, 104
Adams, Howard, 3, 32, 50
Africa, Native perspectives in literature of, 131–32
Albuquerque Indian School (AIS), ix, x
Alexander, Linda, 147–48
Alfred, Gerald Taiaiake: colonization and imposition of definitions on indigenous peoples, 6; on hybridity and Native perspective, 28, 31; on importance of Native critics and criticism, 17, 78n42, 192; nationalism and use of word "sovereignty," 44, 45, 71–72, 78n38, 82n106–107;

on postcolonialism and erasure of Native agency, 26; as social critic and advocate of nationalism, 77n33, 181–82, 208–11; and tradition in contemporary Native discourse, 213; on writing with sense of indigenous consciousness, xiv
Allen, Chadwick, 18, 39–40
Allen, Paula Gunn: and concept of sovereignty, 73; and inclusion of Native voices in criticism, 195–96; and nationalist approaches to Native literature, xx, 2; and Pulitano's critique of separatist approaches to Native literary criticism, 19, 20, 95, 98, 106, 107, 129, 132, 134–35, 164
American Indian Community House (New York), 186
American Indian intellectual history, 197
American Indian literary nationalism. *See* nationalism
American Indian Quarterly, 140
American literature: Native literature and canon of, 163–64; and values of Native literature, 17; and world literature, 41
Anderson, A. T., 83n113
Anishinaabe, 33. *See also* Ojibway
Anzaldua, Gloria, 136
Aoteoroa (New Zealand), 184
Apess, William, 33, 171
Appiah, Kwame Anthony, 21, 111, 131–32
Aquash, Anna Mae Pictou, 204, 205
Arafat, Yasir, 216
Arendt, Hannah, 70

dissent, Said on importance of,
179, 184
Drowning in Fire (Womack), 74,
166–67
Du Bois, W. E. B., 37
Durham, Jimmy, 108

Eagleton, Terry, 100, 172
Eastman, Charles, 186
Elliot, Michael, 11
Ellison, Ralph, 104
Engels, Friedrich, 119
Erdoes, Richard, 84n123
Erdrich, Louise, 53, 55–56, 64,
182, 186
essentialism: and study of Native
American literature by non-
Natives, 10, 11–12; and
Womack's response to Pulitano's
critique, 96, 97, 99, 101–3, 106,
129–30
Eurocentrism, and Pulitano's critique
of Womack, 99, 100, 103, 128,
129
Europe, influence of Native peoples on
cultures of, 119
exile, Said's self-conception of, 192
existence: cultural consciousness and
identity of indigenous people,
xi–xiv; and oral tradition in
indigenous cultures, viii–ix
experience, Native perspective and
definition of, 133

Fanon, Frantz, 27, 180, 201
Faulkner, William, 52–68, 104
feminism: in Navajo context, 211–12;
and Native American Studies,
134–35, 173, 182–83
Finkelstein, Norman, 217–18
fishing rights, and Abenaki Nation of
Missisquoi, 226
Forbes, Jack, 73
Foreman, Grant, 104
Fort Jackson, Treaty of (1814), 58
Foucault, Michel, 130

Franco, Jean, 189

Garcia Marquez, Gabriel, 104
Gardens in the Dunes (Silko), 241–43
Garroutte, Eva, 184, 213, 214
Gasque-Molina, Enrique, 104
Gates, Henry Louis, 21
gathering, and knowledge in Native
American literary nationalism,
244–45, 248–49n19
gay and lesbian studies, and queer
theory, 147
Genet, Jean, 187
Ghost Dance, 35
Gibson, Charles, 148
Gide, André, 187
Glass Mountains (Oklahoma), 9
globalization, and Indian tribes as
living studies of modern nation-
state, 127
Goins, R. Turner, 184, 213
Goldie, Terry, 13, 30, 32
Gough, Julie, 7, 29, 30
government: and federal policy on
definition of "Indians," xii; and
political activism in scholarly
nationalism, 174; Womack on
Creek forms of, 113–14
Granger, Farley, 104
Gray, Janet, 20–21
Green, Michael D., 104
Griffiths, Gareth, 15, 18
Guevara, Ernesto Che, 70

Hames-Garcia, Michael, 122
Hall, Bob, 259
Harjo, Fus, 148
Harjo, Joy, 88n158, 104, 232, 238
Hartman, Geoffrey, 108
Havelock, Eric, 104
Hawai'i, and native peoples, 218
Hays, Harry, 104
Heckwelder, John, 57
Hemingway, Ernest, 104, 187
Henderson, James (Sákéj) Youngblood,
41, 42, 213

oral tradition and nationalistic character of Native American literature, 257–58; on power of words, 225
Montezuma, Carlos, 186
Mooney, James, 105, 138
Moore, Thomas E., 148
Morgan, Lewis Henry, 119
Morrison, Scott, 118
Moss, John, 32, 48–49, 57
Moya, Paula, 122
Mufti, Aamir R., 181, 203, 216
multiculturalism: and concept of multicultural literature, 41; conservative criticism of, 27–28; and non-Native study of Native literature, 12
Munif, Abdelrahman, 187
Musgrove, Mary, 75n6
Muskogee Nation, 88n158. *See also* Creek

naming, colonialism and power of, 6–9
nationalism, and Native literacy criticism: and Abenaki Nation of Missisquoi, 225–46; and communitism, 15–50; and cultural authenticity, 253–60; and current status of scholarship on Native literature, 1–14; meaning of within contemporary scholarship on Native literature, xv–xxi, xx–xxi; and postmodernism, xx; and Womack's response to Pulitano's critique of *Red on Red*, 92–151; and quest for new person, 68–74; *Red on Red* and meaning of tribal literary nationalism, 151–68; Said and relationship of Warrior's *Tribal Secrets* to, 179–220; tenets for compassionate theory of, 168–74. *See also* separatism; sovereignty
Native American Religious Identity (Weaver), 39

Native American Studies: and American Indian Literary Nationalism, 6, 43; graduate programs in, 4–5, 152–53, 235; and jurisdictional issues, 173–74; liberalism and non-Native scholars of, 199; and Native perspectives, 131; and "translation problem," 145
Navajo, 183, 211–12
New, W. H., 9, 11, 16–17, 26, 35–36
New Echota, Treaty of, 63
New York, Native literature and culture in 1980s, 186–87
New Zealand, and Aoteoroa, 184. *See also* Maori
Nicklin, Jim, 105
Niewenhuys, Rob, 49
Noley, Homer, 146
North American literature, and Native literature, 41. *See also* American literature
Norton Anthology of World Literature, 40–41
novel: Native peoples and development of, 119; and Pulitano's analysis of traditional cultures, 117

Occom, Samson, 33, 121, 231
O'Connor, Flannery, 98, 105
Ojibway, 138–39. *See also* Anishinaabe
Oliver, Louis, 159
O'Neil, Eugene, 105
Ong, Walter, 37, 105
"On Lost Causes" (Said), 216–20
oral tradition: and academic approaches to Native literature, 154, 155; and cultural authenticity as issue in nationalism, 256, 257, 259; and cultural identity, xi; "survivance" as postmodern form of, 89n168; and writings of Indigenous peoples, viii–ix
Ortiz, Alfonso, 84n123
Ortiz, Mamie & Joe, ix

Tiffin, Helen, 15, 18
Tohe, Laura, 183, 211–12, 213
"Towards a National Indian Literature: Cultural Authenticity in Nationalism" (Ortiz 1981), xvi–xx, 2, 33–34
Toward a Native American Critical Theory (Pulitano), xx, 92–151
transformation: and concept of hybridity, xix, 160, 240–44, 246; of literary forms in Native literature, 160
Tribal Secrets: Recovering American Indian Intellectual Traditions (Warrior), xv–xvi, 20, 22, 38, 76n22, 99–100, 105, 109, 115, 179–220
trickster, and Native literary studies, 116, 155
Tuggle, W. O., 105
Turtle Goes to War (Weaver), xvi, 43, 46
Twain, Mark, 63, 105

Union Theological Seminary, 185
Universidad Autonoma de Madrid, 41
University of California at Davis, 152
University of Georgia, 152
University of Lethbridge, 121–22
University of Nebraska Press, xx
University of Oklahoma, 95, 101, 110, 122, 152, 156
University of Saskatchewan, 3
University of Trent, 152
"upbuilding" project, and Abenaki Nation of Missisquoi, 229, 233
Utemorrah, Daisy, 68–69

Velie, Alan, 11, 46, 169
Vermont, and Missiquoi Abenaki, 225, 227–28
Vizenor, Gerald: and concept of "survivance," 89n168; and "dialogic" approach, 78n48; and Faulkner, 56, 63, 67; and pluralist separatism of American Indian literary nationalism, 73;

and postmodernism, 31, 186; and present status of Native American literary criticism, 4; and Pulitano's critique of nationalism in Native literary criticism, 21–22, 95, 96, 107, 115, 125, 138–39; relationship to theory, 165–66; and use of language in Native literature, 33; and use of non-Native genres and forms in Native literature, 87n154; and use of term "paracolonial," 39

Walk in Your Soul: Love Incantations of the Oklahoma Cherokee (Kilpatrick and Kilpatrick), 137, 138
Warrior, Robert: and concept of intellectual sovereignty, 38, 45; on gathering and dispersal of knowledge, 244; influence of on Brooks, 233; influence of on Womack, 155; and nationalism in contemporary scholarship on Native literature, xv–xvi; on Native American literary nationalism in context of history, 245; and oral tradition, viii; and Pulitano's critique of Native literary criticism, 19, 20, 22, 95, 97, 98, 99–100, 105, 107, 108, 109, 110, 112, 115, 130, 131, 164–65; and pan-Indian approach to American Indian literary nationalism, 50, 76n22; and reading of Mathews's *Sundown*, 127–28; on revitalization of Native culture, 251–52n29; on scholarly nationalism and political activism, 174; and status of graduate programs in Native American Studies, 4–5; on works of Native authors as "firsts," 80n81. See also *Like a Hurricane: The Indian Movement from Alcatraz to Wounded Knee; Tribal Secrets: Recovering American Indian Intellectual Traditions*